INTEGRATED SOCIAL
POLICY

A REVIEW OF
THE AUSTRIAN EXPERIENCE

ORGANISATION FOR ECONOMIC CO-OPERATION AND DEVELOPMENT

The Organisation for Economic Co-operation and Development (OECD) was set up under a Convention signed in Paris on 14th December 1960, which provides that the OECD
shall promote policies designed:
- to achieve the highest sustainable economic growth and employment and a rising
  standard of living in Member countries, while maintaining financial stability, and
  thus to contribute to the development of the world economy;
- to contribute to sound economic expansion in Member as well as non-member
  countries in the process of economic development;
- to contribute to the expansion of world trade on a multilateral, non-discriminatory
  basis in accordance with international obligations.
The Members of OECD are Australia, Austria, Belgium, Canada, Denmark, Finland,
France, the Federal Republic of Germany, Greece, Iceland, Ireland, Italy, Japan, Lux-
embourg, the Netherlands, New Zealand, Norway, Portugal, Spain, Sweden, Switzerland,
Turkey, the United Kingdom and the United States.

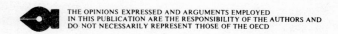

THE OPINIONS EXPRESSED AND ARGUMENTS EMPLOYED
IN THIS PUBLICATION ARE THE RESPONSIBILITY OF THE AUTHORS AND
DO NOT NECESSARILY REPRESENT THOSE OF THE OECD

HN
405.5
.P6512
1981

Publié en français sous le titre :

LA POLITIQUE SOCIALE INTÉGRÉE
Le cas de l'Autriche

.

The examination of Integrated Social Policy in Austria is part of a broader study of integrated social policies for which France, Germany, Japan, the Netherlands and Yugoslavia have prepared studies. It was undertaken by OECD, on the basis of negotiations with the Austrian authorities, with a view to contributing to the discussion of related issues in Austria and to providing other OECD countries with an opportunity to learn from Austria's experience.

The examiners appointed by OECD were:

M. Jean Daney de Marcillac, Deputy Director-General, Société d'études pour le développement économique et social, Paris.
Dr. Rudolf Meidner, former Head of Institute for Labour Studies, Stockholm.
Prof. Dr. Pieter Muntendam, former Secretary of State for Public Health, the Hague.
Mr. Werner Steinjan, Head of Social and Employment Policy Division, Ministry of Economic Affairs, Bonn.

The Austrian authorities commissioned in 1977 twenty-two background studies on key topics ranging over the large area of policy known as "Integrated Social Policy". The examiners visited Austria in October 1978 and January 1979. They discussed issues and aspects of Austrian policy, to which they wished to devote particular attention, with Federal Ministers and officials of the federal authorities concerned and of two Länder, leaders and experts of employers' and employees' organisations, members from the political parties represented in the Federal Assembly and members of a wide range of research institutions. The Examiners' Report was prepared in the course of 1979 and early 1980 in close collaboration with the OECD Secretariat. The Secretariat arranged for the preparation of Annex I on "Austria's Political System" and a "Statistical Overview of Recent Economic and Social Trends" (Annex II). Readers unfamiliar with Austria's political system may wish to begin their reading of the report with Annex I.

A Special Review Meeting of the Manpower and Social Affairs Committee of OECD was held in Vienna on 7 - 8 October 1980 to discuss the questions and issues raised by the examiners in their report. Delegates from twelve Member countries attended this meeting and contributed to the discussion. The Austrian Delegation was composed of the Federal Minister of Health and Environment Protection, Dr. Herbert Salcher; the Secretary of State in the Federal Chancellery, DDr. Adolf Nussbaumer; the Secretary of State in the

Federal Ministry of Finance, Mrs. Elfriede Karl; officials from the Federal Chancellery and eight federal ministries; the Secretary-General of the Federal Chamber of Industry, Commerce and Trade (Bundeskammer der Gewerblichen Wirtschaft), DDr. Karl Kehrer; the Executive Secretary of the Austrian Federation of Trade Unions (Österreichischer Gewerkschaftsbund), Mr. Erich Hofstetter and officials of employers' and employees' organisations.

The statement of the Secretary of State DDr. Nussbaumer, made at the opening of the Review Meeting, the conclusions drawn from the Examiners' Report and the discussion at the review meeting are included in this publication.

The Examiners' Report and Annex I relate to developments up to the first half of 1980. Annex II includes data available up to the middle of 1981.

The examiners wish to express their grateful appreciation to all whose assistance and co-operation made this report possible. The opinions expressed are, however, the sole responsibility of the examiners.

Also available

TOWARDS AN INTEGRATED SOCIAL POLICY IN JAPAN (May 1977)
(81 77 02 1) ISBN 92-64-11638-8   50 pages   £2.20   US$4.50   F18.00

Prices charged at the OECD Publications Office.

THE OECD CATALOGUE OF PUBLICATIONS and supplements will be sent free of charge on request addressed either to OECD Publications Office,
2, rue André-Pascal, 75775 PARIS CEDEX 16, or to the OECD Sales Agent in your country.

CONTENTS

THE EXAMINERS' REPORT

Part I

MAIN CONDITIONS FOR SOCIAL POLICY INTEGRATION

Part II

SOCIAL PARTNERSHIP IN AUSTRIA

Part III

CO-ORDINATION AND INTEGRATION OF VARIOUS AREAS
WITH SPECIAL EMPHASIS ON REDISTRIBUTIVE ASPECTS

Part IV

TOWARDS A COMPREHENSIVE HEALTH POLICY

Part V

REFORM PRIORITIES AND PROBLEMS FOR THE FUTURE

8

THE EXAMINERS' REPORT

Part I

MAIN CONDITIONS FOR SOCIAL POLICY INTEGRATION

A. DEFINITION OF "SOCIAL INTEGRATION"

We must first make clear what we mean by "social integration".
The term covers much more than the integration of social policy
measures and is rather to be understood as an <u>integrated policy for
society as a whole</u>(*) involving the co-ordination of socio-political
measures in the broadest sense, i.e. social policy and policies for
employment, finance, health, housing, transport and education.

This definition broadly coincides with the meaning of the term
<u>Gesellschaftspolitik</u> frequently found in the German-language liter-
ature on the subject. Thus, Hubert Voigtländer speaks of "Gesellschaftspolitik" as "an overall term embracing all the individual partial policies ... which influence social relationships and conditions"(1). Reithofer understands "Gesellschaftspolitik" to mean "the
appraisal of individual policy aims in relation to overall social
goals"(2). Pfaff speaks of an "integrated review of all programmes"(3),

The concept of integrated social policy must not however be understood simply as a multiplicity of policy measures and their co-
ordination at various levels (between different policy areas, between
the different central authorities responsible for those areas, between
federal, state and local authority measures, or between the authorities and independent organisations), but also as the expression of
goal-oriented action aimed at an integrated society. "The basic
feature of integrated social policy is therefore the direction of
the individual measures of individual partial policies towards the
shaping of society on the basis of a future-oriented policy with the
maximum degree of consistency" (Voigtländer). Integrated social
policy, concludes Voigtländer, must never be understood as a policy
for maintaining the status quo, but as a constant effort to reshape
social structures and processes.

Social policy integration is therefore both the process of integration of various policy areas according to common goals, and a
form of society in which social stratification, segmentation and
isolation are kept to a minimum, and equality of opportunity (and,

(*) To be referred to hereinafter as "integrated social policy".

as a further implicit goal, the ability to take advantage of such
opportunity) to participate in the economic, social and cultural
development of society is, if not guaranteed, nevertheless constantly aimed at.

Pfaff-Voigtländer(4) postulate several conditions for an integrated social policy:
- the pursuit of a goal of a part-programme must not endanger
  the achievement of the goals of the overall system;
- undesirable consequences such as programme overlapping,
  gaps, inefficiencies, inadequacies and unfairness must
  be avoided;
- the pursuit of partial interests and the exercise of power
  by individual organised groups must not interfere with the
  aims of the system.

Even if this definition of the concept is too broad and demanding to serve as a basis for the following description of integrated
social policy in Austria, we nevertheless felt it would be useful to
preface our report with it. The features we describe as needing reform and meriting criticism must be viewed in the light of the high
level of demands implicit in our interpretation of the basic concept.

B. THE EXAMINERS' TASK AND THE METHODS USED

The broad outlines of the examiners' task emerge from our definition of the concept of social integration. The examination has to
start from the basic historical and political characteristics of the
country being examined, and in the case of Austria this means giving
special significance to the institutional peculiarities of the
country. The social policy goals must be identified from government
statements, party programmes and official documents of the main organised economic interest groups. Then important sections of social
life are examined, more by means of examples than by a systematic
review, to see where gaps exist and whether these gaps are attributable to insufficient provision of resources or to inadequate co-
ordination of measures, and what recommendations can be made for
better ways of achieving the goals formulated by the decision-makers.
Finally the examiners have to consider, when evaluating what they
have learned, in what respects and to what degree their findings -
favourable or unfavourable - could be applicable to other countries.

This twofold task of the examiners - to make their findings useful both to the country itself and to other countries - raises the
question as to whether the enquiry should concentrate on specifically
Austrian features of social development or whether priority should
be given to identifying and analysing phenomena with a certain

general validity for highly developed welfare states. Too much concentration on Austrian peculiarities would reduce the value of such
a report to other countries. Conversely, too much insistence on
general problems of the welfare society, exemplified by Austria as
a typical case of an advanced welfare society, would lead to a neglect of more specific features and thus reduce the report's usefulness for the country in question.

In practice the question in Austria's case does not present itself as a clear alternative necessitating a difficult choice. A
compromise offers itself in that Austria's integrated social policy
goals, insofar as they are officially formulated, closely resemble
those of other West European welfare states, but their achievement
in Austria is being attempted in a framework which differs from that
of other countries and is indeed almost unique. Bringing out these
particularities stresses the need for caution in applying Austria's
experiences to countries whose history, traditions, and political
and economic development have led to the emergence of different institutional structures. The favourable role which Austrian institutions must be considered to have played in the solution of social
problems is, however, an indication of the direction in which reforms
should be sought for institutions in other welfare states. Let us
say at once here that we are thinking in the first place of social
partnership, which is admittedly a phenomenon which Austria's history
has bequeathed to it, but which also contains features which could
be of interest for the development of relations between the social
partners in industrial countries with strong, independently organised
economic interest groups.

The very broad terms of reference set for the examination cannot,
if only for reasons of time, be anything like comprehensively covered
by an analysis of the available material. The Federal Chancellor's
Office presented in autumn 1978 a large volume of material under five
main headings, produced in the main by academic institutions. The
chief subjects dealt with were the basic framework of Austrian integrated social policy, the distributive effects of various policy
measures, and social partnership and health policy. Within these
areas the examiners' group itself selected particular points of emphasis which either concerned specific Austrian conditions or seemed
to be of general significance for the problems of an integrated
social policy. With this approach it was, of course, not possible
to cover the whole area of integrated social policy in the broad
sense in which we defined it earlier. In particular, in the choice
of the basic framework features to be dealt with and the recommendations, it is clear that the report could do no more than provide
examples, and this may well have led to the neglect of essential
questions.

C. AUSTRIAN HISTORY AND TRADITIONS AS A BACKGROUND
TO PRESENT INTEGRATED SOCIAL POLICY

This background description can and is intended to be only very cursory, especially since Professor Pelinka's study on the political system of Austria is appended in annex to the report. A few decisive features of Austrian development must however be brought out to provide a better understanding in particular of the institutional framework of the present integrated social policy. We are thinking here on the one hand of the "Josephinisch" reform traditions, elements of which can still be seen today: "reforms from above", the great importance, which emerges quite early, of the professional civil service and the readiness to resort to state intervention. We are also thinking of the egalitarian reform efforts of the liberal bourgeoisie and the "Christian anti-capitalism" of the XIXth century, and also of the peculiar features of Austro-marxism (described in Professor Karl Stadler's study on structural conditions for integrated social policy in Austria as an intermediate position between reformist revisionism and revolutionary orthodoxy).(5)

In all the literature, however, the most recent history of Austria, in particular the events of the inter-war years and the second world war, is considered as decisive for the political and institutional structure of modern Austria. From the political and social confrontation of the thirties, which ended in civil war and the collapse of democratic institutions, lessons were learned which found their expression in a far-reaching "concordance" kind of thinking. Experiences of occupation and war gave birth to an awareness of Austrian independence which was much stronger than in the inter-war years when the widespread idea of "Anschluss" (union with Germany) prevented the emergence of a genuine feeling of national independence. Austria's international status as an alliance-free "Kleinstaat" between East and West reinforces this independent role and contributes from outside to the country's stability. One way of interpreting events would be to say that external developments forced a certain role on a small country, and that the people had to adapt themselves and their institutions to that role. That interpretation could, however, be too narrow and incomplete. It would be more correct to say that a general willingness already existed consciously to play the role of a stable welfare state through a consensus of parties and economic interest groups, and to refer back to national traditions in the construction of new institutions.

Austria's progress in the post-war years to a highly developed welfare state was helped by vigorous economic growth. But the remarkable successes of the social integration policy which makes Austria an especially interesting subject for any comparative country study of social policy integration cannot in the main be explained by

16

a higher-than-average growth rate. The main preconditions for this development into an integrated welfare society can be perceived in the historical development of the country, in the revulsion from confrontations induced by experiences of traumatic intensity, in the determination to find common solutions even if that means accepting a highly inflexible system, and finally in the ability to create and develop institutions for achieving these goals.

The peculiar features of Austria find their expression in concepts such as "Austro-marxism" and "Austro-fascism," specifically Austrian forms of worldwide ideological movements. It would be almost equally justified to talk of an "Austro-welfare-society" whose "concordance" ideology and the institutions corresponding thereto make it a special form of the modern welfare society.

D. THE INSTITUTIONAL FRAMEWORK

Of the many institutional conditions for the progress of societal development and political life we shall select here only a few which seem to us important:

- The simultaneously federalistic and centralistic structure of Austria.
- Some main features of the economic structure, in particular the strength of the small- and medium-sized enterprise sectors, and the great importance of the non-private sector.
- The "chambers" system, and economic or social partnership.

a) Federalism and centralism

On this subject, which should be of great importance for the problem of social policy integration, not much material has been available to us. Kostelka and Unkart, in their contribution to Fischer's work on Austria's political system, give a summary of the country's system(6). They explain the historical reasons why the position of the federal Länder in the state structure as a whole is weak, and that the main responsibility for fulfilling objectives is incumbent on the Bund (the Federal Government). Pelinka finds that the position of the federal Länder, compared with that in other federal countries, is not very strong, and points to the weak position of the Bundesrat (the Federal Council, on which the federal Länder are represented)(7). Kelsen speaks of a "centralistic unified state".

The dominant position of the Bund stems from the division of powers and public finance responsibilities. Legislative power is exclusively a matter for the Bund, although the Länder have certain powers to enact implementing legislation. As regards taxation the overwhelming superiority of the Bund is clear. The Bund decides the distribution of federal tax revenues between the Bund and the Länder, and possesses a "pre-emptive right to taxes". Finance equalisation procedures and political negotiations determine the redistribution of revenues between Bund, Länder and communes. The Bund is also in a dominant position in administrative matters. Since 1945 changes in the Constitution have strengthened the powers of the Bund in important areas like education, economic planning, labour law and finance. Moves in the opposite direction were initiated by the Länder in their "1976 Claims Programme", but according to Kostelka and Unkart this had little effect on the tendency towards centralisation.

From the viewpoint of social policy integration Austrian-style federalism seems to present no obstacle, but rather an advantage. The Länder authorities act for the Länder but are also agents for the Bund. At Bezirk and Länder (county and state) levels "there is much greater readiness and ability to see things in the round and organise co-operation between the various branches of administration than can possibly be the case between the specialised central departments of the Bund" (Kostelka-Unkart). There are also the Verbindungsstelle der Bundesländer (liaison office of the federal states) and the Landeshauptmännerkonferenz (Conference of Federal States' Presidents) which enable the Länder to cross-communicate with each other. Another factor which limits federal powers is the existence of linkages between the political parties and the Chambers of Commerce and Labour, which also facilitates cross-connections across the boundaries of the federal Länder.

For the foreign and, of course, insufficiently informed observer the Austrian variant of federalism seems a particularly suitable form of government to put general social policy priorities into practice. The centralistic tendency, the sine qua non for the formulation of priority goals, is unmistakably present in the system. On the other hand a high degree of independence of the Länder is guaranteed, and a relatively large number of communes (2,300 in all, of which 25 per cent with less than 1,000 inhabitants and 50 per cent with less than 1,500) are responsible for their own administrative tasks. The balance between centralisation and decentralisation is also aided by the fact that the Chambers and Verbände (associations) are organised on a Länder basis. This regionalised type of organisation constitutes a counterweight to the centralistic decision-making processes practised by these bodies. In regard to the Austrian pattern of government, therefore, it would again not be very wide of the mark to speak of a specifically Austrian form of federalism, an "Austrofederalism", which pragmatically accepts the centralism required for the modern welfare state, but tries to avoid the many disadvantages associated with it in other countries.

b) Special features of the Austrian economy

i) Small businesses and small farming

Small businesses and small farming are more important in Austria than in the majority of comparable countries in Western Europe. In 1975, 12.5 per cent of the labour force were employed in agriculture and forestry, compared with 7.3 per cent for example in Germany, 6.6 per cent in the Netherlands and 6.4 per cent in Sweden(8). According to the 1970 census, nearly 43 per cent of agriculture and forestry enterprises were less than 5 hectares in size, and 61 per cent less than 10 hectares. It is true that these small farms occupied only about 11 per cent of the total cultivated area under agriculture and forestry, whereas the few large farms (1.7 per cent with more than 100 hectares) occupied 47 per cent of the total cultivated area(9). To say that small farming is the predominant form in Austria is correct if one is referring to the large proportion of small farms, but less correct if one considers the areas of agricultural and forest land being cultivated by small farmers.

Of the total of 280,000 non-farming establishments (1973), only 400 employed more than 500 employees and no less than 85 per cent employed less than 10 employees. In particular, establishments in commerce and the hotel and catering trade are predominantly small or very small, tourism naturally playing a large part in this.

Of the total of 229,000 establishments (1977) with personnel covered by health insurance schemes, 173,000 had up to 5 employees, and 195,000 (85 per cent) less than 10 employees. There were 2,650 medium-sized establishments (100-500 employees), while large establishments (over 500 employees) numbered less than 400.

The predominance of small establishments is clear from the following table, which gives for various industries the percentage of establishments with up to 5 employees.

Establishments with up to 5 employees as a percentage of total number of establishments (1977)

Hotel and catering	78.1
Clothing, bedclothing, footwear	70.8
Food and drink	62.6
Manufacture of textiles	55.3
Manufacture and processing of metals	53.2

Austria has less than 75 large industrial establishments (with more than 1,000 employees). Austrian industry, as the Advisory Council for Economic and Social Questions points out in its study "Suggestions for industrial policy"(10), is predominantly medium-sized, and has no large international companies domiciled on its

territory (like Sweden or Switzerland, for example). In 1964, only
32 per cent of the industrial labour force were working in establishments employing more than 1,000 workers, and these were mainly in
mining, iron and steel, vehicles and electrical engineering. In the
study referred to, the medium-sized structure of Austrian industry
is judged to be a good thing, since it makes possible a greater
adaptability in production and speedier in-establishment communications systems. In spite of quite a flurry of merger activity the
size structure of industry had not changed significantly up to the
mid-seventies.

ii) Ownership structure of industry

One characteristic of the Austrian economy is the size of the
non-private sector which, whether in public enterprise, co-operative
or other social enterprise form, constitutes one third of the whole
economy. Important components of this high proportion are traditional factors such as the predominance of public enterprises in public
utilities supplies (97 per cent), non-profit-making housing schemes
(40 per cent), consumer co-operatives in the grocery trade (23 per
cent) and public ownership of forests (20 per cent). A special feature of the Austrian economy is the state predominance in banking and
insurance (70 per cent) and above all in large-scale industry (nearly
one quarter of total manufacturing production, one-fifth of the industrial labour force).

If one turns, for lack of statistical data on the state share in
really large-scale industry, to a survey covering the 50 largest
enterprises in Austria (including firms outside the manufacturing
sector), it appears that in 1971 domestic private capital accounted
for only 11 per cent of turnover and 12 per cent of employment,
foreign capital for 16 and 17 per cent respectively(11).

The high percentage of large-scale industry in state hands, the
influence of state banks on a further part of industry (here, too,
there are no figures available), the large and increasing part played
by foreign firms, and consequently the fact that, compared with other
countries, only a small part of Austria's industry is privately owned
by Austrian entrepreneurs, are important elements in the framework for
Austrian economic and social policy.

The vigorous development of the non-private sectors and the
nationalisation of large-scale industry have been carried out pragmatically and with a consensus of the political forces. The nationalisation of Austrian large-scale industry is not to be seen as a
result of ideological efforts, but goes back to the political situation in the period immediately after the war, when "ownerless"
German property was taken over under the Nationalisation Acts passed
in 1946 and 1947. The preamble to the legislative texts makes clear,

however, that this was not simply an emergency solution: "The attached draft law thus represents the first step in the creation of a healthy, crisis-free economic constitution guaranteeing full employment ..." In the 1966 Act setting up the ÖIAG(*) (Österreichische Industrieverwaltungs-Aktiengesellschaft), the Act instructs the central holding corporation for the nationalised industries to exercise its participation rights in such a way as to promote the interests of those enterprises and of the workers in them and also of the economy as a whole. Particular attention must be paid to the principles of efficiency and the need for co-ordination measures". (Our underlining).

The extraordinarily important and, for the assessment of Austrian economic and social development, perhaps decisive question is now whether the large role of the non-private sector and in particular the nationalisation of basic industries and banks has essentially changed the character of Austrian society. Many judges of conditions in Austria take the view that it has.

In Thesen der Arbeitsgemeinschaft der Österreichischen Gemeinwirtschaft (1979) (Propositions of the body for institutionalised co-operatives of the Austrian non-private sector) which gives the views of an interest group connected with the non-private sector, it is argued that a strong non-private sector also makes an important contribution to social partnership. A close relationship has developed with trade unions and Chambers of Labour which are also members of the Working Party. Publicly-owned enterprises, in the Working Party's view, contain elements of economic democracy. In times of crisis, when those enterprises have had to make sacrifices, they have helped to maintain jobs, and in times of boom they have pursued a compensatory employment policy. The role of the non-private sector, it is argued, is not to change society but to be a dynamic component of the economy.

In an essay on the nationalised industries in Austria, Ferdinand Lacina instances a number of circumstances which can be considered as structural features of nationalised industries(12). State enterprises, he argues, can take a longer-term view of profit maximisation and therefore have greater continuity in employment, enterprise growth and investment policy. Another structural feature is the fulfilment of macro-economic goals in their pricing policies (through low raw material prices state enterprises can make an important contribution to the reconstruction of the manufacturing and processing industries). The strong position of the unions in the nationalised industries has strengthened trade union influence on enterprise decision-making but not led to overhigh wages in the public

*) Central holding corporation for the nationalised industries.

21

sector. Lacina concludes that the nationalised enterprises, in particular through their employment and investment policies, have had a stabilizing influence on the development of the Austrian economy.

Other stabilizing aspects of the nationalised industries have frequently been emphasized by persons actively engaged in the public sector. Oskar Grünwald points out for example that "the object of all efforts is and must continue to be the consolidation and extension of a group of industries which in essence, i.e. in management and ownership, is Austrian. It thus constitutes a counterweight to the still growing foreign influence in our economy and is at the same time an instrument in the service of Austrian interests on the turbulent energy, raw material and capital markets"(13). And the same author, who is Director-General of the ÖIAG (Österreichische Industrieverwaltungs-Aktiengesellschaft), says in another context that the Austrian model of the mixed economy with its balanced relationship between competition and government intervention, is "the only one with which it will be possible to solve the problems of the coming decades"(14).

The statutory obligation of the nationalised enterprises to take into account the interests of the workers and of the economy as a whole has clearly not led to the neglect of efficiency considerations. According to the figures given in the Yearbook of the European Centre for Public Enterprises for 1978 the productivity of the nationalised enterprises increased by almost 40 per cent from 1970 to 1975, and value added was much higher than the overall average for industry (the structural differences between the nationalised and private industries should be remembered here).

We have dealt at some length with the nationalised sector in Austria and quoted the admittedly frequently subjective assessments of Austrian experts. In our opinion the size of the non-private sector must be considered to be an essential feature of the basic framework for Austria's economic and social development.

c) The "Chambers" system and social partnership

The Chambers system and social partnership are dealt with in detail in Part II and also described and analysed in Annex I. These two institutions and their interconnections are however such important and, for Austria, such specific components of the social system that an introductory chapter on the basic framework for an integrated social policy must include more about them than just references to other parts of the report. It is after all these institutions which mainly serve as the instruments of such an integrated policy or at least make it easier to apply. The basic features of this unique system must therefore be presented in the introductory chapter.

The Chambers system has deep historic roots, but it has only been playing its special role as part of the social partnership system of the Second Republic. The interconnections of self-governing bodies based on statutory provisions and compulsory membership with autonomous economic interest group organisations based on voluntary membership is an Austrian peculiarity which can only be understood in the context of the recent history of the country. Without government intervention, and on the initiative of representatives of freely organised economic interest groups and a self-governing Chambers' organisation, a system has emerged which under changing political and economic conditions has assumed part-responsibility for the stabilization of the economy.

Such a system can only be effective if it is firmly founded on some basic agreement in approach by the participating groupings. This basic agreement is the conviction that differences of interest and conflicts can be settled in the framework of such a system. The rule that decisions of the Joint Commission (Paritätische Kommission für Lohn- und Preisfragen) and its subsidiary bodies can only be taken unanimously presupposes a far-reaching readiness to compromise, a centralistic decision-making structure, and great confidence on the part of members in their officials. It seems that these necessary conditions are fulfilled in Austria's case.

The quite specific form of Austrian social partnership must not be confused either with traditional forms of "incomes policies", nor with formal consultations between the two sides of industry on the reconciliation of differences between themselves (as for example in the Saltsjöbaden Agreement in Sweden in 1938) or between them and the government, even though it contains elements of both. The Austrian system can only be explained in terms of Austrian relationships - the traditions of the Chambers system, the difficult experiences of the occupation and war years with their destruction of all democratic institutions, the strength of the voluntary associations, the close interconnections between associations and political parties, and finally the need for the war-weakened Austrian economy to survive in the post-war world of international competition.

One of the main propositions of this report is that the system of social partnership has been the most important basic factor enabling Austria to achieve a post-war economic and social development which can compare favourably with that of any other country. As will be shown in Annex II, the Austrian economy's growth rate was higher than the OECD average, wage and price increases more moderate than in other Western countries, and full employment has been successfully maintained. The Austrian economy has proved extraordinarily resilient in the present crisis. These achievements were themselves pre-conditions for the development of the socially integrated welfare state, in which it is clear however that a system based on

consensus gives higher priority to stability than to redistribution.
The question will have to be considered, therefore, whether a social
partnership system which has proved itself a stabilizing factor in
a period of growth, and capable of resistance in the present crisis,
can also, in the longer run and above all under conditions of a long-
term trend towards slower growth, contribute to social integration
in the sense of an equitable redistribution of income, wealth and
opportunities.

E. OBJECTIVES OF INTEGRATED SOCIAL POLICY IN AUSTRIA

We have already stated in our introductory remarks that we wished
to interpret the concept of integrated social policy not simply as
the co-ordination of policies, but as the expression of goal-oriented
action, the directing of individual measures towards the reshaping
of society on the basis of a future-oriented socio-political approach.
As Martin Pfaff(15) puts it, progress towards the achievement of the
goals of an integrated social policy can be divided into three successive "solution-phases":

1. The "little" solution consisting of improved co-
   ordination of selective programmes.
2. The "intermediate" solution consisting of strategic
   concepts going further than the extension of the
   present social system and offering a genuine alter
   native to the existing system.
3. The "big" solution going beyond economic, financial
   and social policies as at present conceived, and
   more strongly oriented towards an overriding conception of a humane and just society.

The lack of official pronouncements on goal concepts has given
our group a certain freedom to decide on what phase of integration
our attention should be focused. The first phase in the above tabu-
lation is of a technico-administrative nature, which a group of
examiners from other countries has to put aside because they do not
possess the required knowledge of the administrative process. The
choice was therefore between the "intermediate" and the "big" solution phases. The responsible Austrian authorities explained to us
that a complete concept of "integrated social policy" could neither
be provided from the Austrian side nor put forward by the examining
group. What we were to examine was rather a series of individual
policy developments which had emerged as a result of general goal
concepts, but by a pragmatic process. The problem of conceptual
elaboration would really arise out of this report itself.

We interpreted this statement of position as, in the words of
Karl Popper(16), <u>rejecting</u> "utopian social engineering" and a complete recasting of the social order to replace the present system,
but <u>in favour of</u> a "social technique using a step-by-step approach"
("piecemeal engineering"). According to Popper "the piecemeal
engineer" may have some ideas as to the ideal society "as a whole"
- his ideal may be one of general welfare - but he is not in favour
of reshaping society as a whole(17). If this is the correct interpretation we ought to direct ourselves towards an integration phase
lying somewhere between Pfaff's "intermediate" and "big" solutions.

Our method has therefore been to examine government statements,
party programmes and statements of the organised interest groups to
see what they contain in the way of explicit goals for integrated
social policy. Predominant among these must be the government statements, which naturally for the period after 1970 largely coincide
with social democratic goal formulation.

In the government statement of 1975 the main priorities are a
high level of employment and an improved quality of life. Countering price inflation is given as an important but not a priority aim.
Greater social quality and fairer distribution are considered as
prerequisites for the necessary structural changes. "An improved
quality of life" is defined more precisely as better quality housing
conditions, better living conditions for the farmers, better environmental protection, anticipatory space planning, equality of opportunities in education and health matters, equality for women and better
protection of all citizens by means of social policy. The government statement speaks of social partnership as an important extension of co-operation in the economic field and the term "balance of
interests" ("Interessenausgleich") is used in this connection.

This shows a certain shift in priorities compared with earlier
government statements. In 1971 the fight against poverty was put
first, with an estimate of 450,000 disadvantaged Austrian citizens.
In the first Kreisky government's statement in 1970 education and
research policy was given priority, but there was also an indicative
list of aims for budget policy: promotion of economic growth, a
socially just distribution of incomes, maintenance of full employment and price stability.

In many respects the government statements coincide with the 1978
SPÖ (Austrian Socialist Party) programme. As an ideological programme for the longer term this goes beyond the government statements
in some respects. The demands for doing away with the class society,
reforming decision-making and property relationships, a fundamental
transformation of existing economic relationships towards a democratically planned society are examples of such further-going
suggestions for reforms. This brings out the difference between the
broad terms of a party programme and the short- or medium-term

government programme of that party - the party programme aiming at "a complete reshaping of the social order replacing the present system", the government statement using the "piecemeal social engineering" method. There need be no contradiction between these two dimensions. But we as examiners must naturally concentrate our attention on the shorter-term goals.

The ÖVP (Austrian People's Party) aims were set out in the Salzburger Programme. The most important goal for present-day social policy is an improved quality of life. Social partnership is approved as a basis for the peaceful solution of conflicts. But the ÖVP rejects total government involvement in all aspects of life and stresses the importance of the efforts of individuals. The biggest difference from the socialist programme is the belief in the "social market economy"("soziale Marktwirtschaft") and the freedom of entrepreneurial decisions. The demands for new forms of profit-sharing and for the promotion of individual wealth formation are also expressions of a basically different ideological approach to economic policy.

The belief in the social market economy and a society based on rewards for individual efforts (Leistungsgesellschaft) comes out even more clearly in the FPÖ (Austrian Free Party) manifesto. Growth is explicitly given priority over redistribution. Nationalisation and the planned economy are rejected. The development of the "Kammerstaat" (i.e. the increasing involvement in government of the Chambers of Industry, Trade and Labour) is considered as a degeneration of democracy. It seems that, in its programme at any rate, the FPÖ does not fully subscribe to the consensus which exists between the two large parties concerning the role of the Chambers, the nationalised industries and a number of social policy goals.

Certain programmatic statements on general social policy goals have also been made by some of the organised economic interest groups and Chambers. At the 8th Federal Congress of the ÖGB (Austrian Trade Union Federation) in 1975 one of the items dealt with was the report on "equality of opportunity through social policy"(18), in which social policy was defined as part of a general policy for changing the structure of society, and improving the quality of life was declared to be the main goal. In concrete terms this means:

- the establishment of social justice;
- the abolition of all forms of discrimination;
- the creation of conditions affording equality of opportunity in education, further education and career possibilities;
- material security through full employment, guaranteed incomes and social security;
- transformation of the social position of the workers through co-determination.

The longer the world recession lasts the more pressing the problem of full employment becomes. Thus a resolution of ÖGB Central Committee of 15 February 1979 states: "The top priority of the ÖGB continues to be the maintenance of full employment".

In 1978 the Handelskammerorganisation (Chambers of Trade and Industry Organisations) agreed on a basic programme(19). The Organisation considers stability and full employment to be equally important and in the long term mutually dependent goals. Other goals are economic growth and a better quality of life. The Organisation considers the most appropriate form of economy to be the social market economy, the basic conditions for which are liberty, efficiency, private property, competition, private initiative and social justice. Other conditions are a decentralised decision-making structure, incentives for personal effort and the possibility of profit and success. "Undifferentiated social and economic equality", the orientation of social activities by means of central planning and a "defensive structural policy" ("konservierende Strukturpolitik") are rejected. Social partnership is accorded a conciliation role. The organisation of the economy cannot accept any further nationalisation, which must be interpreted as an acceptance of the nationalisations carried out hitherto.

We now come to the difficult but important question of what sociopolitical concepts our further considerations should be based on. From the overview given above it emerges that, as far as long-term goals are concerned, there exist important differences which are hard to bridge between the Austrian Socialist Party and the Austrian Trade Union Federation on the one hand and the Austrian People's Party, the Austrian Free Party and the Chambers of Trade and Industry on the other. The main differences concern the economic system, the role of state planning and intervention, the concept of the individual's role in society (Menschenbild) and the extent of the social security system. However, these differences lie more in the "utopian" pictures each side has of an ideal future society than in the shorter-term goals which matter most when it comes to "piecemeal social engineering". Another important consideration is the fact that almost all the parties and organisations accept as given the main features of the Austrian social structure, i.e. the extensive nationalised industry sector, the predominantly small-producer economy based on private ownership, and social partnership.

In his book "Die ausgleichende Gesellschaft" (The Compensatory Society)(2), Hans Reithofer has tried to see where the three main tendencies in Austrian social policy - conservatism, liberalism and socialism - agree as to basic objectives. He comes to the conclusion that high level employment lies within the area of basic consensus. The same is true of the postulate for an appropriate rate of growth. Further points on which he considers there is a basic consensus are "socially-oriented" efficiency and <u>the taking into account of social considerations in income distribution and life opportunities</u>. Finally he believes that <u>a gradual shift towards non-economic interests in life</u> is also a feature of the general consensus. We can adopt these well-documented findings of an expert on Austrian conditions and use the goals he enumerates as a starting point for our reflections.

Part II

SOCIAL PARTNERSHIP IN AUSTRIA

A. DEFINITION OF SOCIAL PARTNERSHIP

a) <u>A pragmatical system</u>

In Austria the field of economic and social policy is dominated
by the system of social partnership built up over the course of two
decades. Austrian "social partnership" - the workers' side would
prefer the concept, in their view more comprehensive, of "economic
partnership" - means more than it does in many other countries which
use the same term. It is not only a programmatical concept but an
extensive, smoothly functioning system of co-operation between the
main employers' and workers' institutions. It was developed after
the second world war in the co-operative climate then prevailing in
the settlement of wage and price questions. In the view of the ÖVP
it is the realisation of an idea contained in Christian-social doctrine. The SPÖ is less explicit in its support. The FPÖ generally
approves, but criticises "degenerate" forms of it. By its organisational structure, social partnership is integrative in effect,
whereas the political parliamentary system depends on identifying
and hence emphasizing differences.

After the Verfassungsgerichtshof (constitutional high court)
had forbidden as unconstitutional the setting up of an economic
directorate to institutionalise the co-operation which had meanwhile
developed, the Paritätische Kommission für Lohn- und Preisfragen
(Joint Commission for Wage and Price Questions) was set up as a substitute in 1957. A special feature must be noted here already:
there was no actual "act of foundation" or other legislative decision
(such as for example the Stability and Growth Act for "Concerted Action" in Germany), but simply an exchange of letters between the
then Federal Chancellor and de facto representative of the Federal
Chamber of Commerce, Trade and Industry (Bundeskammer der gewerblichen Wirtschaft) Julius Raab and the then Chairman of the Austrian
Trade Union Federation Johann Böhm. In addition to the exchange of
letters there is also as a matter of fact a Council of Ministers'
decision which is similar in content. The Joint Commission, one of
the most important institutions in Austria, not only has no statutory

29

basis but is not even referred to in any Austrian law. References
are made to the four economic partner organisations responsible for
running it - the Federal Chamber of Commerce, Trade and Industry,
the Chairman's Conference of Austrian Chambers of Agriculture, the
Austrian Chambers of Labour Conference and the Austrian Trade Union
Federation, Österreichischen Gewerkschaftsbund, ÖGB. When it comes
to sanctions for the non-observance of procedures before the Joint
Commission, reference can only be made to the declarations of the
four organisations.

b) Necessary conditions

    What "fundamental consensus"(2) exists in fact as a basis pre-
disposing the partners to engage in pragmatic negotiations to settle
their differences? In Austria - as in all Western countries - there
is no consistent system for an integrated social policy. The party
programmes are not much help. They do not seem to have much significance for the practical side of social partnership. This can be
illustrated by the declarations of position in regard to the market
economy.
    Austria has "a mixed-economy system with market-economy condi-
tions"(5) with important government and social regulations. The
economic processes are mainly guided by markets, and government economic policy interventions still leave sufficient substance and room
for market-economy behaviour.
    In the Salzburger Programme the ÖVP declares its faith in the
social market economy. From the point of view of what we are now
discussing that presents no problems. But the SPÖ programme makes
the well-known socialist criticism of the capitalist economic system,
which is blamed for all the problems of the industrial society and
all international difficulties. The programme calls for the reform
of decision-making and property relationships. The chapter entitled
"Towards a human economy"(20) contains the following propositions
which are of importance for what we are now discussing:

    - The efficient production of desired goods and services
      can only be guaranteed if the economic process is demo-
      cratically determined by a planned society.
    - A change in conditions of ownership does not necessarily
      mean a change in the direction of democratic socialism.
    - Failures of the market economy do not necessarily always
      have to be corrected after the event; production and
      investment decisions need not necessarily depend solely
      on profit considerations; the market is not a value in
      itself, it is only one method of organisation among
      others for running the economy.

- The alternatives are: economic crises which destroy
  freedom and lay waste whole regions, or a democratically
  planned society.

It might be expected that this rejection of the market economy
would adversely affect co-operation in an essentially market economy
system. If two partners (to put the question thus simply for the
moment) start out with such opposed views of the system, it might be
supposed that co-operation between them would encounter many more
difficulties than is in fact the case. The reality is in any case
different. The intellectual superstructure seems at any rate in
particular fields to have freed itself from the economic base. This
seems also to be true for tendencies usually attributed to the ÖVP,
as reflected in the statement by catholic social theoreticians
suggesting "the development of a decentralised democratic economic
system with framework-planning elements"(5). In fact, practical
considerations gain the upper hand.

It is therefore only logical that there should be no jointly
formulated theory of social partnership, but only programme statements on concrete points. There is little probability of a revolutionary outbreak when all those in positions of political responsibility in a system based on voluntary support concentrate on finding
peaceful solutions to concrete differences. This general attitude
of a moderate, pluralistic exercise of power, the belief that what
is needed is an appropriate, normal rate of growth of the economy
and above all a high level of employment(2), practically excludes
any rejection of the market economy which is the basis of present-
day prosperity. And this means that the requisite conditions for
the smooth functioning of the market economy must not be jeopardised.

The achievements of the Austrian economy are due in no small
measure to the fact that there have neither been nor are there now
any distribution disputes associated with labour troubles. The criticism of sociologists that the structure of the incomes pyramid has
hardly changed ("Report on Inequalities")(21) is clearly not a spur
to action. The responsible people in both camps attribute great
importance for example to the fact that even this year a moderate
wages policy in line with trends in the economy is being pursued.

Since 1950 there have been many periods when income differentials have lessened or widened, but also many when they have simply
developed in parallel. Since 1972 it is believed that there has
been some increase in inequality, although one would rather have expected the opposite under a SPÖ government. Viewed long term, the
incomes pyramid has however been very stable. It is in fact very
doubtful whether there is a majority in favour of a levelling of
incomes. When "we want more" is what everyone says, changes in
relative levels are difficult to make. They only occur when the

underlying factors, in particular supply and demand on the labour market, have changed significantly, and even then they occur only slowly. Dirigiste interventions provoke active or passive resistance from those concerned and cause frictional losses.

The desire to avoid disturbances is very widespread in Austria, however. This perhaps explains the scant interest of the negotiators in the income structure and redistributive processes, although statistical material for better information is available. More attention is paid to keeping the system in good working order and ensuring economic growth than to trying to bring about an "equitable income structure", which is difficult to define, by means of interventions which jeopardise the economy. Economic growth is regarded as a top priority because it is a necessary condition for full employment, but also for successfully accomplishing social tasks. This approach is accepted without argument in both camps. This shows that considerable progress has been made towards a convergence of views. Apparently, more than two decades of responsible working together have produced an agreed assessment of economic interrelationships which is rarely brought into question any more, even if it is perhaps not so openly admitted. It is nonetheless astonishing when representatives of the labour side say that they are in favour of a hard currency, stable prices and, as an important instrument for achieving these, low wage increases.

Participation in power has not come without participation in responsibility. When asked what would happen if there was a serious economic setback with perhaps even economic retrenchment giving rise to higher unemployment, only one of our partners in the discussions considered that that would jeopardise social partnership, all the others taking the view that that would be just the time really to put social partnership into practice.

For social partnership, economic growth is both an end and a means; an end because both camps want increased prosperity, a means because without prosperity the support of the rank and file would be endangered. Social partnership - like many another political system - is condemned to succeed. Its success must be measured mainly in economic terms, even though it has considerable social consequences.

c) The twofold parity of representation

A further peculiarity of the Austrian system is perhaps the fact that most texts do not refer to "members" of the Joint (paritätische) Commission, but simply say that in the Commission there are regular "meetings" between the members of the federal government and the chief officials of the four big economic organisations. This, too, shows that under social partnership what matters

most are the factual aspects of a process, only limited regard being
had for formal, institutional aspects. The basis on which social
partnership is practised is clearly the already mentioned fundamental consensus in favour of a moderate collaborative approach to resolving conflict and exercising power. In such a system what is
important is that the power groups involved are prepared to work
together, that their representatives are empowered to reach decisions, and that those decisions - even if only to preserve the prestige of the representatives - are almost invariably respected. This
has so far always been possible in Austria.

The success of the system does not depend only on co-operation
between the top officials of the economic associations. A further
very important element is the practice of so-called "twofold parity"
(doppelte Parität). The top officials involved in social partnership are usually also members of Parliament (the Nationalrat) and
functionaries in their own parties. Formally, neither the political
parties nor Parliament have any role in social partnership; but
because of the dual or multiple roles of the individuals concerned
(Personalunion) they are in fact constantly involved. This is
true, although to a lesser extent, even for members of the executive
branch, at least as far as the Länder governments are concerned, in
which social partnership functionaries have posts. Here, instead
of a separation of powers principle, we have what might perhaps be
called a personal interlocking of powers principle. Is this a revival of a person-related government power as in former times,
instead of the functional, institution-based structure of the modern
state? It must at once be admitted that the personality of the
office-holder plays an importznt part in both systems. The peculiarity of the Austrian system is that two levels of institution,
namely state and society, are represented in one and the same person.

It is precisely this interlocking which seems to be important
for the political balance. The twofold parity exists between employers and workers who are each closely involved in one or other of the
two large parties. Because of the Fraktionsystem (sub-groups based
on membership of one or other of the political parties) in the social
organisations, the more or less bourgeois Austrian People's Party is
predominant in the Federal Chamber of Trade and Industry and Chairmen's Conference of Chambers of Agriculture, and the Austrian Socialist Party in the Chambers of Labour Conference and the Austrian Trade
Union Federation. The same balance could also be found among the
representatives of the executive during the period of the Great Coalition. When in 1966 the People's Party formed a one-party government, the parity principle was available for use. It was therefore
quite logical, from the social partnership point of view, that the
then Federal Chancellor Klaus abstained on behalf of the government
members from using their vote in the Joint Commission. In 1970, the

Socialist Party in its turn formed a one-party government, and Federal Chancellor Dr. Kreisky, with equal logic, observed the same rule.

Academic experts(22) say however that this carefully balanced parity might be upset by the emergence of additional organisations and political forces. That is not necessarily true. Social partnership works on the unanimity principle. Neither a group nor an individual exponent can be overriden by a majority vote. All Austrian experts on social partnership, however, stress the great importance for the functioning of the system of the long-lasting personal contacts between the leading personalities. These personal contacts produce a high degree of intimacy and hence avoidance of publicity which can go as far as the holding back of data. Practical considerations are much more important than formal obligations. The government and the social partners have in all less than 20 persons representing them on the Joint Commission; newcomers are rare; they have known each other for years.

This field of relationships would be upset by the entry of additional organisations. It is however conceivable that any opening up of the exclusive social partnership club would leave it almost defenceless against an endless stream of new membership demands. Experience with "Concerted Action" in Germany, which began in 1967 with a group that was hardly any bigger, but numbered almost 80 at its meeting in July 1977, shows the difficulties that can arise once exclusivity is relaxed.

The procedure social partnership has to use makes it decidedly conservative. Once unanimity has begun to emerge, it must be preserved. Changes are only possible if the balance is preserved, and that is a complicated process, since everyone must always agree. Interestingly enough, this system in Austria has certainly not ruled out the possibility of reforms. Examples like the reduction in the working week, or the Labour Constitution Law with its first steps towards co-determination, are proof of the contrary. All changes were brought about in a consensus which respected the interests of those represented. This means that the social partnership élites, in spite of the high degree of independence they enjoy mainly as a result of the confidentiality accompanying the decision-making process, cannot simply forget their rank and file when they negotiate. Nevertheless, the system of non-publicity, as opposed to the publicity principle applied in parliamentary matters, makes it easier for them to take unpopular decisions, or at least to refrain from making sacrifices to popularity ("wooing the electorate").

d) The outsiders

Only the four large groups are allowed to take part in formal
social partnership activities: excluded are all the smaller "Chamber" organisations and many free associations. Even such an important organisation as the Vereinigung Österreichischer Industrieller
(Association of Austrian Industrialists) participates only indirectly, insofar as its officials also hold posts in the Federal Chamber
for Trade and Industry. Any of the small groups a majority of whose
members sympathise with one or other of the two big political parties
can also of course feel that they have some sort of representation.

There is a special problem in the case of the workers' organisation of the Austrian People's Party - the Österreichisches Arbeiter-
und Angestelltenbund (Blue-collar and White-collar Workers' Federation). Although the ÖAA Federation contains the biggest single
block of People's Party voters - over 50 per cent of People's Party
voters are workers - it is only weakly represented in social partnership. In the Advisory Council for Economic and Social Questions, the
third Committee of the Joint Commission (see below, section B), one
of the three representatives of the Chamber of Commerce, Trade and
Industry is from the Association of Industrialists, and one of the
three representatives of the Chambers of Labour is from the ÖAAB.
But the position of the ÖAAB representative is particularly difficult
because he has not got at his disposal any apparatus which deals on
a continuous basis with the internal affairs of the Joint Commission.
In the Chambers of Labour there are Socialist Party majorities which,
because of the multi-level system of election, completely dominate
the Chambers of Labour Conference, although about a quarter of the
workers vote for the People's Party. Participation in the Advisory
Council also means participating in a number of other negotiations,
e.g. on social legislation. Furthermore, the Association of Industrialists is also represented on other advisory councils, such as
the one on labour market policies, so that its participation rights
are in practice greater than would at first appear to be the case.

The position is still worse for the FPÖ, the Austrian Freiheitliche Partei. It is not in a decisive position in any of the large
associations. The FPÖ recognises social partnership to be a successful instrument for preserving good industrial relations, but is
naturally particularly critical of its incomplete democratic legitimation. This is especially true of economic representation. According to the FPÖ the Chamber of Commerce, Trade and Industry represents only 70 per cent of the economic groups. Since in addition
under the dual parity system large areas are also dominated by one
or other of the two big parties, the minorities are gravely disadvantaged at all levels up to and including the allocation of leading
positions. The FPÖ is thus not recognised as an independent group

in the Austrian Trade Union Federation because of the high quorum requirements, even though it is represented on the Federation's management committee and is treated in fact like a Fraktion (political party group).

The disadvantageous position of the small groups is the inevitable result of the basic conditions for social partnership. Collaboration on such personal terms can succeed only if numbers are restricted. Social partnership is by no means an economic and social council, a "second parliament" with parliamentary representation and parliamentary rules of the game. In this context a small opposition finds it difficult to make itself heard, to say nothing of "tipping the balance". Social partnership, in an era when we are governed by anonymous mammoth organisations, is a highly successful throwback to an earlier age when personalities mattered.

The question of the outsiders does not only arise in formal terms. We have to ask ourselves whether under the social partnership system it is at all possible to come to grips with the problems of unrepresented groups. A test case for this could be the so-called "new social questions" now being discussed in Germany. In the extensive system of social protection in Austria there are also gaps, safeguards found to be unsatisfactory by those whom they are intended to protect. Social critics are also talking of a "new poverty" by which they mean not only inadequately covered basic material needs but also social disintegration. In spite of considerable imprecision in the definition it certainly cannot be denied that there are new poverty groups in which the "old poverty" (low income) is combined with the "new poverty" (social disintegration).

The question now is whether under the social partnership system there is a likelihood of initiatives being undertaken to tackle such problems. The majority of the members of the big organisations are themselves hardly affected. The functioning of social partnership depends precisely on the satisfaction of the large majority with their own personal well-being. Such a position would also arise in a similar economic situation even without social partnership. The question boils down to this: are the top officials of the social partners who are less dependent on majorities more capable of taking action which is not politically motivated - on ethical grounds for example - than the top officials of the major political parties? For the moment there is no answer to this question. The politically decisive forces must be aware of the discussions of which the "Report on Inequalities" is a typical example. Measures to improve the social situation are an obvious part of the programme of a welfare state. Whether beyond that it will come to special action being taken, it is not yet possible to say. So far there is not even a sufficiently concrete definition of the problem on the basis of which a programme could be worked out.

e) Social partnership as a problem of constitutional law

Under constitutional law social partnership must conform to society: it is not a state within a state. Social partnership decisions must either be formalised by the state in laws, or at least be backed up by possible state sanctions before they can be promulgated. Only wage policy is formally an autonomous field (as it is, incidentally, in many countries); collective agreements apply to all workers, including those who do not belong to trade unions. The participants in social partnership thus require the formal co-operation of the state to implement their decisions. Viewed in this way, no objections need be raised against it on constitutional law grounds.

In fact, however, the sovereignty of the state is limited in the field occupied by social partnership. The legislator serves as a formalising instrument of political decisions. It is quite unthinkable that a matter decided by the social partners should be defeated in Parliament or because the government is opposed to it. Social partnership is so powerful a factor in constitutional reality that it would be perfectly in order to ask for it to be given a basis in constitutional law. Social partnership is not merely a source of social legitimation, like for example a concerted action or a tripartite conference. Decisions taken under a concerted action or by a tripartite conference (if there are any such decisions) will not be ignored by the state. A strong government, a self-assured Parliament, can however decide otherwise, even though naturally in any system the state is in certain respects also the formal expression of society, and, like a tree, cannot be independent of its roots. Social partnership is however more than a source of social legitimation. It is already the decision-maker; as has frequently happened in the past, the decisions are already formalised within its organisation. Economic and social laws and regulations are formulated in the two categories of "chambers", processes which in other countries are the responsibility of the ministries or parliamentary committees.

This practice constitutes a serious potential challenge to the democratic state. Here the state is functioning through the mediation of the social groups dealing directly with each other. State and society are almost identical. The constitutional norm is thus largely undermined by constitutional reality. The demand for a constitutional basis for social partnership seems to follow as a natural consequence. Against this it can be argued that social partnership could not, without distorting its present structure(23), be fitted into the decision-making system laid down by the Constitution. The constitutional system is based on the idea of Parliament as the only body empowered to take decisions, and provides very precise control mechanisms to ensure that this is so. Every

action by government bodies must be able to stand the test of justification in law.

If this principle were extended to cover social partnership, then
social partnership would have to abandon its reliance on persons and
transfer its tasks to institutions.

The modern constitutional state (Rechtsstaat) vests the exercise
of authority in the institution, the present holder of an office.
Social partnership also speaks in the name of organisations, i.e.
institutions, but it speaks through their leading personalities.
This is precisely what gives it its great flexibility, and this
would be lost by any formalisation process.

This conflict between legitimacy and flexibility cannot be solved
if the advantages of the system are to be preserved. Institutionalisation would establish a state within the state. Social partnership
would become the third Chamber and probably very soon deprive Parliament of its powers in the field of economic and social policy, but
also perhaps increasingly in other fields. It would seem better not
to push this usurpation of responsibilities further by institutionalisation, but to accept, as Austria does, a position of unstable equilibrium. This is only possible in the long run if the main protag-
onists exercise a high degree of self-restraint. Voluntary restraint
in the exercise of power, consideration for minorities - these must
be, as they have been in the past, essential prerequisites for the
continued functioning of social partnership.

The problem of legitimation naturally arises within the associations too. According to the understanding of Western European democracy, such a strong concentration of power in the hands of a few
leading officials is hardly to be tolerated. But the effectiveness
of the system depends precisely on the ability of the leading personalities to decide on a matter quickly, without having first to
engage in a long and wearing process of persuasion. One has only
to look at areas with highly institutionalised and multi-level decision-making processes to recognise the considerable disadvantages
of far-reaching democratic formalisation compared with a personal-
ised decision-making procedure. Not only do the processes go on for
years without end, they often break down altogether in a stalemate
of irreconcilable views. Complicated economic and social problems,
which can often be understood only by specialists, must ultimately
in any case be decided by those specialists, even if the formal political decision and responsibility are taken by politicians. The
more complex the matters to be decided, the more important the self-
control of the leading groups who, under the Austrian system of
social partnership have to take the decisions.

In Austria's case it is argued that within the various camps
there is a remarkable loyalty between the leadership and the rank
and file. This is obviously in large part due to the small size of

the country, which facilitates personal contacts. The importance of supervision through public opinion should also not be forgotten. And finally there is certainly in social partnership in Austria a phenomenon which is of great importance for the modern democratic industrial state - the built-in control of officials by officials. This presupposes a high degree of awareness of responsibility and state obligations on the part of officials, who can after all no longer be effectively supervised from outside. The checks and balances of the democratic state need to be extended to the realm of the experts. Like all control procedures, this would not be cheap, but the costs of an evenly balanced decision-finding procedure are perhaps less than the costs of an uncontrolled monopoly of power whose mistakes in decision-making invariably only become obvious at a very late, sometimes already catastrophic stage.

In connection with the social partnership system another problem must be mentioned. In the modern **industrial** state there is a growing tendency, perhaps as a result of the possibilities offered by information techniques, for decisions to be taken at the top. Instead of decisions being delegated from the top downwards, decisions are increasingly being left to those at the top. This leads almost inevitably to overwork and excessive strain on people in leading positions. Admittedly social partnership, with the Joint Commission and its committees, is also a centralistic institution, but it does make it possible virtually to finalise in the pre-parliamentary stage one area of governmental responsibility and decision-making. Alongside the concentration of power at the top of a modern state it provides a second centre of power which can be useful as a democratic counterweight.

B. REPERCUSSIONS OF THE SYSTEM IN CERTAIN FIELDS

a) Economics

The generally favourable attitude to the market economy has already been dealt with briefly in Part I. The question now arises as to how competition - one of the basic elements of the market economy - can be combined with a system of deliberate convergence inspired by the interests of the economy as a whole. The participants in this system are, on each side of the table, representatives of certain economic interests. Does this not give rise to serious conflicts between individual interests and the general interest, both of which have to be borne in mind simultaneously? Clearly these conflicts are resolved without obvious damage in the process of social partnership, but it is not possible to say whether the results obtained in each case correspond to an optimal allocation of resources.

Institutionally speaking, in any case, the shifting of final decision-making on to the shoulders of the big organisations is a useful thing. They are thereby compelled to consider not only the interests they represent but also the mutually conflicting interests within their own organisation. Almost inevitably they must confine themselves to general considerations, so that dirigiste interferences with the detailed working of market process remain limited to few fields and cases. They must endeavour to arrive at tolerable compromises. Such compromises between opposing interests are not necessarily always in the general interest. It is perfectly possible to agree to exploit a majority interest, for example employers and labour in the same industry at the expense of the consumers. The temptation to do this will be all the greater the more the producers find themselves in a favourable market position, or have a monopoly of supply, as is the case for the railways or the post office, or the nationalised banking system in Austria. It depends therefore very much whether and to what extent the decision-making functionaries are themselves actuated by a general responsibility vis-à-vis the community and bear in mind - and are able to bear in mind - the general interest in taking such decisions. Presumably such decisions are made easier by the fact that, for example, the rejection of proposals to the Federal Chamber of Trade and Industry does not have to be justified, and that the way in which decisions are reached is not revealed to the public.

This would incidentally seem to be a further reason for not laying down hard and fast rules for social partnership. The bureaucratic dirigisme which is one of its characteristics cannot function without considerable freedom of discretion. In complicated economic processes such as wage and price formation or resource allocation, the desire for democratic control comes up against the limits of practical feasibility, as does the proposed direction and control of enterprise activities on the model of parliamentary or even plebiscitary democracy - in the name of economic democracy. Wherever direct control has to be used instead of indirect control by price - and the enterprise is a classic example of this - the same problems seem to arise.

The relatively large measure of freedom in economic policy decision-making is perhaps one reason - certainly not the only one - why it was possible very early on, i.e. in 1974, to make a start on countercyclical financial, economic and employment policies to combat the growing depression. Large budget and foreign payments deficits were accepted in order to endanger as little as possible the central goal of full employment. This policy was adopted, and has so far been maintained, with the aim of tiding over a crisis period until a new self-sustaining recovery occurs. It has, as already mentioned, led to large deficits and could therefore, in spite of

40

the improvement in the foreign payments balance in 1978 (with a still considerable but much reduced deficit on current payments), get into trouble if the hoped-for sustained, vigorous recovery does not occur. An adjustment crisis would then ensue which could well be the severest test social partnership has ever had to face.

These considerations prompt the question as to whether in the long run the costs of settling conflicts are not too high under the social partnership system. Of course, the economic advantages of assured industrial peace must be set off against the economic disadvantages of an allocation of resources which is not fully rational on economic grounds. A certain slowdown in growth can be observed. The necessary adjustment to changing markets is taking place slowly; this is the result of the pressure exerted in the name of full employment to postpone until very late, if not indefinitely, dismissing redundant labour. The "right to a job" as a political, if not yet legal, demand is holding back adjustment measures, especially if they involve closures.

The repercussions on investment behaviour (and hence in the long run on employment policy) are difficult to assess. Yields on shares are not very encouraging, additions to capital and new issues are not satisfactory, although there is a bewildering variety of reliefs and allowances for enterprises. It was interesting to note that representatives of the non-private sector spoke of the extraordinary zest for innovation of foreign enterprises. Does this mean that a vacant space in the economy is gradually emerging which will attract more foreign firms? It must also be remembered that in the state-run sector of the economy, profitability suffers because in the name of full employment personnel who were laid off in other sectors of the economy have been taken on, and naturally dismissals on rationalisation grounds rarely occur in the state-run sector. And in the opinion of people we spoke to on the workers' side the very far-reaching promotion of almost risk-free saving (short-term funds, real estate) is affecting people's readiness to invest in risk capital.

b) Employment policy

Repeated reference has been made to the importance of full employment for the whole social system of Austria. This behaviour, bearing the imprint of the nationalised and other non-private sectors of the economy, like a sort of unwritten law, has clearly had repercussions on all sectors of the economy. This is the only way to explain how a behaviour not determined by the market - indeed running counter to it - can be practised. Group dismissals cannot be justified vis-à-vis public opinion. The only thing to do is to try to carry on, and hoard labour in enterprises.

The connection between productivity improvements, growth and employment is in Austria generally the same as in other countries. The deliberate policy of keeping on the workforce naturally holds back productivity increases: technical progress overall is somewhat slowed down. This perhaps also explains why, in Austria, for a comparatively low expenditure on employment-creating measures - in relative terms it is roughly of the order of 1/3 of the expenditure in Germany - a bigger employment effect is achieved. There are also a number of special factors:

- Since the recession there has been a catching-up effect in the services sector. In the boom years the public administration showed considerable restraint and was now able to catch up at the expense of the public finances; there was a margin of slack for countercyclical employment policy, which has in the meantime in any case been taken up.
- A wages policy aligned on what the economy could bear enlarged the employment-effective margin for deficit financing. The employment effect per unit of deficit financing was consequently increased. Besides a "reallocation of labour" there was a reallocation of wage increases.
- This also made room for bigger reductions in working hours.
- The numbers of foreign workers were also quietly reduced. Priority, sanctioned by law, is given to the employment of Austrian workers, without there being much need in fact to push out foreigners. In this respect, because of the employment structure, there is unlikely to be any large cushion left for the future.
- Finally, on general policy grounds, structural changes have been slowed down. In this regard, as with the hoarding of labour, the question arises as to how long such a policy can be pursued. In view of the importance of foreign trade to Austria's economy, these policies could cause serious problems in the future.

If a reorientation in the direction of speedier structural adjustment were to become necessary, this could give rise to serious conflict for social partnership - as was already pointed out in the previous section - because the basis for co-operation would be affected. It would no longer be a question of agreeing on measures to maintain full employment at almost any price. If the costs could no longer be borne, then for a time the political burden of higher adjustment unemployment would have to be borne jointly. In such a period the workers' organisations would be the first to bear the brunt, but ultimately all the political organisations would feel the strain. It is possible that the present lower unemployment due to delayed structural adjustment will have to be paid for in the future by correspondingly higher unemployment. Full employment by means of hoarding cannot be maintained in the long run.

Insofar as this diagnosis is correct, it might be necessary, while maintaining the goal of full employment, to initiate partial adjustment measures, even if frictional problems could not be fully avoided, and so achieve with less drastic disturbances a level of employment appropriate to future structures. It would be the responsibility of labour market policy to help in such an adjustment.

This would mean making difficult choices between present and future burdens.

c) Wages policy

Much has already been said about wages policy. There are only one or two additional things to be said on this subject here. The main point is that the two parties in wage questions obviously take it for granted, as it were, that they must respect underlying conditions in the economy. Social partnership has triggered off a successful process in the direction of economic reasonableness. In doing this the close links existing on both sides of the negotiating table between the specialist sections of the employers' Chambers of Commerce, Trade and Industry, and agriculture and the industrial unions on the one hand and their respective top federal organisations (Spitzenorganisationen) on the other, presumably play an important role. The consensus in top level discussions as to what is at any given time economically reasonable filters down as guidelines for current concrete negotiations. No one in Austria can avoid the call to contribute to full employment by pursuing a moderate wages policy. That is the necessary corollary to an employment policy by enterprises which exceeds their immediate economic requirements. A further requirement is the acceptance of regional wage differentials (e.g. the decline from West to East) - because they are regarded as something which cannot be changed - so that regional unemployment brought about by general minimum wage levels remains limited.

The wages sub-committee of the Joint Commission in practice limits itself to influencing the timetable for wage negotiations. The proposals for increasing wages and salaries in collective agreements, and for changing framework or umbrella collective agreements, put forward by the Austrian Trade Union Federation on behalf of its constituent industrial unions, must be passed down by the wages sub-committee for free negotiation. In certain cases the sub-committee can decide to allow only an exploratory testing of the ground between the responsible specialist organisations of both sides with a report

to the sub-committee. The time-lag thus imposed can have a certain
moderating effect and can also influence the timing of individual
decisions. This procedure cannot however be described as a control
of wage policy. The parties to the wage negotiations remain autonomous in deciding wage rates and working conditions. This method is
not even a practical application of moral persuasion in wage policy,
as might perhaps have been said of the wage guideline data of the
early years of "concerted action" in Germany (e.g. 1967, 1968). In
this respect, too, therefore, orientation remains largely indirect,
and reliance is placed on the responsible behaviour of the negotiating partners.

d) Prices policy

The prices sub-committee of the Joint Commission deals with the
prices of goods and services produced by the member firms of the
Federal Chamber for Trade and Industry. Its actual influence on
price trends is therefore limited. Almost a quarter of all consumption expenditure is spent on goods and services which in one form
or another come under official price regulation; a third is spent
on goods and services whose prices are dealt with by the sub-
committee(2). Not subject to control are imported goods and goods
subject to rapid fashion and technical changes, and also most services. Experience has shown that the astonishing variety of goods
and services supplied in a market economy cannot be brought under
bureaucratic coverage and control. It is still perhaps of symboli-
cal significance that for example the prices charged by two Viennese
firms which are important suppliers of works canteens are subject to
the procedures of the prices sub-committee. In any case the decisions of the prices sub-committee cannot be simply ignored. Public
authority contractors only recognise price increases which have been
acknowledged by the Joint Commission. Given the large relative size
of the public sector, this undoubtedly has some disciplinary effect.
A very important factor is the constantly renewed decision that retail percentage markups must not be changed. The question arises
as to whether it is right to fix for all time retail margins which
applied at a given time in the past. Naturally such fixed margins
constitute a vested interest. They are therefore attacked from the
workers' side, and with similar logic the Federal Chamber for Trade
and Industry, under the influence of the large number of retailers,
has so far rejected any change. From the economic viewpoint there
is perhaps here a certain analogy with minimum wages. Just as minimum wages can be a cause of unemployment, so guaranteed margins can
be a cause of misallocation of resources and hold back rationalisation. On the other hand, price controls are in the final analysis
just as lacking in stringency as the fixing of wage rates. The

44

prescribed prices are maximum prices: they can be underbid. And
there is also plenty of opportunity to take evasive action and con-
ceal price increases by changes in quality or in the product. It
would seem that the arsenal of price supervision in partial sectors
of the Austrian economy, a supervision carried out with very modest
machinery (in the Federation of Trade Unions only two persons),
amounts overall more to moral persuasion than to actual control. Its
importance may perhaps in the final analysis also reside in the fact
that a wages policy which is based on respect for general economic
conditions needs a political counterweight in the form of some element of price policy.

e) General effect on economic and social questions

For the economic and social policy aspects of integrated social
policy, the third social partnership institution, the Advisory Council for Economic and Social Questions, is probably of greater importance in spite of - or perhaps just because of - its much less precise mandate. The Advisory Council has neither a permanent headquarters, nor an established secretarial staff, nor a budget of its
own. Its affairs are run by two general secretaries lent by the
Federal Chamber of Commerce, Trade and Industry and the Chambers of
Labour to do this work in addition to their normal duties in their
own institutions. The Advisory Council is composed of three representatives each from the four big organisations on the Joint Commission, one of the three from the Federal Chamber of Commerce, Trade
and Industry being a representative of the Austrian Industrialists'
Association, and one of the three from the Chambers of Labour being
a representative of the Austrian Blue Collar and White Collar Workers'
Federation (ÖAAB), the workers' wing of the Austrian People's Party.
The Chairmanship of the Advisory Council rotates every six months
among the constituent institutions. Finally, the head of the Austrian Institute for Economic Research attends all meetings as a permanent expert. The reports are usually drawn up by working parties
on which experts from areas outside the big four economic organisations are also co-opted. This membership gives an interesting combination of committed and independent expertise, and there are also
present two important institutions not represented in the other two
Joint Commission bodies.

The Advisory Council's studies are held in high regard, probably
precisely because they are the result of co-operation between independent experts and experts with political connections. They are
saved by this from the fate of many free-ranging reports by completely independent experts, namely to hit the headlines, but to
have no impact on policies. There is always a good prospect that
the Advisory Council's studies will be translated into political

practice since they are backed up not only by expert opinion but also by the influence of the top officials of the big organised interest groupings. Many of these studies have had considerable influence on Austrian financial, economic and social policies.

All this is rounded off by the comprehensive participation of the employers' and workers' organisations in all aspects of economic and social policy up to and including the formulation and implementation of legislation. The Chambers of Industry and Labour thus have the right to submit systematic commentaries on government bills before they are laid before Parliament. This can go so far that the first drafts of bills are worked out not in the ministries but in the offices of the big four organisations. In the execution of many laws, before making up his mind, the minister concerned must hear the advisory bodies of which the chambers are members. The de facto involvement of the social partners in ministerial responsibility is thus largely ensured.

C. SOCIAL PARTNERSHIP AS INTEGRATED SOCIAL POLICY?

As in all countries there is in Austria no formulated concept of integrated social policy, but only a process, set in motion at considerable expense, towards a more conscious integration. But it is impossible to say whether this aim is actually being achieved, since the profusion of contributions made so far do not add up to an internally cohesive system, and no concept which would ensure such a synthesis has so far emerged.

It would however be wrong to say that an integrated social policy, which is what we were supposed to examine, simply does not exist. After all, integration takes place wherever people live together in an ordered state or social community. Even without a comprehensive systematising concept, institutions and people must constantly adjust their behaviour to each other, and find ways of balancing conflicts and interests. Individual cases of integration are therefore constantly occurring.

The problem of a complex society is however that these individual adjustment cases are not always compatible with each other. Decisions are taken in ignorance of other decisions, or without due consideration of them. It thus happens that the results of official transfer policies are often the opposite of those intended. The oft-quoted "Report on Inequalities" seems to confirm that this is so. The undoubtedly beneficial pragmatism of Austrian policies in government and associations can go so far, but no further. As guiding "concept" there are really only general declarations of the intention to preserve social peace, and only one goal with anything approaching a clear definition, namely full employment. Whether the intention declared by the overwhelming majority of organised social forces of reducing the inequality that has been diagnosed really amounts to a concrete political goal cannot be discerned from what has happened so far. And finally the goal of achieving greater prosperity through economic growth is at the present time a fairly generally supported goal. Nevertheless it is a goal which calls for concrete action. But in Austria there is no economic planning and equally no social planning. Concrete individual goals are declared, worked towards and often indeed achieved, but there is no system for integrating those goals. Even the "Report on Inequalities" is no more than a lengthy catalogue of critical observations; it does not reveal any underlying system held together by its own internal logic.

The question as to whether a system which depends so much on pragmatic negotiation can continue to be practised indefinitely remains open. Can one be certain that the basic consensus in favour of a moderate, and largely pluralistic exercise of power aimed at preserving social peace will always give rise to an unformulated and, since it does not exist concretely, quite unformulable concept of integrated social policy? The undeniable fact that this is what has happened in the past is no guarantee for the future. A growing discussion concerning social interrelationships, and not least the programme we are now engaged in, are grounds for supposing that on this question a new policy awareness could develop.

What role could social partnership play in this? What role must it play? Could there be the re-parliamentarisation which Pelinka(24) considers possible and hence a qualitative change in social partnership? The answers to these questions can only be speculative. Social partnership itself, which is not only aimed at social peace, but also depends for its existence on a situation of social peace, could lose its ability to function if conflicts between the two groupings, but also within those groupings, were to accentuate. It is therefore in the interests of the social partners not to brush aside conflicts which arise, but to face up to them. If they do not do that, then effective decision-making powers will inevitably drift away elsewhere. Since a basic democracy à la Zwentendorf(25) can only be an episode, never a system, in an industrial state, this would in fact set the re-parliamentarisation process going. The social partners should therefore also get to grips with the question of the system, including the question of greater participation for those who have so far been almost entirely excluded.

The point made by Pelinka(24) that, in the opinion of the insiders in social partnership, the Advisory Council for Economic and Social Questions - a particularly important body in the search for solutions to such problems - has declined in importance since 1966, does not mean that it cannot be re-activated. Such a renewal could involve not only better participation of those who have so far not been allowed to participate but also an inner reform of the system in the sense of stronger links with government decision-making centres. It is in any case hardly conceivable that after a generation of steadily improving co-operation between the social partners, the working out of a concept of social integration would be linked with a simultaneous drastic shift in emphasis towards the parliamentary system.

It is true that democracy depends on competition - one can even say conflict - between the groups. The balance of power grows out of the opposition of interests. But it is also true that the amount of conflict our increasingly complex industrial societies can cope with is steadily decreasing. Their sensitive mechanisms work best when conflict is least. It only requires occasional disturbances for great damage to be done. The satisfaction of the citizen is therefore not only the state philosophy of the Second Republic in Austria(24) but also a pre-requisite for the harmony needed by every industrial state.

It is not simply by chance therefore that the developed industrial states have extensive systems for resolving conflicts. One field in which success in the resolution of conflict still varies very much from country to country, the field of wages policy, is in Austria - thanks precisely to social partnership - very well managed, although the obligation imposed on employers to continue to pay their workers' wages even during lock-outs raises doubts as to whether equality of armament between the two sides still exists. The "right" of the stronger is however in Austria very extensively rationalised. Such a style of wage settlement is only possible in a system that is something more than "only another way of expressing class conflicts"(22). Social partnership is nevertheless based on a dualism of that kind; it is a two-pillar system(24), which with much oversimplification can be looked on as a two-class system. And it probably works precisely because of this oversimplification which ignores the pluralistic reality. On the other hand it is equally certainly something more than simply "an attempt to consider the struggle about income trends as a limited conflict", as Josef Taus once put it.

What can be done, therefore, to cope with the reality of a constantly changing society? Does not social partnership which has proved so flexible up to now, offer the possibility of coping with the task of integration by developing further the symbiosis between the two decision-making centres of state-and-parliament and social partnership, at the same time ensuring a closer involvement of new forces in a pluralistic approach?

The open situation of the present time compels us to conclude this section without attempting answers to that question, and indeed to the many other detailed questions which need not be repeated here. It is not for the observer from outside to formulate and propose concrete reforms. We believe that the Austrian system is capable of reform, and we are confident therefore that the necessary steps will be taken.

D. CONCLUSIONS

Social partnership in Austria thus appears to be a system operated by the large economic groupings which on the whole works well, and which has so far always achieved its declared aims of industrial harmony, full employment and an appropriate measure of economic growth and the consequent improved living standards. Any significant change in the system cannot therefore be recommended.

In the concept of integrated social policy, social partnership is seen to be an inductive system which, by practising the principle of agreement (Konkordanz) in the fields of economics and social insurance, has achieved integration without there being any commonly accepted and formulated concept of integration. Integration is evidently - and the Austrian example proves it - possible even without such a concept. Whether this pragmatic approach is viable in the long run, without at least a simultaneous attempt to evolve a concept of integrated policy, would however seem to be doubtful. The discussion which this programme has aroused in Austria should therefore be continued within the social partnership institutions.

No solution seems to have been found concerning the participation of groups which have so far been excluded. It would seem necessary to look for ways of increasing their involvement. In the recent past it has become clear that the feeling of noteworthy groups that they are not represented can lead to spontaneous campaigns of significant political importance. Since any extension of membership of the social partnership "club" is not possible if co-operation is to remain a practical possibility, efforts might be made to ensure greater involvement of unrepresented interest groups in advisory councils or similar bodies which can be regarded as intermediate stages in the decision-making process.

Much closer attention needs to be paid to the problem of indefinitely postponed structural changes since this is an area in which dangerous potential conflict material could build up for the future. In co-operation with the social partners it ought to be possible not only to make a realistic analysis but to agree on possible unpopular courses of action. Experience justifies the exception that it should

be possible in the framework of social partnership to achieve a
limited change of course of this kind.

Social partnership also presents a problem for constitutional
policy. Social partnership must faithfully reflect the society in
which it exists and, in any case, is formally not a state within
the State. Its decisions must be formalised by the State through
legislation and to be implemented must at least have the government's approval in the background. In actual fact, however, the
sovereignty of the State in the economic and social area occupied
by the social partnership system is limited. It is, for example,
quite unthinkable that a matter decided on by the social partners
should be rejected by Parliament or through opposition from the
government. Not only is social partnership itself the decision-
maker, but its institutions themselves formulate the laws and ordi-
nances. It is tempting to demand, therefore, that social partnership should also be given an explicit basis in constitutional law.
Against that it can be argued that social partnership could not be
brought into line with the decison-making process as provided for
in constitutional law without distorting its present structure,
which depends on co-operation on a personal basis. This conflict
between legitimacy and flexibility cannot be solved if the advantages of the system are to be maintained. Institutionalisation
would mean creating a state within the State, social partnership
would become a third chamber. It is therefore probably better to
accept the present imprecise balance of power. But that means that
all those involved must continue in future to exercise their powers
with the same high degree of self-restraint that they have shown in
the past.

Part III

CO-ORDINATION AND INTEGRATION OF VARIOUS AREAS
WITH SPECIAL EMPHASIS ON REDISTRIBUTIVE ASPECTS

A. INTRODUCTION

Once the goals of an integrated social policy have been adopted, integration consists in finding the optimal organisation of all the means available to the public authorities in the various areas in order to achieve those goals. The desire to achieve maximum efficiency at the least cost for the community means almost always having to rely on a complex combination of means; integration consists in putting those means to work in as consistent a way as possible. Thus defined, the integration of social policies is an ideal which is not really achieved in any country.

It is when the goals aimed at are medium- or long-term goals that integration is most necessary: the diversity of administrative or institutional powers, and the frequent insufficiency of information, can, in the absence of such integration, lead to inconsistent, sometimes incompatible projects, and at the very least to a waste of public money.

For shorter time-horizons, the inertia of social phenomena is sufficient to reduce the need for integration to a simple co-ordination of short-term policies.

a) Constraints tending to prevent a real integration of social policies in Austria

The attitudes of the social partners in Austria, but also the peculiarities of the Austrian federal Constitution, explain why, in the absence of overall economic and social development planning, there can hardly be integration of social policies except in certain limited fields.

i) The social partners

As has been demonstrated in Parts I and II, the social partners are more concerned with the maintenance of employment in the short term than in participating in reflections on integrated social policies. The successful way in which the Austrian economy has been able to weather the crisis, keeping unemployment down to a particularly low rate (2.1 per cent in 1978) and keeping inflation under control (the annual rate of increase in the consumer price index was of the order of 3.5 per cent at the end of 1978), justifies perhaps the almost exclusive attention which the machinery for concertation between the social partners has paid to problems of regulating the economy.

The widespread awareness that the expansion of the last twenty years has benefited all categories of the population is another explanation - less convincing the closer one looks into it - for the scant attention paid to monetary redistribution or to the redistributive aspects of specific social policies.

ii) The federal Constitution

Austria is a federal state. Its Constitution enumerates the powers of the Federation in a limitative way, and this would make it difficult to introduce any unforeseen central function such as planning:

- the Federation has powers to legislate, and to execute such legislation in the following areas among others: higher education, secondary education, railways, waterways, air transport, federal trunk roads, post-telegraph-telephone, industry and trade, mines, forests, water and watercourse rights, drainage and irrigation, installation of high tension cables for the transport of electricity, the protection of monuments and population censuses;
- the power to legislate belongs to the Federation, whereas the execution of the law is the responsibility of the Länder, for example in matters concerning the habitat;
- the power to legislate belongs to the Federation, whereas the passing of the implementing laws and the execution of those laws belongs to the Länder, in the following fields among others: demographic policy, health and health care establishments, thermal and mineral springs and agrarian reform.

This complicated overlapping of responsibilities would seem to more than justify the institution of a body which could ensure a minimum of consistency between the medium- and long-term projects of those who prepare the laws and those who execute them, but there is in fact no institutional arrangement whereby this can be done. At the most there is since 1971 a ten-year investment programme of the federal government, which lays down, without financial commitment, priority budget directives and the effects they are expected to have on structural development, taking account of a summary fore-cast of the Federation's expenditures and revenues. But this pro-gramme, which was submitted to Parliament, does not seem to have given rise to any real discussion, either among the public authori-ties or with the social partners.

b) Plan for the following sections

In spite of these constraints, however, it is possible to find in Austria concrete cases of integration of social policies for the achievement of particular medium and long-term objectives. Section B gives three examples: the first two concern regional planning and regional development, and the third the campaign against poverty.

Integration results here from the need to employ over a long period various means controlled by different territorial authorities and by several federal ministries.

Apart from these cases which thus appear as exceptions, general practice consists much more usually of a simple co-ordination; it would be difficult to link the themes studied in the other sections of this part of the report to any overall blueprint for the develop-ment of Austrian society.

The following two sections are devoted to the redistributive aspects as regards incomes: Section C examines from a global view-point the primary distribution and redistribution of incomes; Section D presents in more detail the main elements of the redistri-bution system, taxes and compulsory contributions on the one hand, and payments and services distributed by the authorities on the other.

Section E describes the practices, co-ordinated among themselves to varying degrees, employed in the definition and implementation of policies in certain important areas of the development of society: transport, housing, education, health and environment (of which Part IV will give a more detailed analysis).

Section F briefly presents some conclusions and recommendations.

B. SOME EXAMPLES OF AN OVERALL INTEGRATED SOCIAL POLICY APPROACH

Regional planning and development on the one hand and the cam-paign against poverty on the other, are two types of cases in which social integration seems likely to be achieved, even if it was not explicitly sought for as such to begin with. In both cases it is a question of relatively recent attempts; practical achievements have begun to get beyond the stage of intentions, but proof has still not been provided that they will stand up to the wear and tear of time and financial constraints.

a) Regional planning and development

Three examples will be given to show how different areas of policies are integrated in regional planning: the first example covers the whole of the Federation, the second a large region (three Länder in Eastern Austria), and the third a limited geographical area (Aichfeld-Murboden = 120 square kilometres).

i) Regional planning in Austria

A very interesting document, published in several languages by the Austrian Regional Planning Conference (OROK) on the occasion of the 4th European Conference of Ministers Responsible for Regional Planning at Vienna in October 1978, contains much information on the legal bases and organisation of regional planning; it describes the role and activities of the OROK since its creation in 1971.

Regional planning (Raumordnung) as a concept is not recognised in the Austrian Constitution. Consequently no public authority has specific competence in the matter, each public authority being able to plan its activity in the field for which it is responsible. The communes can thus draw up their local plans, and the Länder can adopt development plans without the Federation having to know about them. The compatibility of these plans for any given area is not something which can be taken for granted.

The geographical situation of Austria is very unusual. Stretched out across the heart of Europe, it is crossed en masse, in spite of the alpine character of more than half of its territory, by incessant north-south flows of goods and tourists; its population is very unevenly distributed, and is affected by a strong tendency to drift away from the areas bordering on the Eastern European countries with which her trade flows have shrunk considerably. Austria's capital city, situated very much off-centre, was conceived at the beginning of the century for 4 million inhabitants, but now has only 1.6 million (just over one-fifth of the total population of the Federation). All these reasons, several of which are bound up with the history of the country itself, argue in favour of a unitary approach to regional planning.

The Constitution was amended in 1974 to allow the Federation and Länder to conclude state treaties concerning matters falling within their respective fields of competence. Even before the new provisions, the Federation, Länder and Communes had agreed, in 1971, to set up a permanent joint organisation for co-operation in the regional planning field, the Austrian Regional Planning Conference (OROK) already mentioned. Besides the Federal Chancellor, all the Federal ministers and the elected governors of all the Länder (Landeshauptmänner) are members, plus one representative each from

the Rural Authorities Communes Association (Gemeindebund) and the
Urban Authorities Association (Städtetag). Associated with them,
on a consultative basis, are the Chairmen of the Federal Chamber of
Commerce, Trade and Industry, the Chambers of Labour Conference,
the Trade Union Federation, the Conference of Chairmen of the Chambers of Agriculture and the Association of Industrialists.

Deputies of the Conference members prepare the work and are divided into sub-committees on a permanent basis for dealing with long-
standing subjects, or on an ad hoc basis for dealing with current
regional planning problems.

It is in these institutions that the integration of social development policies finds its broadest expression in Austria. The
first years of operation showed the difficulty of working out a common language and basis for assessing starting situations, extrapo-
lating past trends, particularly in population matters, and the
establishment of overall or sectoral projections. Account had also
to be taken of the decisions already taken by the territorial authorities who had not waited for the setting up of the OROK to draw
up their development programmes, and an attempt made to fit those
decisions into a common perspective.

Procedures for co-ordination were progressively laid down. Technical assistance provided by the Austrian Institute for Regional
Planning should make it possible to establish "planning variants"
for the geographical distribution of jobs, housing and equipment by
homogeneous geographical areas (from 50 to 100,000 inhabitants) in
relation to the transport system and the functional specialisation
of the individual areas (agriculture, industry, tourism, protected
area, etc.).

It does not seem, however, as if the process has yet arrived at
the point where financial arbitration between the federal budget and
the Länder and commune budgets will become necessary.

It is true that the fundamental question of financial equalisation of public revenues between the various territorial public authorities has been explicitly excluded from OROK discussions at the
request of the Länder themselves. Nevertheless, the financial equalisation of public revenues between the Federation, the Länder and
the communes tends to favour the status quo and consolidates acquired
rights, whereas a deliberate policy for regional planning would necessitate other choices to reduce disparities between rich and poor
communes.

The harmonization of the long-term investment projects of the
various public authorities has so far only been discussed in theory
by one of the sub-committees set up by the Committee of Deputies,
which has published preliminary expert studies on this subject. It
also seems significant that the exact title of the sub-committee is
"the possibility of harmonization" and not harmonization itself.

However that may be, a process has been begun, and has already led the officials of the Federation, Länder or communes to reflect with the social partners on the many interactions which can be seen between the various fields of an integrated social policy: employment, housing, transport, training, leisure pursuits, sport, culture, etc., and to be more aware of the need for a common view of a possible future for the Federation as a whole and each of its constituent parts.

The breadth of scope and novelty of the problems with which the OROK is confronted no doubt explain why it has not been possible for the moment to go further with a global approach. Regional planning work relating to smaller areas is in this respect more advanced, even though it too does not seem to have been able to go as far as a complete taking into account of the financial aspects.

ii) Eastern Region Planning Association

The three Länder of Eastern Austria are closely interconnected. Vienna, formerly the capital city of an empire, is situated in Lower Austria. The seat of government of Lower Austria has remained in the city of Vienna. The political majorities of these two Länder – which formed only one land before 1921 – are different. As for Burgenland, which became Austrian in 1921, it has always been a border region. Still predominantly rural, it experienced a very high rate of emigration (particularly to the United States) in the 1930s. The regions near the Eastern frontier, where economic trade flows shrank considerably, were being depopulated at an alarming rate. Early successes were achieved in getting the population to stay put by creating industrial jobs, a systematic policy of commuting, daily and weekly, and developing areas for recreation and secondary residences for the Viennese.

In spite of very great differences in size and wealth, the three Länder reached the conclusion that there were many disadvantages in continuing to draw up separate programmes, without taking account of the possible repercussions of the measures taken by the one on the others. They agreed that on the contrary they had every interest in getting together, in particular in their dealings with the institutions of the Federation, whose headquarters was also in Vienna.

Instituted by a state treaty between the three Länder, the main object of the Association is to carry out joint research and to attempt harmonization with a view to joint planning. Another object is to ensure joint representation of the three Länder vis-à-vis the Federation. The experts come from the three regional planning services (with rotating chairmanship).

The basic conception which led to the setting up of this Association embraces many aspects of an integrated social policy: ageing

56

of the population, imbalances between urban areas and sparsely popu-
lated rural areas, significant additions to the incomes of many farmers through non-farm work, an inadequate network of collective
infrastructures, and so on. It is not surprising, therefore, that
the first measures studied show the beginnings of integration of
policies concerning various aspects of social development. It is a
question in the main of adopting a policy of "decentralised concentration" which makes it possible to reduce the distances travelled
daily along particular routes and around secondary centres (with
30,000 to 50,000 inhabitants) possessing a satisfactory network of
secondary schools, technical schools, cultural, sports and health
institutions, and also involving a minimum of industrial job creation.

The transport network is central to such a policy. A scheme for
rapid short-distance transport serving a large part of the environs
of Vienna is being built up with the participation of the Federal
Ministry for Transport. This has got as far as the implementation
stage, that is to say they are now battling with the financing difficulties. The city of Vienna, unlike the other two Länder, owns
large transport enterprises for which it fixes the tariffs; it also
receives a subsidy from the Federation for its underground railway
system. The inequality of the partners has complicated matters,
especially as regards the sharing of the transport deficit between
the three Länder (and the communes). But procedures have been found
which seem to satisfy those concerned. The objective now is to
achieve a single pricing system allowing people to travel with a
single ticket on various modes of transport in a given area.

A similar problem arises in regard to health, but the three
Länder have not solved it yet. It is relatively easier to agree on
a graded network of health care services, and even to share in the
financing of the building of a new hospital, thanks in the main to
a federal co-operation fund for hospital matters, than subsequently
to decide how to share the operating deficits. This, it seems, is
what is happening in the case of a regional hospital now in course
of construction in Vienna.

The wide powers of the communes - which have been greatly reduced
in number over the last 20 years, mainly by means of mergers between
rural communes - make it easier to adjust the supply of social facilities to the needs of the inhabitants, but the Länder have almost
no means for correcting the financial disparities which continue to
exist between communes. They have to rely for this on the financial
equalisation carried out by the Federation, whereas the communes,
for their part, try to attract jobs by means of fiscal measures
which ultimately reduce their resources.

The following example shows how regional planning applied to a
restricted area has made it possible to overcome such difficulties.

iii) The Aichfeld-Murboden Regional Programme

The Aichfeld-Murboden Region extends over 120 km^2 in Upper
Styria. It has 65,000 inhabitants. It is a region with a very
old mining tradition, since coal had been mined there for more than
300 years. Iron and steel plants had grown up around the mining
activities. There are also paper-pulp and paper mills, the location
of which is explained by the nearby forests. The exhaustion of the
mines and the decline of the other industries caused a severe shortage of jobs for men in the 1960s. Inadequate school facilities,
the very poor quality of the environment (the thermal power station
and the pulp and paper mills), the disadvantageous siting of dwell-
ing houses and factories all helped to accentuate the drifting
away of the population which began during the 1960s. The 17 mayors
of the communes concerned set up an "Association for the Promotion
and Planning of Aichfeld-Murboden" and set about seeing what could
be done.

At the beginning of the 1970s this Association applied for
assistance to the federal government. On the initiative of the
Federal Chancellor a meeting was organised between members of the
federal government and the Land government of Styria, the mayors
of the communes of the region and the heads of the national enterprises concerned and the representatives of the two sides of industry.

Agreement was reached in 1971 on a number of measures: improvement of the transport infrastructure (roads), building of houses,
the setting-up of new technical schools and training centres for
adults. The final decisions were taken in 1972, and the programme
began to operate in 1973: 3,000 new industrial jobs were created,
which resulted in further job creation in the tertiary sector, so
that a total of 4,500 new jobs were created in addition to the
25,000 jobs initially existing.

Finance was provided mainly by the Federation, but as broad a
margin of activity as possible was left to private initiative. A
complete financial balance sheet has apparently never been made.
It is clear, moreover, this programme preceded the setting up of
the OROK, a good illustration of the pragmatic attitude of the
Austrian authorities. The concentration of the effort made on this
area, which shows a very concrete integration of social policies
on the ground, could probably not be repeated in many areas at the
same time, especially in a period of slow growth. Difficult choices
will no doubt be necessary; the financial situation of the country
as a whole probably excludes the possibility of there being many
such examples.

The OROK report quoted mentions a case of the same kind, which
it was decided in 1976 to implement for the former copper mining

region of Mitterberg. The report also mentions - though the programming is not so far-reaching in this case - the existence of co-
operative regional programmes for border areas in the East and South-
Eastern parts of Austria, based on co-ordinated promotion measures
for farming, industry and tourism, and improving the technical,
social and cultural infrastructures.

*

* *

More generally, it would indeed seem that the federal regional
development programme for the "Programmregionen" (programme regions),
like the programmes of the Länder themselves, or of the largest
cities, reflect a real concern to integrate social policies by combining various means relating to the collective services as a whole.

Intervention by the Federation is, however, limited by the
Austrian Constitution itself: each of the various regional planning
and development questions comes under the competence of the particular territorial authority responsible for the regulation of the administrative field concerned.

It is true that the successive modifications made to the Constitution to enable regional planning to take place by combining the
means of the various territorial authorities concerned have made it
possible, in a very empirical way, to reconcile the constraints of
a federal-type organisation with the need for a joint approach. But
it must be pointed out that in the three cases described above, what
was involved was more physical planning than a real integration going
so far as to take the financial aspects into account. But public
resources are not indefinitely extendable, and it would be difficult
to attempt so much everywhere at the same time.

These examples show, however, how Austria can progress towards
an integrated social policy.

Other examples can be found, this time based on an approach by
population category, instead of a spatial approach. The policy for
helping the handicapped or the campaign against poverty bear witness
to this. It is the latter example which we propose to say more about
here, since the way in which it has been treated reflects a more far-
reaching search for consistency between the various fields of integrated social policy.

b) The campaign against poverty

Working parties meeting in the Ministry for Social Affairs, made
up of representatives of a number of ministries and Länder, academic
experts of the disciplines concerned, the social partners, and also

representatives of the private associations concerned and the churches were instructed to draw up a programme for the campaign against poverty in present-day Austria.

A first report was circulated at the beginning of 1978; a second appeared in autumn 1979. It is based on various empirical studies made over the last decade on the initiative of Chambers of Labour, the Länder and the Ministry for Social Affairs, studies commissioned, among others, from the Institute for Empirical Social Research (IFES), and also the empirical studies made by the European Centre for Social Welfare Training and Research. The report follows a procedure similar to that followed by Sweden in the 1960s, but it goes further since the studies made have led to the formulation of a programme of complex measures which is now going to be put into effect.

While the old kind of poverty, defined in terms of incomes, has practically disappeared, except perhaps in agriculture, a new kind of poverty has emerged which is characterised by accumulations of handicaps: physical and mental illnesses, segregation, lack of contacts, alcoholism, drug addition, criminality, which are symptomatic of a deterioration in the conditions of the social life of the groups in question.

Illnesses, chronic bad health, unemployment, irregular living, the lack of a fixed abode, result in the emergence of new "substructures", in which individuals and families find themselves "outside society" (immigrant workers are particularly affected).

To fight against this poverty, monetary assistance is indispensable, which means making special adjustments in social security or social assistance. But that is not enough. In addition the authorities have to take a combination of actions in the health, social and cultural fields to improve the living conditions of those concerned. The need to co-ordinate these measures leads to the setting up of teams of social workers who can anticipate the most difficult cases, and use to the full the possibilities of prevention and rehabilitation. Model projects are going to be launched, as part of a very broad programme embracing many detailed measures whose achievement and co-ordination will pose many problems.

This example shows, in an extreme case, both the need for an overall integrative approach to social problems within the framework of an integrated social policy and the capacity of the Austrian institutions to take into account such integration when the facts demand it, basing their efforts on appropriately adjusted information and very broad consultations with all those concerned. But what seemed obvious in regard to poverty is only a particularly clear example of what should be the general approach in social policies: this combination of means, this co-ordination, which the campaign against poverty demands, would also have positive effects if

it were practised more generally for the whole population. Not that
such amounts of financial means would need to be mobilised in dealing with all problems of individuals or families, but because certain interventions by the public authorities are necessary in any
case and would be more effective for a given cost, or less costly
for a given effectiveness, if they were more articulated, co-ordinated,
integrated, in an overall project.

However, since there is no overall concept of integrated social
policy for the country as a whole, such as would result from overall economic and social development planning for example, no attempt
is made to take an overall view either of incomes or of collective
services. The most that can be seen are, in certain cases, apart
from efforts to ensure short-term co-ordination, certain bilateral
contacts between institutions working towards a common objective.

C. PRIMARY DISTRIBUTION AND THE REDISTRIBUTION OF INCOMES: GLOBAL PRESENTATION

This section is based not only on the available statistics but
also on what we have been able to learn of the practices of the
various public and private agencies involved, during the interviews
arranged in Vienna in January 1979, which had themselves been prepared by study of precise, detailed and voluminous prior documenta-
tion.

The intention here, therefore, is not to analyse programmes or
repeat speeches, but, while keeping to the logic of this part of the
report, which is devoted to co-ordination and integration between
the various fields of social policies in particular from the point
of view of redistributive aspects, to say simply what has appeared
to us to be the present situation as it strikes outside observers
who have been as well informed as possible and who have benefited
from all kinds of facilities to meet and question in all freedom
and with very great frankness the various parties concerned: members
of the government, members of Parliament, civil servants from the
federal ministries or the Länder, representatives of the parties or
the main social partners, university academics and researchers.

In any country an approach of this kind would be bound to highlight a wide divergence between declarations of intention and everyday practices. This section, like the following sections, remains
deliberately empirical.

For most of the Austrians we were able to meet, the distribution
of income does not seem to raise any major problem; nor does the
redistribution of incomes. It is true, all the economic and social
partners are convinced that tax reform is necessary, but the main
objective seems to them to be to reconcile the appearances of marginal

tax rates with the reality of average tax rates, and not a priori
to improve redistribution. The Hauptverband der Sozialversicherungsträger (Federation of Social Insurance Institutions) seemed to
us to show admirable confidence in the managing of its expenditures,
and assured us that it would not be necessary to envisage any significant increase in contribution rates. As for the benefits provided,
reforms of particular points find defenders here and there, but,
after the recent reform of family policy, no overall project is under study. In brief, the status quo seems to be accepted on all
sides.

How, therefore, does the Austrian system function so that its
representatives do not appear to have strong feelings about problems
which have become burning questions in almost all the other developed
countries, whether it be income differentials, the steep increase in
social expenditures or the effectiveness of redistribution? The
questions put in order to try and understand what appeared to us to
be a social and economic miracle hardly found any satisfactory answers, for lack, it is true, of any confirmed overall information.
Austria is far from being the only country in which income statistics are insufficient, but in many other countries the desire to
improve information is linked to the determination to correct at
least some aspects of income distribution. Perhaps the positive
view the Austrians take of the status quo explains why interest in
improving statistics has hardly developed. The steep increase recently in the number of studies on these subjects would seem, however, to suggest that a change in attitude is about to take place(26).

a) Primary distribution

All the economic and social partners whom we were able to question felt that vigorous overall growth had been of equal benefit to
all categories, so that the distribution of the incomes has grosso
modo remained stable since the beginning of the 1960s. This assessment is probably correct as far as wages and salaries are concerned,
but is not necessarily true for income from property and entrepreneurship, about which not much is known.

i) Available statistics

There are, in fact, no direct data on the incomes of households,
but only data on certain incomes of individuals. As for households,
the only possible indirect approach consists in referring to surveys
of consumption made every 10 years by the Statistical Office. These
surveys, based on representative samples of 8,000 households, show
a total for consumption spending higher than declared income, but

it is possible to draw conclusions from them about the trend in real income, on the assumption that that trend is parallel to the trend in total consumption spending.

Existing surveys do not reveal any significant reduction in the overall dispersion of incomes, although the lowest incomes have increased faster since the mid-1960s. There is a wide spread of differentials within each of the groups shown: wage and salary earners in the public sector, blue-collar and white-collar workers in the private sector, individual entrepreneurs, liberal professions. A certain relative shift has occurred, however, between the average incomes of the various groups, at the expense of certain categories of the self-employed (small farmers, small traders, etc.), although the liberal professions are still favourably placed.

To these data, which in fact make it possible to compare the disposable incomes rather than the primary incomes of households, it is only possible to add the indications that the IFES deduces from the answers to the questions it regularly puts on incomes at the end of its surveys of households (30,000 interviews per year, on subjects of every kind). As in many other countries these questions are put rather vaguely, since their object is not to observe income as such; the vague replies obtained are used as a classification variable in the processing and interpretation of the surveys. The results of these surveys also do not seem to show any narrowing in the overall spread of the disposable incomes of households.

As in many other countries, moreover, one has to be content with statistics on individual incomes, with little hope of finding out how the various partial incomes received by a household are combined. Several sources can be used:

- Tax statistics, although slow in compilation, are more useful than the data mentioned above. They are taken at source and therefore, in theory, correct for wage and salary earners. For incomes from property and entrepreneurship, on the other hand, they simply reproduce the individual statements of those concerned, which makes them very unreliable (better however than the surveys mentioned above). Comparisons made with national accounts show that tax statistics make it possible to reconstitute a large proportion of wage incomes, but a much lower proportion of non-wage incomes. In spite of everything, and on the assumption of stability over time in deviations from reality, these statistics have shown a very great constancy of dispersion since the 1960s, whether measured on the basis of interdecile differences or a Gini coefficient, and in spite of large differences in tax policy or pricing policy (income of the self-employed) during the period.

- <u>Statistics on wages and salaries</u> by the Federal Chamber
  of Commerce, Trade and Industry are published twice a
  year for blue-collar workers and once a year for white-
  collar workers. They give results by group of qualification for wage-earners in industry which are quite
  independent of the previous source. In this restricted
  field, the results are quite comparable to the previous
  ones: they also show a very great constancy in the
  dispersion of wages for each qualification since the war.
- An additional source can be found, at least as far as
  large enterprises are concerned, in the statistics of
  <u>daily allowances</u> paid by employers to wage and salary
  earners absent through sickness (known through the application of a mechanism of compensation between enterprises).
  The distribution of these allowances shows, in addition
  to a fairly high degree of average stability over time,
  more cyclical movements of a narrowing of the spread
  in a period of recession and of opening out again in a
  period of more rapid growth. In the long term, the
  highest incomes seem rather to have improved their position
  in relation to the average, but the lowest incomes have
  also increased thanks to a minimum wage policy.
- The statistics on wages provided by <u>Social Security</u> by
  bracket of wages on the basis of the contributions paid
  are the most rapidly available. They give no indications
  as regards the highest wages and salaries, because of the
  ceilings which limit their contribution base. They do
  not cover civil servants at their various levels. Another
  difficulty, which will shortly be remedied, is that a
  worker who has two jobs is counted twice. These statistics show a fairly considerable widening between 1953 and
  1960, followed by stability in the 1960s, and then a
  slight increase in differentials between 1970 and 1980.

It is not easy to draw a clear conclusion from all these statistics. The overall impression is, however, that of a fairly great
stability in relative differentials.

ii) <u>The attitudes of the main social partners</u>

The union for each industry is responsible for the negotiations
leading up to wage agreements for that industry. The general recommendations formulated by the Gewerkschaftsbund (Trade Union Federation) as part of their "solidaristic wages policy" include a certain
margin for wage increases. The individual unions then negotiate
with the representatives of the employers minimum rates of increase

for the whole of their industry and also the increase in real wages, which are higher ("Ist-Löhne"). The resulting increase is usually higher than that which would result from the strict application of the initial recommendation.

In certain parts of the economy it may happen that above-average increases are recommended; this is above all the case for industries in which real wages are very close to the minimum wage.

Within a given industry, negotiations then take place on an establishment basis. The "wages actually paid" which result from these ("Effektivlöhne") are higher than the "real wages" negotiated through collective bargaining for the industry as a whole ("Ist-Löhne"). The increase in wages actually paid in an enterprise is not accepted by the Trade Union Federation as an argument for higher costs when it is taking part in the discussions of the Joint Commission's sub-committee on prices. If, nevertheless, that argument is advanced, the Trade Union Federation, which controls the time-table of negotiations on prices, can still prolong the duration of the previous price agreements by delaying the opening of a new nego-tiation before the Joint Commission. The basic rule of the "soli-daristic wages policy" is, in fact, that wage levels should remain in harmony with the general economic situation. It is hardly pos-sible for enterprises to cheat as regards the incidence of wage in-creases since the results of collective bargaining are highly publi-cised.

All those taking part in these negotiations are aware of the poor quality of the statistics on wages and salaries, but believe nevertheless that the wage differential structure has been more or less constant. It would certainly be useful to improve statistics on wages and salaries but, in the opinion of the representatives of the wage and salary earners, it would be even more useful to improve the statistics on non-wage incomes.

The difference in wages between men and women is large, although the principle is "equal wages for equal work". This difference hard-ly changed between 1964 and 1977.

A working party of the Advisory Council (Beirat für Wirtschaft und Sozialfragen) to the Prices and Wages Commission has published "recommendations for improving statistics on income distribution". According to the Finance Ministry, these recommendations have not been acted on for the time being (apart from a few exceptions), because of the difficult institutional situation, and of psycholog-ical and technical problems, and certainly also because of the fact that it is difficult to convince those concerned with collecting these data of the need to establish a detailed data base. These somewhat embarrassed explanations confirm the impression that, be-yond the general consensus as to the satisfactory nature of the status quo and the constancy of distribution, nobody is really concerned to push for clarification, everybody being more or less consciously afraid of the reactions that would be provoked by any modification of relative positions. It is, therefore, hardly surprising that even the term redistribution was hardly used by the people we spoke to during the interviews in January 1979.

b) Global redistribution

Without knowing the precise distribution of primary incomes, it is impossible to say how the fiscal and social levies, and the subsequent reallocation of funds (to say nothing of the preferential use of certain public services by privileged categories), modify the initial distribution of incomes. A statement of this kind is incidentally not only true of Austria but could, no doubt, be applied to many other countries. In the absence of overall data, no one can say for certain what the overall redistributive effect of all these interventions is. Many believe that the most probable answer is that the sum total of the individual collective measures hardly changes the final distribution, which seems to them to be constant. But many recognise also that there are special cases in which "redistribution" in fact favours those who have least need to be protected. But, they hasten to add, none of that is very clear, there are many other more urgent problems, and in any case it would be wrong to think that official intervention can compensate for everything.

Others also believe that it would be pointless to pursue a policy of reducing inequalities, even though such a policy is part of the traditions of Social Democracy, and of Social Christian doctrine, by trying to go against the trends of the market economy, according to which access to a given service is a function of the price that the person concerned is capable of paying for himself. For example, in health matters the legislation lays it down that adequate "basic services" accessible to everyone shall be provided. Why should attempts be made to prevent the development of the best services, due to technical progress, from becoming more accessible to the wealthier sections of the population, thanks to the mechanisms of complementary insurance? These same people forget to add however that such mechanisms, accessible only to the better off, are also favoured by tax exemptions.

The experts who have looked most closely into these problems add that some redistribution has nevertheless been achieved in favour of the lowest incomes, thanks to various guaranteed minimum mechanisms. A number of measures have in fact been taken in favour of economically disadvantaged groups: higher-than-average increases in minimum pensions, which benefit in particular the economically disadvantaged and farmers; the steps now being taken to remove the differences between certain allowances paid to blue-collar and white-collar workers, for example for holidays or for daily allowance payments in cases of absence due to illness (allowances which were originally reserved to white-collar workers), etc.

Most of the people we interviewed considered that the main problem was above all psychological: the marginal rates of income tax are in theory high, but a large number of tax exemptions leads in practice to much lower rates. Tax-payers imagine that they are paying very heavy taxes, whereas in fact this is not so. Hence the need for a tax reform which simultaneously reduces apparent rates and exemptions. Some of our interlocutors added that the burden of indirect taxation should also be reduced, since this had increased too much in recent years.

The Social Security specialists whom we met considered that a certain barrier had been reached as regards the burden of compulsory contributions, because "people" were no longer willing to forego increases in their own income to help pay for social benefits for everybody. Further pressure might lead to an increase in moonlighting. According to these specialists, however, there is no objective limit to redistribution; no one can give an unequivocal answer to the question as to how much he would be prepared to give up of his income for the benefit of others. This, they believe, is a psychological problem: the amount is not necessarily limited if adequate explanations can be given to those concerned; moreover, the total tax and compulsory contributions burden in Austria, which is about 40 per cent of Gross National Product, is more or less average compared with industrial European countries.

Officials of the Federal Ministry for Finance consider that it is not possible to fix an a priori limit for the overall tax burden: every time this had been attempted, it had subsequently been found that the limits announced had already been exceeded. Tax policy is only one component of a whole package of redistributive effects, and to contribute to redistribution is only one objective for fiscal policy among many others (raising revenue, countering the business cycle, to say nothing of special policies in regard to transport, energy, etc.). It is moreover very difficult to intervene with a tax structure whose origins are mainly to be found in history. And there are not in any case large groups of the population for whom no tax measures can bring any benefit at all. The repercussions of the measures taken do not always coincide with those intended, because market conditions affect them. Taxes paid by wage earners finance a large part of the transfers received by households: there is "redistribution from one pocket to another", but, because of "asymmetry in evaluation", the pain of the tax outweighs, and is more immediately felt than the pleasure of the benefit received. Moreover, direct taxes do not necessarily produce a better distribution than indirect taxes, since differentiations in the VAT rates can attenuate the regressive income effects of indirect taxes.

As to social security contributions, say these same officials, they are less resented than taxes, and yet more than a quarter of the expenditures on social security is financed by the federal budget, and therefore out of taxes. The overall redistributive balance sheet is difficult to draw up. It seems nevertheless obvious that it leads to a redistribution at the expense of the active members of the labour force and in favour of retired people and certain socially disadvantaged groups, above all among the self-employed and farmers: the latter benefit in particular from a guaranteed level of income which is very important for the equilibrium of the country.

Several of the experts in research institutions stressed that it was probably no accident that the political parties or trade unions have so far confined themselves to general statements as to the need to reduce excessive disparities. The postwar recovery phase led to improvements in the situation of all Austrians, and all of them are aware of this. But, with the slowdown in growth, redistribution is probably going to become more of a subject for controversy. Then studies will perhaps be considered necessary.

To this review of the main opinions put to us during our interviews in Vienna we feel we should add a point which seemed to us to be significant: the Advisory Council of the Joint Commission on Prices and Incomes, which has the necessary academic resources to go to the root of the matter, has not chosen to include the theme of redistribution in its programme. Is that because it is aware that it might endanger the consensus which is the basis of the official philosophy of Austria? Or is it simply because the social partners are responsible for dealing jointly with primary distribution, whereas the discussions on tax policy and Social Security policy take place largely outside the social partnership system (although their results have an increasing impact on disposable incomes)?

While it would be foolish to try to provide from outside any firm answers to these difficult questions, it is at least possible to examine in turn the main features of the "redistributive" system now in force.

D. MAIN FEATURES OF THE REDISTRIBUTIVE SYSTEM

There can be no question here of presenting in detail all the transfer elements, negative or positive, which affect income. This section examines first of all the main taxes paid by households; it then describes the benefits paid by the Social Security funds and the way they are financed; and finally it gives indications of the main allocations from the federal budget.

a) Federal taxes

It should be remembered that taxation in Austria is predominantly a federal matter. The Länder and the communes have hardly any machinery for raising local revenues; a law defines the financial equalisation procedure for redistributing a major part of tax revenues - 37 per cent - to the Länder and the communes. Many studies on this subject have been made, giving rise to very keen discussions between the various levels of public authorities. But the emphasis thus put on certain "redistributive" aspects of the public finances (redistribution in this context having a spatial connotation) explains perhaps why the study of redistribution between categories of households has been rather neglected. It is true that this aspect concerns (almost) exclusively the Federation, which in any case levies almost all the taxes.

Given the relatively minor role played by taxes on wealth (1.1 per cent of Gross National Product in 1977), our examination will be confined to direct taxes on incomes and indirect taxes on goods and services.

A very detailed study, written on the occasion of the procedure leading up to this report by Mrs. Edith Kitzmantel, an official of the Finance Ministry, was published in 1979 by that Ministry under the title "Taxes: Who pays them and who bears the burden" (Steuern: Wer sie zahlt, wer sie trägt). The preface by the Vice-Chancellor, the Finance Minister, underlines its importance at a time when a commission on tax reform with a broad mandate was about to be set up. This is the only study which exists at present on the redistributive effects of the taxation system. It should help considerably in informing the deliberations of the Commission, as it has helped the writers of this report to make certain brief observations here from the point of view of integrated social policy.

Taxes with a typically redistributive impact represent in Austria a relatively small share of total tax receipts (including social security contributions): in 1976, 25 per cent for taxes on income and 3 per cent for taxes on wealth. On the other hand, the proportion derived from indirect taxes (35 per cent) and from social security contributions (29 per cent) are relatively high. International comparisons show that fiscal pressure in the usual sense of the term (including amounts raised for the family burdens compensation fund) is relatively high (27.6 per cent of GNP in 1976) whereas total fiscal pressure, including social security contributions, is slightly above average (38.9 per cent of GNP in 1976). More than half of the funds thus raised are redistributed in the form of monetary transfers (either to households or to enterprises). Thus in 1974, households themselves financed almost the whole transfers paid to them and 90 per cent of the subsidies paid to enterprises.

i) Income taxes

There are two forms of income tax:

- the tax on wages and salaries (Lohneinkommen), which applies to the wages and salaries of the dependently employed and also the pensions paid to former wage and salary earners;
- the tax on gains and profits (Gewinneinkommen), which applies to incomes other than wages and salaries, that is to say:

  - incomes of households carrying on personal businesses (non-public companies), mainly members of the liberal professions, farmers, artisans, traders,
  - but also incomes derived from the possession of capital,
  - and also incomes derived from public companies.

During the period 1955 to 1977 there was a considerable shift between these two large categories of tax, the tax on wages and salaries becoming much more predominant for the following reasons:

- there was a profound change in the breakdown of categories of employed people, i.e. a large shift in favour of wage and salary earners;
- the distribution of non-wage incomes is more concentrated towards the upper end of the range of incomes than that of wages and salaries; the result is that the effect of the progressivity of the tax as a function of the general increase in incomes leads automatically to a lower tax yield for non-wage incomes than for wage incomes;
- tax reliefs for enterprises to encourage investment have been considerably increased since 1965;
- the increase in private investment since the end of the 1960s has led to greater use of these tax incentives.

Between 1965 and 1976, total taxation on wages and salaries increased by 231 per cent, whereas total taxation on non-wage earnings and profits only increased by 126 per cent.

While the income tax scale as a whole (whether on wage or non-wage incomes) is in theory intended to have a redistributive effect, since the marginal rate of tax increases from 23 to 62 per cent, there exist many legal provisions which allow for considerable deductions and in practice attenuate very significantly the real progressivity of the tax.

Certain reliefs relate to the tax base, others to the amount of tax itself. The former reduce the progressivity of the tax more than the latter: a relief on the tax base leads to a larger reduction in tax on higher incomes; but a relief on the tax itself benefits all tax-payers equally, so long at least as the initial tax is greater than the relief. In any case no relief - whether it applies to the tax base or to the tax itself - can be of benefit to those who do not have any tax to pay (for example people receiving unemployment benefits or social assistance). Such a defect can only be eliminated by adopting a non-fiscal mechanism of positive assistance for those whom it is intended to help. The changes in family assistance policy made by Austria during the last ten years show that at least in this field the above criticisms have been taken into account: initially, the reliefs based on the number of children were applied to the tax base; then from 1973 onwards they were replaced by reliefs on the tax itself; and finally, since 1978, they have been replaced by an increase in family allowances.

But many tax reliefs still exist. Their effect is to lead to very significant reductions in real rates of taxation compared with the theoretical rates which would result from the direct application of the basic scale: this explains the wide differences between the effective burden of the tax on income and the potential yield of that tax.

Besides the incentives for investment, already noted, and which help in particular housing construction, there are many other possibilities for relief - for savings, voluntary contributions to sickness insurance, or even for calling in a tax consultant. Such reliefs bring greater benefits the higher the incomes of the tax-payers, which incidentally also enables them to save more, and to contribute more for better health protection insurance.

- The tax on wages and salaries

In the case of the tax on wages and salaries (and the pensions of former wage and salary earners), the reduction in rates, according to calculations made for 1970 and for 1973, has been of the order of two-thirds: i.e. if the theoretical progressive tax scale had been applied to the gross base (without relief of any sort), the yield of the tax on wages and salaries would have been three times

71

as high as it actually was after taking into account the reliefs provided by law. It should be noted however that if the general deductible amount applicable to all tax-payers is considered as an integral part of the general tax scale, the abolition of the other (personal) abatements would have doubled (not tripled) the yield.

Some of these reliefs particularly favour those receiving the highest incomes, and thus in fact have a negative redistributive effect. This is the case for savings for private insurance. Others are linked to certain forms of remuneration (for example additional remuneration attributed to a salary earner for a "fifteenth month", or for overtime). In the case of white-collar workers with one child, for example, it seems that a quarter of the tax reliefs can be attributed to an individual erosion having negative redistributive effects and three-quarters to general effects which nevertheless provide room for a net positive redistributive effect.

For the year 1973, the overall effect of all reliefs led to an approximately proportional reduction (as a percentage of gross income) for three-quarters of wage and salary earners liable for tax whose incomes came within the lower and middle brackets of income distribution. For the top quartile, i.e. the higher incomes, the reduction is smaller in relative value (in relation to gross income or in relation to the fictional burden of the theoretical tax) the higher the income. In absolute value, however, the relief increases with income.

These conclusions are drawn from the interesting study quoted above, and are based on a tax incidence model of which Table 1, for the year 1973, is an example.

From 1970 to 1977 the ratio between tax actually paid and the wages and salaries to which it applies remained practically constant, following the reforms made meanwhile and which made it possible to cancel out the effects due to inflation. But significant differences in this respect exist between the various socio-economic groups: the rate of taxation diminished for people drawing pensions and for unmarried tax-payers and those receiving low incomes.

- The tax on non-wage earnings and profits

In this case too there is a considerable gap between the real burden and the fictional burden which would result if only the theoretical tax scales were applied to real incomes without any reliefs. The main reasons for this are the fiscal incentives for investment (which for example in 1974 reduced the taxable base by 40 per cent in the case of companies), and the application of privileged rates for the taxation of profits distributed by companies (in 1974, this led to a reduction of 22 per cent in the amount of corporate taxes).

The study of the Austrian fiscal system made by Mrs. E.Kitzmantel clearly shows that there is progressivity in the tax on non-wage earnings, but this is on the assumption that the tax is not passed on in prices. Such an assumption, considered unrealistic when it is a question of the corporate tax or even more the tax on trade activity (Gewerbesteuer), is also equally unrealistic for income tax in the case of the self-employed (tax on the profits of personal business). It is unfortunately impossible to compare the tax paid and the corresponding incomes since no acceptable statistical breakdown of the incomes of the self-employed is available.

The tax on non-wage earnings and profits results on average in a significantly heavier burden than that of the tax on wages and salaries. In 1973, the burden was 32.5 per cent of declared profits, and 16.5 per cent of the economic estimate of profits (national accounts base). In the same period the fiscal burden (in the strict sense, excluding social security contributions) was 9 per cent for wages and salaries. The explanation for these differences is that non-wage earnings are on the whole higher than wages and salaries and are also more unevenly distributed: the top decile of non-wage earnings accounts for half of the total amount of declared earnings, whereas the top decile of wages and salaries only represents a quarter of total wages and salaries.

As for the tax on corporations to which moral persons are subject, this represented on average in 1974 a burden of 40 per cent on declared profits. But it must be said that 97 per cent of companies were taxed at a lower than average rate, and that for 65 per cent of them the burden was on average 20 per cent.

ii) Indirect taxes

The most important of these is the tax on turnover, which became the value added tax (VAT) in 1973, and which accounted for 62 per cent of the total of indirect taxes in 1977. The share of indirect taxes in total taxes and compulsory contributions remained steady for a long time at about 25 per cent mainly due to a reduction in customs duties; it has increased since the introduction of VAT in 1973 and stood at 28.6 per cent in 1977.

From 1973 to 1977 there were two VAT rates: the normal rate, which was 16 per cent up to 1976 and 18 per cent from 1977 onwards, and the reduced rate of 8 per cent applied to food products and to a number of services (rents, passenger transport, etc.). Since 1978 a third rate of 30 per cent has been introduced. It applies to goods considered as luxuries, such as motor-cars, antiquities, jewellery, etc. At present about 43 per cent of the volume of goods and services subject to the tax come under the reduced rate of 8 per cent,

Table 1

TAX RELIEFS PER INCOME BRACKET IN 1973 FOR WAGE AND SALARY EARNERS

	Gross Yearly Wage (1) in A.Sch.	Tax Paid per capita (2) in A.Sch.	(3) in % (2)/(1)	Theoretical Tax per capita (4) in A.Sch.	(5) in % (4)/(1)	Tax relief per capita *(6) = (4)-(2) in A.Sch.	*(7) in % (6)/(1)
1st Quartile	50,000 - 60,000	2,040	3.7	12,840	23.2	10,800	19.5
Median	70,000 - 80,000	4,160	5.5	18,740	25.0	14,580	19.5
3rd Quartile	100,000 - 120,000	8,370	7.7	30,490	27.9	22,120	20.2
	200,000 - 250,000	36,330	16.4	78,050	35.3	41,720	18.9
	500,000 - 700,000	170,260	29.6	272,000	47.4	101,740	17.8
	More than 1,000,000	536,000	39.3	738,999	54.1	202,390	14.8

* Calculated on the basis of Table 14, p. 43 of the study quoted Steuern: Wer sie zahlt, wer sie trägt.

74

a little more than 50 per cent are taxed at the normal rate of 18 per cent and about 6 per cent at the higher rate of 30 per cent.

The redistributive effect, in theory negative, of a tax on consumption (which represents a larger percentage of income for low incomes and a smaller percentage for high incomes) is to some extent offset by the application of the three different rates. By comparison with gross incomes, the burden is still slightly regressive, but by comparison with disposable incomes (gross incomes less taxes plus benefits), the preparatory studies made in Austria came to the conclusion that the burden was more or less proportional, at about 10 per cent.

b) Social transfers

Over the period 1970 to 1977 transfers paid to private households more than doubled. The proportion of social incomes in the total incomes of households is high in Austria by comparison with other countries: the protection of the elderly, sickness insurance and compensation for family burdens have become very important. In 1974 Austria, with Belgium and France, was at the top of the table of industrial European countries for assistance to families. The main emphasis of this assistance (especially since 1978) is on large families with low incomes. For a household whose income is equal to the average, family assistance (in the form of tax reliefs and positive benefits) increased in real terms by 30 per cent between 1970 and 1978, more or less in line with national income. For households with low incomes which could not derive full benefit from tax reliefs, the increase can be as high as 124 per cent (because the initial tax reliefs have been replaced by direct transfers).

i) Social insurances properly so called (pensions and sickness)

Apart from a very small number of occupational groups, the whole population is now covered by social security. White-collar workers have been covered in principle since 1909; blue-collar workers - apart from agricultural or horticultural workers - have been covered against sickness since 1889 and for pensions and disability since 1939; non-wage earners in farming, forestry and horticulture have been insured against old age and disability since 1957, and against sickness since 1966; non-wage earners in craft trades, commerce and industry have been covered since 1952 or 1958, depending on the case, for retirement and disability, and since 1958 for sickness (except for a few occupational groups which preferred, after a vote on the matter, to keep their freedom to insure themselves against sickness).

The Hauptverband der Sozialversicherungsträger (Federation of Social Insurance Institutions) includes all the social insurance schemes for wage earners and non-wage earners and the insurance schemes covering accident pensions. It does not cover the pension and social benefit schemes for civil servants working for the Federation, the Länder and the communes.

Apart from accident insurance, which is borne exclusively by employers, contributions are made jointly by employers and employees, in varying proportions. For sickness insurance the shares are equal: half by the employers, half by the employees. For disability retirement, a supplementary contribution over and above the "normal" contribution was introduced in 1978. This supplementary contribution was of the order of 2 per cent of the contribution base in 1978 and 1979, of which 0.5 per cent was borne by the employee and 1.5 per cent by the employer. In 1980 the supplementary contribution was raised to 3 per cent, of which 1 per cent by the employee and 2 per cent by the employer. In the case of retirement contributions for non-wage earning individual entrepreneurs, the Federation pays a "partner's contribution" equal to the contribution paid by those concerned, but this provision does not apply in the case of non-wage earners belonging to the liberal professions: they pay the full contribution themselves.

The compulsory contributions are deductible from the income tax base; voluntary contributions are also deductible, but only up to a certain ceiling.

The basis for contributions for a given year (n) for non-wage earners in commerce and industry, and for members of their families compulsorily covered by insurance in certain liberal professions, is in principle the income calculated by the finance administration on the basis of the tax on profit made in the year (n-3), grossed up by the rate of inflation recorded over the intervening three-year period. In the case of non-wage earners in agriculture and horticulture, the value declared for insuring the agricultural enterprise is taken as the basis for fixing contributions.

For wage earners, the base for contributions is the gross wage up to a certain level. The "ceilings" are different for sickness insurance and for old age/disability insurance, the ceilings for the latter being higher. The contributions are fixed by law and the ceilings are recalculated periodically at the same time as the benefits. The contributions, insofar as they are calculated on the basis of an income below the ceiling, are proportional to that income. Their percentage then diminishes as the income exceeds the ceiling. The resulting regressive effect partially offsets the progressive effect of the income tax: the highest wages and salaries are subject to a higher fiscal burden but a lower social burden. The overall redistributive effect of income tax and contributions, compared to the effect of the tax alone, corresponds to a significantly higher average rate of taxation but with a considerably attenuated progressivity.

It must be added that the ability to deduct social security contributions from the income tax base accentuates the regressive effect of the contributions. For example, a taxpayer in employment with two children and one earned income equal to the half of the average wage would still have to pay the total amount of his contributions, since he cannot claim against income tax which he does not have to pay. A taxpayer with the same family situation but with a wage equal to the average wage would only have to pay two-thirds of his contributions, the rest being covered by a relief on tax liability. In the case where the wage or salary equals three times the average wage, the person concerned only has to pay 45 per cent of his contributions out of his own pocket.

The total amount of contributions of all kinds to social insurance schemes represented 8.6 per cent of the GNP in 1965. This proportion increased in subsequent years, and levelled out at about 9.5 per cent between 1968 and 1973, and then increased again up to 12 per cent in 1977, or 28.6 per cent of the combined total of taxes and compulsory contributions.

- Pensions

Pensions are calculated on the basis of the contribution base (up to a ceiling) over the last five years and the recognised period of insurance (there must be a minimum of 180 months - 60 in the case of disability or death). The normal age for retirement is (apart from exceptions) 65 for men and 60 for women. Early retirement is possible if the person concerned has been insured for 420 months, from the age of 55 for women and 60 for men. Pensions are adjusted each year by means of a multiplier coefficient laid down by decree by the Ministry of Social Affairs in the light of expert advice from the Advisory Committee for Pensions Adjustment ("Renten" in the case of blue-collar workers, "Pension" in the case of white-collar workers). The Advisory Committee must take account in its expert advice of the economic situation and its expected trend, and of the ratio of numbers of pensioners to contributors. It must recommend for use as a multiplier coefficient either an index derived from the change in the average base for contributions (and hence linked to wage trends) or another factor which it is entitled to propose.

In cases where pensions paid fall below a minimum income (Richtsatz), social security pays a "supplementary allowance" to the person concerned; this is subsequently reimbursed to social security by the federal authorities. In agreement with the social partners, it was decided to use this mechanism to increase more rapidly the lowest incomes of retired persons. The ratio between average pensions and average wages thus rose from about 30 per cent in the mid-1950s to 42 per cent during the period 1962 to 1972(27). In 1978, 336,000 retired persons received supplementary allowances, the total amount involved being A.Sch.5.4 billion. The arrival at pensionable age of age groups who have contributed for longer periods, and who therefore qualify for higher basic pensions, should in future reduce the amount of these supplementary allowances.

The contribution paid by the Federation to pensions is given in the form of a guarantee in case of deficit. This guarantee is fixed, in case of a deficit, as an amount corresponding to the difference between recorded revenues and expenditures, so as to ensure that revenues exceed expenditures by 1.5 per cent. In calculating this amount no account is taken of supplementary allowances or housing allowances. The Federation's contributions to pensions during the period 1965 to 1977 ranged between 14 and 30 per cent according to the year. Since 1978 it has been only about 20 per cent, as a result of various measures taken in regard to social insurance schemes in order to relieve the federal budget.

It was explained to us at the Federation of Social Insurance Institutions that a very sophisticated forecasting system, taking into account in particular demographic factors, made it possible to calculate the future contributions to be made out of the Federation's budget, so that no surprises could occur. The Finance Ministry mentioned however that the sudden change in the birth rate had certainly been underestimated, and that very sophisticated population forecasting is unfortunately not in itself enough to calculate precisely the future contributions to be paid by the Federation. But leaving aside possible changes in benefits, it is above all the general trends in the economy which matter, with their effects on the labour market, which in turn have repercussions on the contributions paid in.

It is the Ministry of Social Affairs (and not the Federation of Social Insurance Institutions) which decides each year, following a proposal by the Advisory Council for Pensions Adjustments, the annual increase in pensions, and which, bearing in mind the trend in contributions, determines the deficit which the federal budget has to make up.

It has incidentally been necessary in recent years to increase contribution rates in order to limit budgetary expenditures. However, the scheme for white-collar workers is the only one to show a surplus. As for the others, in 1977 the Federation financed 37.5 per cent of blue-collar workers' pensions (in the strict sense), 42 per cent of railwaymen's pensions, 83 per cent of miners' pensions, 80 per cent of all non-wage non-farm workers' pensions and 90 per cent of farmers' pensions(28).

All in all the Federal budget paid A.Sch.24 billion in 1978(29)
to pension schemes (or about 10 per cent of total budget expenditure); it would have had to pay 8 or 9 billion more if the contribution rates had not been raised(30).

- Sickness insurance

Part IV considers the organisation of the Austrian health system
from the medical point of view; only some salient financial aspects
are dealt with here.

Compulsory insurance covers almost the entire population (96 per
cent in 1979). Except in special cases (miners, railway workers,
etc) sickness insurance schemes are organised by each Land.

The resources of the social insurance sickness schemes come entirely from contributions, without any financing from the federal
budget, apart from its contribution to the sickness scheme for farmers. It should not be forgotten, however, that the Federation in-
tervenes directly in health matters, in particular through the Hospitals' Equalisation Fund, (Krankenanstaltenzusammenarbeitsfonds)
which is financed, among others, by special taxes (alcohol, tobacco)
and by the recent increase in VAT rates on luxury products.

The rates and ceilings for sickness insurance contributions are
at present as follows (1979):

	Rate	Ceiling(31)
Civil servants	6.4	A.Sch.14 200
White-collar workers	5.0	A.Sch.13 800
Blue-collar workers	6.3 (32)	A.Sch.13 800
Farmers	4.8	A.Sch.16 100
Self-employed other than farmers	7.7	A.Sch.16 100

Wives and children are covered without specific contributions in
the case of wage and salary earners and farmers, but self-employed
other than farmers have to pay contributions to cover them. The
ceilings vary in average level in the same proportion as retirement
pensions.

The basic protection provided by social security is the same for
all wage and salary earners. Insured self-employed contribute directly 20 per cent of all sickness insurance costs concerning them (except
for certain services, such as for example hospital care lasting more
than five weeks or dialysis treatment). A similar regulation is
applied to the costs of treatment in the case of civil servants.

Contributions to private insurance schemes (deductible from the
income tax base for the worker or the corporate profits for the employer) make it possible to increase the insurance protection for
those who wish it... and can afford it. A fifth of the population is

thus covered by supplementary insurance schemes. The proportion of private insurance compared with compulsory insurance has increased significantly in recent years (see Part IV, Section D a).

The aim of the sickness insurance schemes is to provide optimum satisfaction for those injured, within the limits of the possibilities provided by the contributions fixed by law. It is not to provide unlimited benefits and services at no matter what cost. It is thus recognised that all risks cannot be covered without some participation by those insured. Social security is based on its receipts and covers part of the costs. The law stipulates that "adequate care must be provided according to needs, without exceeding the extent necessary". Thus, for example, hospitalisation is not allowed if there is no need to provide medical care (which confronts the doctors with difficult decisions). In particular, for the elderly living in old people's homes, sickness insurance only covers what relates to its primary task, that is to say expenditure on treatment.

The treatment and accommodation provided under private insurance seem to be of better quality, especially in hospitals, but a higher price is charged for them. Costs per day are apparently roughly twice as high for patients under private insurance as for patients under compulsory insurance. Senior doctors in hospitals find it in their interests to receive private fees (financed in part, it must be remembered, by reliefs out of public resources through the mechanism of tax allowances on voluntary contributions). In one Land, Carinthia, a law has been passed fixing a ceiling on the additional income a senior doctor can derive from these arrangements: the ceiling is A.Sch.100,000 per month.

The basic protection includes the right, through a "coupons" scheme, to certain benefits and treatments whose value is fixed by negotiation between the Sickness Insurance Institution, the regional Chamber of Doctors and the Austrian Chamber of Pharmacists (the Social Security system is "self-administering", but subject to the supervision of the Federation).

Patients are free to choose their doctors, subject to various restrictions as to the number of visits (per patient and per doctor), it being understood that there are different categories of fees depending on the choice freely made by the doctor:

- some independent doctors do not have contracts with any social security schemes; their fees are not subject to any regulation;
- others sign individual contracts with one or more schemes; their fees are subject to a general agreement decided on by the Chamber of Doctors and the social security schemes;
- yet others are employed by one or other of the sickness insurance schemes.

As for <u>medicines</u>, these must be registered by the Federal Ministry, which fixes reasonable maximum prices. The Federation of Social Insurance Institutions also makes a selection of medicines to decide which are reimbursable: for example, certain placebo medicines, vitamins or tonics in particular, are not reimbursable. According to the Austrian Chamber of Doctors, these would be quite pleased to be able to refuse useless medicines on these grounds.

- Prolongation of wage payments in case of illness

When a wage earner is ill, his employer continues to pay his wages for a certain period which, moreover, varies according to whether he is a white-collar or a blue-collar worker, and which depends on the seniority of the person concerned. In the case of white-collar workers, the enterprise itself bears the risk of having to continue to pay a salary without any compensating contribution. In the case of blue-collar workers, this risk has been transferred to a fund: the Law on Prolongation of Payment of Wages adopted the solution of an insurance: a special fund of the Social Insurance Schemes, financed by flat-rate contributions, makes it possible to equalise risks between the various enterprises. The mechanism employed results, according to studies made on the subject, in the large enterprises (more than 100 workers), in which absenteeism is high, being subsidised by the small firms (less than 10 workers).

Social security contributions corresponding to the wage paid had in the past to be taken on charge by the employer, in addition to the wage paid. From 1979 onwards, it has been decided that the Fund would no longer reimburse the larger enterprises for wages paid to workers on sick leave.

Beyond the maximum period for the prolongation of payment of wages, blue-collar and white-collar workers receive a daily allowance (Krankengeld) paid by social security and amounting to just under 50 per cent of the last wage used as a basis for calculating contributions. This 50 per cent is increased up to 60 per cent in the case of prolonged illness; there are also supplements for family responsibilities.

ii) Other main benefits

Unemployment, disabilities, families.

- Unemployment benefit and assistance for the unemployed

The protection of workers who have lost their jobs is the responsibility of the Federal Ministry for Social Affairs and is regulated by the Unemployment Insurance Law (Arbeitslosenversicherungsgesetz).

The costs of unemployment insurance benefits are covered mainly by contributions which are shared equally between employers and wage earners. These contributions amount at present to 2 per cent of the base for sickness insurance contributions(33); the base taken into consideration being calculated on a calendar basis (and not per days worked) up to a fixed ceiling (A.Sch.460 per day in 1979).

When it becomes evident that the revenue would no longer cover the foreseeable expenditure, the contribution rate may be raised by nature of a joint decision of the Ministry of Social Affairs and the Ministry of Finance. Conversely, the rate may be reduced provided the disposable assets in the Revenue Fund exceed the average revenue from contributions for the last five years.

All expenses are advanced out of the federal budget according to regulations which, incidentally, are not peculiar to Austria, and there is accounting for the contributions received. Eventual surpluses are transferred to the Revenue Fund and eventual deficits are, in the first instance, covered out of this Fund. Deficits not recuperable in this way because of the exhaustion of the Fund are financed provisionally by the Federation and reimbursed in subsequent years out of contribution receipts.

Unemployment benefit is only paid for a certain period, after which the unemployed person has a right to public assistance, for which, however, his own incomes and those of his near relatives must be taken into consideration, at least beyond a certain limit.

The Budget had at certain times in the course of the 1950s a credit of A.Sch.2 billion with the Reserve Fund, and the Fund was able to reimburse this debt subsequently in a period of strong growth. No one knows what would happen if unemployment, particularly low compared with most European countries, should increase for a lengthy period. The connection between the Fund and the budget, and a certain flexibility in fixing contribution rates, would no doubt make it possible to make certain adjustments for a certain time, but just how long could this go on, and what would the consequences be for the budget? Apprehension on these grounds must, it is true, be tempered by the fact that Austria, unlike a number of other industrial countries, has been able to contain unemployment within very low limits (on average 2.0 per cent since the recession of 1975), thanks to an active employment policy which considers the maintenance of full employment as the most important objective of the federal government.

- The disabled

The Federal Ministry for Social Affairs plans to strengthen cooperation between the Federation, the Länder and the Social Security Funds so as to improve the rehabilitation of the disabled, in particular by setting up sheltered workshops, and to clarify the method of coverage by social security of medical expenditures on the disabled. A working party has been set up for this purpose between the Federal Ministry, the Länder and the Social Security Funds (see Part V, Section B).

c) Family allowances

Various measures taken in recent years to reinforce perinatal protection are described in the following Part IV which deals with the health system. We shall only deal here with measures concerning financial compensation for family burdens.

In Austria these measures come directly under the federal budget, and not social security. The general provisions have been readjusted several times in the course of the last ten years, as has already been briefly indicated above in connection with the redistributive effects of social transfers.

Before 1973 the provisions were based on positive direct transfers (varying with the number of children) and on reliefs on the income tax base. A first reform in 1973 consisted in replacing these reliefs on the income tax base by abatement of the tax liability itself, which is less regressive from the point of view of redistribution, but could not be of any help to families too poor to pay income taxes.

A further reform, in mid-1978, abolished these tax allowances and replaced them by a considerable increase in direct positive transfers, irrespective of the level of family incomes, which restores the balance in favour of large families with low incomes.

These allowances are granted for each child under 18 and up to 27 years of age for children still in education or training.

As at 1 January 1979, the monthly amount of these allowances was as follows:

1 child	A.Sch.910
2 children	A.Sch.1,860
3 children	A.Sch.2,930
4 children	A.Sch.3,900 (+ 1,010 per additional child)

An additional monthly allowance of A.Sch.1,100 was also paid on each handicapped child.

These allowances are financed by levies for the Family Burdens Compensation Fund. These levies, which are not legally taxes, are paid by the employer and represent (since 1978) 5 per cent of the total wage bill.

Besides the above allowances, the Family Burdens Compensation Fund also finances birth allowances, allowances for transport of children to school or university, school books, the "mother-child passbook" scheme, and improved pensions for mothers.

The present system is undoubtedly much more redistributive than the previous systems, and this puts Austria ahead of other countries.

d) Reforms envisaged

The foregoing indicates the diversity of the mechanisms for social protection now existing and the connection between them, but also suggests that the degree of redistribution which they can make is probably rather limited. The taxes on income are much less progressive than the theoretical marginal rates would lead one to suppose. Indirect taxes have, no doubt, a slight regressive effect; at best they are neutral. The social security contributions are subject to ceilings (that is to say they are no longer proportional to income once the income exceeds the ceiling) and the Federation directly bears part of the costs of these for many non-wage earners. Basic health protection is supplemented by private insurance schemes favoured by tax reliefs which offer greater comfort to wealthier patients. Assistance to families is the most redistributive because it is independent of income and financed by a levy which is not subject to a ceiling.

Naturally these various provisions owe their existence to historical reasons, and to the gradual building up of a network of social protection, the initial purpose of which was not redistribution. Naturally also, it is certainly not possible to proceed rapidly with the changes which would make the system as a whole more redistributive.

This does not mean that a general reflection on reforms necessary should not form part of any real attempt at integrated social policy. However, while the need for a reform of the fiscal system is clearly perceived, all the indications are that it will be studied on its own, without thorough consideration of the other mechanisms for raising revenues, even though the financial connections between social security and the federal budget are numerous, complicated and very important to the total picture.

It would be regrettable therefore to limit attention to a reform of the taxation system. It is true that no limits have been fixed a priori to the agenda of the commission which is meeting on this subject. The Minister of Finance is not in the chair, and its membership is very wide: the field is wide open for reflections, initiatives and negotiation by the social partners. These seem to be thinking above all of reducing the optical effect which makes tax-payers believe, through the intense publicity given to marginal rates which are in theory very high, that they are bearing a crushing burden. The administration for its part would like to obtain greater transparency, a simplification of management and a narrowing of the gap between the subjective impression of the burden of taxation and the objective burden itself. It also hopes the proposals for reform will take into consideration an equitable redistributive effect while at the same time leaving open the possibility of using taxation for counter-cyclical purposes: the reform will have to preserve the neutrality of tax revenues, and not reduce the financial resources necessary to the public authorities for the accomplishment of their tasks.

But will the real discussions over the coming year take place in the commission on reform, after serious preparation in the customary concertation system, or in Parliament, which finally votes the taxes? What will be the real degree of progressivity sought for, and what means will be provided for checking statements and preventing tax evasion?

E. INTEGRATION PRACTICE IN SOME GOVERNMENTAL ACTIVITIES

The examples given in Section B showed how, in regional planning or the implementation of regional development programmes, and also in the campaign against poverty, those responsible for the conception and implementation of specific policies bearing on various aspects of integrated social policy could achieve real social integration, combining various means of intervention in the service of joint medium- or long-term objectives.

But there is no real overall economic and social development planning at federal level, with the result that the management of the government activities which are now going to be mentioned gives rise to a short-term co-ordination between related functions rather than to real integration aimed at joint medium- and long-term objectives. Overall co-ordination between ministries is formally, according to the law, the responsibility of the Federal Chancellor.

As was indicated in Section A of this part, the division of responsibilities for regulation and implementation between the Federation, the Länder and communes is precisely defined for each of the government functions by the Constitution. This division of powers and responsibilities differs from one function to another; and this gives rise to important differences between co-ordination practices, depending on whether the function concerned is highly centralised in conception and execution or on the contrary highly decentralised.

The importance of transport for regional planning, but also the strong centralisation of the legislative and executive responsibilities in this field explain why the Ministry of Transport, and the Ministry for Construction (insofar as the road network is concerned) are among the federal ministries most concerned with integration, within an overall picture of the medium or long term, of the organisation of the national territory. The other functions studied - housing, education, health and environment - are, it seems, coordinated rather than integrated into an overall perspective of policy for society as a whole.

a) Transport

The example of the Eastern Region Development Plan given above is a good illustration of the role played by public transport systems and the road network in improving commuter flows between home and work, in revitalising border areas which are being depopulated, and, more generally, in organising social life around towns and village centres possessing a minimum of collective infrastructure (education, health, sport, leisure, culture). It also exemplifies the difficulty of finding a balanced way of sharing the financing of transport companies' deficits between public authorities of unequal size and power.

The competence of the Federation in transport matters is more pronounced than elsewhere, but not exclusive. Through-roads, motorways and federal highways come under the Federal Ministry of Construction and Technology, the Länder and communes being responsible for the secondary road network. The Federal Ministry of Transport is responsible for railways, and for post and telecommunications. The two Ministries seek to interlink as closely as possible economic and social objectives with financial constraint without confining themselves to immediate short-term problems, but trying to adopt an active approach oriented towards the medium and long term. The aim is gradually to build up an infrastructure which will improve social well-being,in the knowledge however that ultimately someone has to pay, and that he who pays is not always the one who uses the equipment.

A continuous process of concertation between the partners concerned takes into account various criteria: the relative importance of the areas concerned, profitability, transport safety, regional planning, environment protection, a formalised transport model. Federal officials are aware that a balanced concertation process presupposes certain precautions, since the economic and technical interests are organised: their representatives, experienced in negotiation, know how to put over their cases, whereas broad categories of people are hardly heard at all in the discussions in which they are only partially represented (people without cars for example). However much is done to correct this imbalance; the public authorities know that they must adopt a realistic attitude.

The pluri-annual programme drawn up as a result of this process by the Ministry of Transport is finally promulgated as a Law. The

Ministry of Construction for its part establishes every five years (the last one in 1975) a list of priorities for road construction, which it submits to Parliament. Priorities for the federal network have moreover varied, and those for 1975 are not quite the same as they were in 1972. The highest priorities concern high-speed transport for commuters and the most intensely used traffic routes. High priority has also been given to serving the border areas and to their links with the large population centres.

The programme drawn up by the Ministry of Transport includes a number of financing measures, sometimes unpopular, such as the introduction of a new tax on automobiles: the product of this tax is allocated to the development of the high-speed, short-distance railway network, financed as to 80 per cent by the proceeds of the tax and as to 20 per cent by the Land concerned.

A new Ministry of Transport programme is being prepared for 1980. Its field will be extended to inland waterways and pipelines (opening of the Main-Danube canal). Similarly, the Ministry of Construction is proposing for autumn 1980 a new list of priorities for the road network.

The example of unprofitable railway lines shows that policy is based on a long-term view: short-term rationality would indicate the closing of about 40 unprofitable lines, which each of the local authorities concerned would like to keep open, of course. It is necessary to examine case by case the potential usefulness, in ten or twenty years' time, of these lines, in the light of the demographic and economic forecasts which can be made concerning the areas served, before any decision is taken.

The assistance provided by the Federal Ministry of Transport in the drawing up of global urban transport plans - these now exist for almost all the large towns - has enabled it to participate in many detailed studies and to acquire broad experience in the matter (for example in organising pedestrian zones). A formalised model, describing the social utilisation of "space - time", based on the Swedish studies of T. Hägerstrand, has been set up and has led to interesting results, in particular for the city of Vienna. It must be said that the low population density in Austria leaves sufficient space available for the constraints met with in this respect to be less than in other countries: more than half the population is in towns with less than 5,000 inhabitants, and the density of the Vienna conurbation is the same as the overall density of the Rhineland.

b) Housing

The Ministry for Construction and Technology is aware not only of the importance of housing in an integrated social policy, but also of the difficulties met with because of the complicated division of responsibilities for housing.

Housing policy is in practice highly decentralised; the powers of the Federation relate only to legislation and regulations, whereas the Länder are responsible for implementation. The urgent need for reconstruction after the war (and the permanent economic crisis in Austria in the inter-war period) made the reconstitution of the nation's stock of housing a priority task after 1945.

For many years the bulk of the reconstruction effort was borne by non-profit co-operatives and the public authorities themselves, especially the communes. The allocation of the accommodation they built or reconditioned enabled the responsible authorities in the Länder or communes to distribute certain favours (a third party was hardly allowed to participate in these arrangements, as the FPO openly complains).

As the economic situation improved, private initiative developed and ultimately took over a dominant share: in 1979, 48 per cent of houses built were commissioned by private individuals, and 9 per cent by "other legal persons" (other than communes or non-profit organisations). Housing construction incentives were re-organised in 1968. The two Federal Funds ("Wohnhaus-Wiederaufbaufonds" and "Bundes-Wohn- und Siedlungsfonds")were replaced by various incentive measures, none of which, as will be seen below, can be considered to be re-distributive. But the Federal Ministry does not think that official action could hope to get rid of all the disparities.

People living in old flats who returned to them before 1968 pay lower rents than new arrivals, but there is no equalisation between old and new tenants. But the law on rents is the responsibility of the Federal Ministry of Justice, and not the Ministry of Construction and Technology.

Modernisation incentives consist of reductions in the annual repayments on loans granted for this purpose. Initially reserved for owners of dwellings, they can also be claimed, since 1972, for modernisation work commissioned by tenants or their dependents. These provisions, which are proving very successful as regards individual houses, are less effective for low-cost categories of housing, less at any rate than the authors of the law had hoped. Later, however, this tendency was attenuated as a result of the following measures:

- the tenants themselves were allowed to apply, under guarantee by the Land (1972 amendment);
- a housing allowance was introduced (1975 amendment);
- low-cost housing was given priority in the allocation of loans (1978 amendments).

In spite of everything, it seems that in the opinion of the tenants the additional charges resulting from the improvement work are still relatively high compared to the original rents. The Ministry of Construction disputes this, pointing out that the loans available are for 10 years at the most, and that the interest subsidies and housing allowances granted to the economically disadvantaged considerably reduce the net cost of the loans.

Building incentives consisted initially of financial assistance to non-profit house building organisations providing rented accommodation. They now consist in the main of assistance to persons or to societies who are building or improving their own accommodation according to procedures which in fact favour the more well-to-do would-be house owners. In 1979, out of almost 35,000 houses which received construction aid, 48 per cent were built by non-profit societies, 10 per cent by the communes, 2 per cent by other legal persons, 40 per cent by private individuals.

Subject to very generous conditions as regards income, any person wishing to build a house can obtain a very long-term government loan ($47\frac{1}{2}$ years) at a very low rate of interest (0.5 per cent) and with a reduced payment of capital for the first twenty years (at a rate of 1 per cent as compared with 3.5 per cent for the remaining years). These loans are granted to at least 45 per cent of total cost (within the limits of a ceiling price) for private individual builders, and 50 per cent of total cost for dwellings built by co-operatives or the communes. The high income ceiling, based on the ceiling for social security contributions, with a large adjustment for size of family (plus 70 per cent for a couple, plus 20 per cent per child) only excludes in fact, according to the tax statements produced, 5 per cent of families. A personal down payment of between 5 and 10 per cent is required: the remainder can be borrowed on the private capital market, with tax incentives which are the more interesting the higher one's income is: repayment on capital for these loans is deductible from the income tax base, up to a limit of A.Sch.10,000 for the head of family, with in addition A.Sch.10,000 for his wife, and A.Sch.5,000 for each child.

To the knowledge of the Ministry for Construction and Technology, no calculation has ever been made of the cost of these provisions.

All these measures (and the low population density) have led to a widely dispersed housing pattern: in the 1971 census, 41 per cent of the stock of housing (without counting farm buildings) was made up of detached or semi-detached houses. According to the 1979 microcensus, 48 per cent of houses occupied were detached or semi-detached. The result is that housing conditions are very uneven according to income categories; half of the economically disadvantaged (especially among blue-collar workers) are dissatisfied with their accommodation, either as regards quantity (superficial area) or above all as regards quality. The total cost of expenditure on housing compared with total expenditure by households is not very high on average, since it does not exceed 6 per cent, but it can be as high as 15 per cent for the lowest incomes.

The above figures must be considered to be provisional: they result from a preliminary across-the-board sorting of replies to a special survey made in 1977 by the Institute for Urban Research of 6,000 households on behalf of the Ministry for Construction and Technology (in the absence of a frame for the enquiry, the selection of the sample was based on electoral lists; adjustments then had to be made to arrive at a sample representative of households and not of individuals). The circulation of these findings should make it possible to stimulate a better awareness of the non-redistributive aspects of housing policy, which might in turn ultimately lead to a greater determination to include housing policy in integrated social policy, bearing in mind in particular the collective neighbourhood services which constitute the primary stuff of social life.

c) Education

The OECD has already devoted several reports to manpower and education policies in Austria(34); it is not necessary to describe here an original and complex system which has given proof of its efficiency. Unlike many other European countries, the percentage of an age class leaving the education system without preparation for a trade is very low. The almost complete absence of juvenile unemployment bears witness to this.

The importance, traditional in Austria, of the social prestige brought by education, which is held in much higher regard than wealth, no doubt explains the abundance of studies available on the effects of education, and the number and quality of documents written on the redistributive effects of education during the preparatory work for this report.

The concern to promote the integration of this sector - which the Austrians, it would seem, consider as an end in itself - into integrated social policy as a whole leads us here, however, to put more emphasis on the difficulties of the system than on its successes.

The considerable development of the education system since the mid-1950s, in particular as regards secondary education, concentrated during the 1960s on the general schools, and from 1970 onwards on technical and vocational schools. This effort has been effective in all the regions. Higher education, which is also regionalised, has experienced an explosive expansion.

The growth of education throughout these years has no doubt powerfully contributed to national stability by allowing people to hope for personal betterment, if not for themselves, at least for their children. Apart from any possible effect on income, education in Austria, more than elsewhere it would seem, improves social status. Greater equality of opportunities has been achieved without creating too many problems between generations. But it is not certain that the important disproportion between what is offered to young people and what the older generation, who finance by the taxes they pay the expenditures on education, have themselves received, would be tolerated for long in a less prosperous period.

For many years the driving force for this development has been employment and the labour market. The growth in education and training was justified by the requirements of economic growth. There was a broader consensus than in many other countries for a training model oriented towards economic requirements. This phase of educational explosion is now over, at least as regards primary education. There will be no return to a policy of quantitative orientation of education and training as a function of employment.

There are several reasons for this. On the one hand, in a period of slower growth a certain polyvalence is necessary in training, so that transfers to different kinds of jobs do not present insurmountable problems when each economic crisis occurs. Moreover, empirical studies have shown, in Austria as in many other countries, that the link between training received and jobs obtained was much less close than was previously thought: wage and salary earners who have received a given technical training are by no means all to be found in the corresponding trades; conversely, in any given trade, wage and salary earners can be found who have received quite different initial training. Since, moreover, population trends are going to lead to a pause in recruitment, the time seems ripe to look for new objectives for education to aim at.

In the medium or long term, the links which existed between education and income seem likely to become more tenuous: the proportion of more highly trained people in any given generation will continue to increase, but henceforward it will be at a more rapid rate than that of jobs requiring higher qualifications, which means increased competition for access to those jobs, and no doubt substitution towards somewhat less qualified jobs, at the expense of those who have had medium-level training who might have expected to take those jobs. There will be a gradual shift in qualification patterns; formal qualifications will be more and more a necessary safeguard, but they will be less and less of a guarantee of attaining certain ranks. University degrees will be increasingly taken for granted among executive staffs. They will have to accept having their professional abilities periodically checked.

It is still possible, it is true, that such a development may be put off for a time and not come about in the immediate future but only in the longer run. In a study financed by the Ministry for Social Affairs(35) the need for workers who have received a general training at least equal to university entrance requirement was compared with the foreseeable supply. On the assumption that the distribution of qualifications (in per cent) in the various qualifications remains what it was in 1976, the number of posts available for university-trained workers would be 125,000 in 1981, whereas the corresponding demand for employment would be 116,000. Furthermore, the Public Employment Service is attempting, by appropriate publicity, to draw the attention of employers to the many possibilities of using university-trained personnel and creating new jobs, with new content, in order to reduce the substitution tendency which threatens to emerge towards jobs demanding lower qualifications.

The education system has so far generated its own development. The time will come when the budgetary cost of this collective effort will be questioned. It is not certain that the present official attitude concerning the absence of any selection on entry into universities can be any longer maintained.

University entry for those with secondary leaving certificates is in fact completely free at present in all specialities, including medicine (for which, according to the Ministry for Social Affairs, requirements are not always met). It is true that the percentage of members of a given age group entering the university is still relatively low: 12 per cent (about 50 per cent of whom complete their studies with a degree), whereas the corresponding figure is 22 per cent in Germany. But the slowdown in growth and in job opportunity may induce an increase in this percentage, a tendency for students to "park" themselves in universities. In any case, even if there is no "parking" effect, higher education will have the consequences of the quantitative policy in secondary education pursued during the last 15 years: the number of students will continue to increase at least until the 1990s; it has already increased by 70 per cent since 1971.

The requirements of greater equality of opportunity would be enough to ensure that this trend will continue: the bases have been created for extending access to higher education to all categories of the population. But social inequalities are far from having been abolished. Whereas almost all children of higher social categories go to universities, only a small percentage (10 per cent) of blue-collar workers' children do so, even though the percentage has doubled in the last ten years (in absolute numbers of students, the increase is still below that of children of the privileged categories). Any restrictive policy now decided would only accentuate the gap at the expense of the underprivileged. It is not possible to stop halfway. Government expenditure on education will continue to increase more quickly than the resources of the Federation.

No doubt the process briefly described above is not peculiar to
Austria, and the same difficulties, which could lead to an explosive
situation, are to be found in many other developed countries. Reflection on the medium and long term, as an integral part of social and
economic development planning, would improve the chances of keeping
these phenomena under control. In any case, it would seem unwise to
deal with these problems only from the viewpoint of short-term co-
ordination.

But these are not the only difficulties suggested by an examination of present education and training policies. Others emerge which
are more specific to the Austrian system. Some have to do with the
division at a very early age (ten years of age) into "upper" and
"lower" careers, with the choice which has to be made between two
types of education; others have to do with the still widely practised segregation of the sexes in the training process; and yet
others are connected with recurrent education practices which have
little to do with initial training.

Vertical separation from the age of ten onwards between senior
primary schools and grammar schools means that, at the age of 15,
about 50 per cent of pupils begin apprenticeship, whereas most of
the others continue up to the school-leaving certificate, either in
grammar school, or in a higher vocational school (commercial, technical, etc.), or in a short-course technical school (two to four years)
providing training equivalent to apprenticeship in several related
occupations. When a child is ten years old, his family plays a decisive role, and there are few opportunities for subsequent correction,
in spite of the theoretical existence of open "bridges" between the
two sub-systems.

It is also true that the most serious discrimination comes from
the employment market itself which, in Austria as in many other
countries, offers lower pay for manual work than for intellectual
work. But the list of different trades for which the training lines
prepare their pupils is still too long in spite of the efforts made
since 1973 by the Ministry for Commerce, Trade and Industry to group
training lines which are "similar by nature".

A large proportion of young people would like to have training
for a definite occupation rather than a more general training.
Nevertheless, the segregative drawbacks resulting from the present
system would be less serious if the common basic education were taken
further, for example up to 14 or 15 years of age.

The de facto segregation of boys and girls, who are supposed to
be being prepared for different occupations, has moreover helped to
produce built-in discriminations in the reality of Austrian life.
In spite of all the encouragement given since 1969 to the training
of girls, the gap has still not been made good.

Discrimination continues, even for girls who do apprenticeships or enter vocational schools: although in the official texts there are no differences in principle between the sexes, schemes which prepare pupils for trades chosen most often by women (for example hairdressing) give a less polyvalent training than schemes which are preparing their pupils for trades chosen more often by men (for example engineering). Moreover, training for engineering is recognised as equivalent for several trades, whereas a girl who has been trained as a hairdresser finds that her qualification is ignored if she takes up another trade. The Ministry for Social Affairs is trying to get rid of the subtle discrimination which still exists in collective bargaining agreements, which for example prevent women from being data-processors because nightwork is forbidden for women.

The Ministry for Social Affairs is also trying to draw the attention of girls to ways in which they can broaden their occupational qualifications, and is taking steps to ensure that employers and parents are better informed on these questions. This is a problem of psychological attitudes rather than legislation, but it does not seem as if the social partners are sufficiently aware of the position in Austria in this respect, which is way behind that in many other European countries.

Finally, insufficient account seems to be taken of recurrent education in the general organisation of the education and training system. Efforts made since the 1960s by the Ministry for Social Affairs and the Ministry for Education and the Arts to improve recurrent education have certainly achieved some success, but it does not seem as if the consequences have been drawn in adjusting initial training programmes. This is still a field in which a better integration of social policies would certainly produce good results in the medium or long term.

d) Health and environment

Health policy has already been mentioned on several occasions, in connection with the Eastern Regional Planning Association and then in connection with health insurance. The next part of this report, which deals with the medical aspects properly so called of the Austrian situation, contains many observations on the scope for co-ordination between the Ministry of Health and Environment Protection and the other federal ministries, the Länder and Social Security.

e) Remarks on statistical information

Integration is difficult to achieve without adequate information. But the responsible people we met in the various ministries in Vienna

do not seem to be aware of the need to establish and use programmes
for developing the statistics necessary for their work. It is true
that a law passed in 1965 strictly limits the statistical responsibilities of the ministries, which it allocates to the Central Statistical Office. Those responsible in the Central Office assured us
that they were in a position to make the necessary co-ordination.

The most favourable case is that of transport and roads. The
Ministry of Transport possesses data on the railways and the postal
services (the latter in Austria are an important provider of road
passenger transport). It makes much use of data derived from censuses or from the "micro-census" carried out by the Central Statistical Office. It has built up models and has the necessary ability
to use them. The Central Statistical Office has worked out a broad
programme for transport statistics which has been reformulated as
a draft law by the Ministry of Transport. For its part the Ministry
of Construction centralises data on road traffic. The results of
traffic counts and surveys by interviews are used as a basis for
working out traffic forecasts prior to drawing up the list of priorities for the construction of roads (done every five years as
pointed out above). The Ministry of Construction is envisaging organising all these data, which have already been published, in the
form of a data bank on roads.

The decentralisation of responsibilities in the field of construction explains why the Ministry of Construction and Technology
does not possess a statistical service of its own. The compilation
of statistics in this field is in fact done by the Central Statistical Office, and the Ministry also makes much use of the findings
of censuses and the "micro-census". The Central Statistical Office
considers this co-operation as exemplary, and preferable to the
elaboration by the Ministry itself of a special surveys system. It
should however be noted that the Ministry has commissioned a special
survey by the Institute for Urban Research, the preliminary findings
of which - highly interesting - have been quoted above.

The Ministry for Education and the Arts and the Ministry for
Science and Research are adequately informed. For example, the 1978
Report of the Ministry for Science and Research contains many useful
tables.

The Ministry for Social Affairs has a statistical service which
is responsible in particular for statistics of employment and unemployment. It has also a special section on social security matters.
Apart from the technical problems it has to deal with, this section
is responsible for collecting statistics on social security, all
established on the basis of instructions given by the Ministry. The
Ministry is also considering broadening the scope of its traditional
annual report (Sozialbericht) and transforming it more into a "social

report" properly so called, which will seek to assess the whole spectrum of social problems.

As for the Ministry of Health and Environment Protection, it supplements the statistics produced by the Social Security Funds with data worked out jointly with the Central Statistical Office, mainly concerning mortality and morbidity and health-care personnel. It is taking steps to improve the co-ordination of the information system, in particular by exploiting the new opportunities provided by the data-processing equipment of the Ministry and the Länder governments.

As for the other ministries, the law referred to above, which gives the Central Statistical Office powers to carry out any co-ordination considered appropriate, did not seem to us to be being used very much. We felt it was significant for example that the people we spoke to in the various ministries never mentioned this co-ordination function during the interviews we had. We also noticed that the federal Law of 1973, which lists the functions of the federal ministries, does not mention the Central Statistical Office, whereas in fact it comes under the Federal Chancellery. The explanation given to us was that the 1973 Law does not give an exclusive list of the functions attributed to the ministries, whereas the 1965 Law had previously laid down the functions of the Central Statistical Office. The heads of the Office add that in their opinion the co-operation of the Office with the ministries goes well beyond the minimum norms laid down by the law and extend in fact to many details, whether it be survey programmes, methods of evaluation, construction of sample surveys plan, etc.

F. CONCLUSIONS

The critical examination made in this part of the report of co-ordination and integration practices between the various fields has made it possible to identify certain avenues of advance which could usefully be explored further, bearing in mind the present state of affairs in Austria.

a) Improving statistical information

Before suggesting some ways in which the body of statistical information could be developed with a view to achieving an integrated social policy, we would like to stress what has already been done by the Central Statistical Office to establish social indicators and the regular publication of "social data". It nevertheless remains true that the establishment of an integrated social policy would require an extensive development of usable information, and this, in our view, will necessitate a considerable increase in the resources of the statistical services of the ministries as well as in those of the Central Statistical Office. The gaps revealed are in fact due less to an insufficiency of co-ordinating powers, or of inadequate use of those powers, than to a variety of weaknesses: technical (in accounting for data-processing equipment), conceptual (in the definition of statistical units), legal (protection against the diffusion of data on individuals), or even institutional (depending on the administration providing the data to be processed). In all countries such weaknesses are causing real difficulties which increase with the complexity of organisation of the public authorities, and which can only be overcome by a process of painstaking, long and costly harmonization.

In spite of the federal organisation of Austria, statistics are fairly centralised. Some Länder, however, have the beginnings of statistical services.

All the primary statistics resulting from the observation of households, by survey or census, come under the Central Statistical Office, and that is its main task. The "microcensus" has made it possible since 1968 to make quarterly surveys of a one per cent sample of households (with sampling rates varying according to region), i.e. 25,000 households, the voluntary refusal rate being at the most 7 to 8 per cent. The questionnaire consists of a fixed part and a variable part, which makes it possible to cover successively a wide series of fields of household behaviour: training, further training, career development, consumption, health, leisure, holidays, etc. A special survey on the social situation and life contexts was carried out in September 1978 in connection with the OECD project on social indicators.

The Central Statistical Office has legal powers to intervene on its own initiative vis-à-vis all the administrative authorities in regard to statistics, and the responsible people in the CSO assert that they make constant use of their powers. As in all other countries, administrative statistics in Austria are produced where the basic data are to be found, usually according to a programme laid down in collaboration between the Office and the responsible administration. But such administrative statistics cannot claim to cover all the aspects of social reality. For example, the Ministry for Social Affairs can only record as unemployed those appearing on the registers of persons seeking employment. To develop a more complete system of information on unemployment would require, besides an already close co-operation between the Ministry and the Office, important human and material resources.

The same is true of statistics compiled for tax purposes. Significant improvements will no doubt very soon be made in the statistics on personal incomes of non-wage earners, on condition of course

that the Ministry of Finance takes the necessary measures, which
means increases in personnel and costs. The Central Statistical
Office has had to restrain its hopes of learning more about household incomes by means of direct sample surveys (micro-census). On
the other hand, it intends to put the stress on income aspects in
the 10-yearly surveys on consumption. In the 10-year intervals between two such surveys, it points out that the data derived from
the micro-census on households' equipment in cars and other durable
goods, and on the possession of certain wealth aspects (secondary
residences, for example) can make it possible to carry out certain
analyses on the gaps between rich and poor, and thus to be used as
substitutes for direct data on incomes. But the idea of grouping
together the personal data (on taxes particularly) on the various
members of the same household seems to have been rejected. We must
however stress how useful it would be to work out a programme for
doing this. The possible obstacle created by the law recently voted
to protect the population against the misuse of data bases is only
an alibi: statistical confidentiality is as important as tax confidentiality, and other countries have found it possible to organise
joint operations by the statistical and taxation services while mutually respecting each other's confidentiality obligations.

Statistics do not grow on trees! They require a great deal of
time, patience, personnel and computer-hours. Without systematic
arrangements for constant inter-ministerial co-ordination and consultation, strongly supported by the Finance Ministry, particularly
when federal budgets are being prepared, there would be little
chance of significantly improving data originating from government
departments or institutions. Without a persistent political determination to improve things, the quality of the data will continue
to depend directly on the immediate interest taken in them by the
administrative service which produces them for its own use, with
its own codes and nomenclatures.

The policies pursued would no doubt give better results if they
were based on less uncertain data. But it would still be necessary
for those who in principle need better statistics to know of their
existence and be able to use them. The development of a better integrated social policy should be of help here, precisely because it
would necessitate closer contacts between decision-makers and stat-
isticians.

b) Developing the regional approach

This is without a doubt the most realistic approach for improving in the next few years the concrete integration of policies as
part of an integrated social policy. The path it opens up seems
promising. But in addition to the physical programming of capital

investment, it will be necessary to do more financial analysis of the policies applied.

c) Approach to specific target groups

The precise report recently submitted by the Working Party on the Campaign against Poverty defines the ways and means for a complex policy(36). It is to be hoped that it will be possible to apply that policy with continuity and determination.

d) Tax reform

Tax reform should be studied from the point of view of a general reflection on redistribution.

Taxes make it possible to finance various social benefits, either directly or through subsidies from the federal budget to supplement the resources derived from social security contributions to the social security schemes. It is certainly urgently necessary to reform taxation, but care must be taken to ensure that the reflections and proposals of the Commission on Tax Reform which has been set up do not neglect the connections between taxes and the other aspects of policies for the development of society, in particular social security contributions.

e) Studying themes for the future

It would seem desirable to make a start now on studying themes for the future, without waiting until all the conditions have been achieved for a veritable planning of policies in the context of an integrated social policy.

This pilot examination under OECD auspices for which Austria has volunteered has provided an occasion for bringing together civil servants and researchers in a variety of policy fields. The fruitful exchanges which have resulted should be followed up, provided with a meeting place in which they can be taken further.

A number of themes are sketched out below. They have been selected from those which deserve priority attention both because they seem to be under-estimated in the current reflections of those actively concerned in social change, whereas they will, or at least could have a significant impact on the development of Austrian society in the medium or long term, and because they would make it possible to advance in the direction of a better integration of policies.

i) Population

The population, already very "old" because of the low birthrates in the inter-war period, has now adopted a fertility behaviour which does not ensure the renewal of the present generations. The general attitude is to neglect this phenomenon. As one representative of a political party put it: "my grandmother had 16 children; we were 4; I have 2 children. Who can say whether we would be happier in Austria with a population of 14 million than with one of 7 million?".

The economic and social partners have a better perception of the serious consequences in the long term of Austrian population trends, but that is hardly their responsibility and there is practically no discussion of the problem.

ii) Inequalities and redistribution

The subject of inequalities, on which a very interesting paper was submitted to the examiners, was not taken up spontaneously by any of our interlocutors during the interviews in January 1979. In spite of uncertainties relating to the overall figures repeatedly referred to above, Mrs. Fischer-Kowalski demonstrates, on the basis of a series of partial indicators, serious inequalities in many fields.

iii) Working conditions

The recent setting up of a Research Institute for Labour Sciences will make it possible to co-ordinate the Federal Ministries for Social Affairs, Health and Environment, Science and Research, and the activities of the economic and social partners, the Social Security Funds and the scientific institutions.

This move would gain by being approached from the integrated social policy viewpoint, taking into account. besides working conditions within enterprises (workshops, offices or worksites), aspects connected with the organisation of social life (in particular housing and transport).

iv) Recurrent education

A better articulation between initial education and the recurrent education throughout life would probably improve the social effectiveness of the education system and would be a concrete theme for integration of policies in the context of an integrated social policy.

Part IV

TOWARDS A COMPREHENSIVE HEALTH POLICY

The broad scope of the health-related problems and policies
dealt with in this review is evidence of the Austrian government's
concern to develop a truly integrated social policy. Until the
1960s Austria shared the optimistic view that the health situation
of the population would further improve through progress in medical
science and increasing public responsibility for health care and
for the equitable sharing of the costs of adequate medical treatment among the various population groups. Infectious diseases
would be eradicated, life expectancy would continue to rise substantially, and inequality in access to and use of optimal medical care
would disappear. Austria has not been alone in discovering, in the
1970s, that destructive forces which have emerged in modern society
are now threatening to offset the factors making for the continuous
improvement of the public health situation; that these forces have
to be identified and counteracted without delay in many different
areas and along many different lines outside the health care system
proper; that the health care system is tending to become less efficient; and, finally, that certain population groups are more exposed to these forces and less likely to benefit from health care
than others, in spite of the progress achieved in access to health
care and in social security.

The structure of supply and demand for health care in Austria
occupies an intermediary position somewhere between the national
health services and the more decentralised systems of other federal
states. The reforms required in the 1970s on the health demand and
health supply sides implied no radical changes. The problems arising
and the measures taken to deal with them were similar to those of
other countries.

Austria's tradition in public health policy dates back to the
XVIIIth century. The legislation which still basically determines
the structure, organisation and responsibilities of public health
administration was adopted more than 100 years ago. The rules which
distribute the legislative and executive powers in health-related
affairs as between the Federation and the Länder were established

after World War I. Social health insurance, now covering 98 per cent
of the population, has evolved since the beginning of the century and
was virtually completed in the 1950s by the inclusion of the self-
employed. In 1960 there were, on average, almost the same number of
hospital beds and doctors per 100,000 inhabitants as in 1980.

There is ample evidence that neither the early legislators and
their interpreters, nor the pioneers of Austrian health policy limited
the concept of "health affairs" (Gesundheitswesen) to health care
in its narrow sense. Hence, Austrian scientists such as L. Teleky(37)
were among the first to study the interrelationship between social
conditions in the widest sense and the health situation of specific
population groups, and to stress that improving social conditions is
if anything more important than making advances in medical science.
The Austrian contributions in the fields of psychiatry and socio-
psychosomatic factors for medical diagnosis and treatment are uni-
versally acknowledged. We also realise how much modern medical rehabilitation owes to progress achieved in Vienna since World War I
(Professor Böhler's work is an outstanding example of this).

In the 1960s there was in Austria a new upsurge of interest in
social prevention, medical prophylaxis, the integration of psychiatry into the health care system, rehabilitation and the reduction
of inequality in health care. This led around 1970 to a broader conception of, and framework for health policy. The most notable result
was the creation, in 1972, of a separate Federal Ministry of Health
and Environment Protection (hereafter referred to as the "Ministry
of Health"). But many other initiatives followed. Some originated
from the new ministry, or from the Ministry of Social Affairs or
the Federal Chancellery, or were instigated by one or more of the
Federal Länder, or the Federation of Social Insurance Institutions.
Some were pressed for by the social partnership organisations. Some
cannot be credited to any single body.

In trying to identify and evaluate these initiatives and their
underlying problems we have come across many approaches - from consistent concepts for social change to haphazard measures. We know
of the barriers to comprehensive change in health care in countries
with a high degree of centralisation. They are even more formidable
in federal states beset as they are with all the problems inherent
in the widespread distribution of competences and power.

Many of the problems and policies discussed in this part are not
peculiar to Austria, but we discuss them at some length because they
are of general interest.

As to the layout of this Part IV, it is presented in eight sections. In Section A we outline the basis and structure of public
health administration in Austria and summarise the Austrian concept
of a comprehensive health policy with a view to providing the context and background for analytical account and evaluation of health

policies which begins with a review of the most relevant achievements
and problems in the field of social and medical prevention (Section
C). In Section B we analyse recent trends in the health situation
of the Austrian population, referring as much as possible to the
underlying determinants and to significant regional and group differences. Section D then deals with a number of key questions concerning the reform of curative health care, the solution of which we
consider essential for the attainment of the Austrian health policy
objectives. Section E concentrates on certain aspects of Austrian
policies for health personnel and for what we call "health science".
We then go on in Section F to make a summary assessment of rehabilitation policies in which we try to identify advances made and gaps
still to be filled and to indicate future directions for action
which would accord with Austrian constitutional conditions and the
Austrian health policy concept. In Section G we appraise the salient features, implications and developments in the field of health
care in the broadest sense from the viewpoints of economic and social
effectiveness and public and private costs, and raise the question
of alternative structures for future health policy design and implementation. Section H consists of a summary of our conclusions.

A. HEALTH AS A GOVERNMENT CONCERN

a) Structure for policy formation and administration

The legislation of the XVIIIth and XIXth centuries and the concept of public health contained therein had established the predominance of central government responsibility in this area. Of equal
importance were the Rechtsstaat ("legal state") principles which implied that government legislation and regulations stipulated rights
and responsibilities for the individual citizens. The Constitution
of the Republic maintained the prime competence of the Federation
for all health matters, but with important qualifications. Competence for hospitals and similar institutions for example rests with
the Federation for framing legislation and with the Länder for detailed legislation and for execution. Matters concerning social
insurance, including health insurance, remain entirely within the
orbit of the Federation. However, the social insurance institutions
are bipartite self-governing bodies associated in the Federation of
Social Insurance Institutions (Hauptverband der Oesterreichischen
Sozialversicherungstraeger). They are under the supervision of the
Ministry of Social Affairs. The Chamber of Doctors, and the corresponding Chambers in each Land, have an influence on legislation concerning health matters, bargain on behalf of doctors with health insurance institutions, and exercise mandatory powers in such matters

as admission to or expulsion from the profession. Another Austrian characteristic is that for the most important social health insurance branch, namely that for wage earners and salaried employees (except those in the civil service and some public and private enterprises), there are different schemes for each Land, an important feature for health policy development and implementation in a federal state.

Since 1972 the Ministry of Health is the supreme authority for the administration of public health. Each Land government is vested with a Public Health Authority (Landessanitätsbehörde), and there are public health offices (Gesundheitsämter) for each county (or bigger town) which are competent for a wide range of public health affairs and employ some 250 public health officers as civil servants. Private practitioners are charged with public health responsibilities at the local level (communes or groups of communes).

In matters concerning social prevention and environment protection there is a division of competences for legislation and execution as between the Federation, the Länder, the counties (Bezirke) and the communes. It would be very difficult within the Austrian legal system to shift the legislative and/or executive competence for health-relevant aspects, say of housing, industry and trade, labour, transport, urban development, etc., from the authorities with the principal competence in these affairs to the Ministry of Health. The same applies to activities closely related to health care, such as social assistance and social services. At the Land and local area levels, we have been told, this dispersion of competences in respect of health-related affairs creates fewer problems. At those levels, either the same authorities would be competent both for health and a number of these other health-related matters, or there is close co-operation with the respective regional or local office of the federal administration. At federal level, however, scattered competences could be a serious handicap. There is, for instance, a separation of competences in respect of health care demand and of health care supply, and the Ministry of Health has only a co-ordinating competence in environment protection matters. The effectiveness of the established mechanisms for consultation, co-ordination and co-operation at the federal government level has proved difficult for us to judge. We confine ourselves to stressing that the implementation of a consistently formulated concept of a comprehensive health policy might meet with many difficulties if the ministry with the prime responsibility is not endowed with the requisite competence.

b) Policy objectives and priorities

We have been impressed by the determination with which the government adheres to the principle that every member of the community has the right to receive, in equal measure and by the same ways and means, the health care he or she needs, including preventive care, rehabilitation in the medical, vocational and social senses, and also protection of health from harmful psycho-hygienic and physio-hygienic environmental influences. We welcome, moreover, the fact that the government has switched from the negative conception of health ("to be free of physical or mental illness") to the positive notion of the World Health Organisation, namely "the state of complete physical, mental and social wellbeing". This implies as the prime objective the solution of the health problems of the population in this broad sense, not merely medical diagnosis and therapy. We can sum up the goal of Austrian health policy as follows: the maintenance and restoration of healthy living conditions, and the provision of an effective and economically efficient system of health insurance, health protection and health care for all groups of the population.

The government ascribes an essential role to research findings and to their application for health maintenance and health care, and this, we understand, includes research not only in physics, chemistry, biology and technology, but also in the human and social sciences such as psychology and sociology. We fully agree with the Ministry of Health in respect of two assessments: first, that the currently most prevalent illnesses cannot be attributed to particular single causes, with the result that it has become very difficult to prescribe a "causal" therapy and to organise co-ordinated measures to combat the causes; second, that the differences in the incidence of illnesses by social classes and groups, age brackets, regions, occupations and living habits reflect the varying spread of health risks, and that these risks are at the origin of the currently most prevalent illnesses, in particular cardio-vascular diseases and mental illnesses. Experiences to date would lead to the conclusion that comprehensive preventive measures (including environment protection and improved conditions for all aspects of life) are, in the long term, the most effective means of diminishing the health risks of the population. To counteract detrimental behavioural patterns, health education, counselling and information, directed to specific target groups and convincingly presented, should be an integral part of preventive health policy.

Concerning medical prophylaxis the Austrian government gives the highest priority to the early detection of specific illnesses, and to a further reduction of infant mortality and infant disablement, objectives which we, too, consider as being of utmost importance in the Austrian context for the reasons given in Section C.

In the field of health care priority is assigned to the reform of the structure of the care system by the application of up-to-date planning and management methods and improved access to all elements of health supply, in particular through an adequate regional spreading of the supply services and their optimal utilisation and accessibility for the population. The Ministry stipulated the following principles for the further development of the health care system:

- Effectiveness.
- Adaptation to the needs of the client population.
- Economic efficiency.
- Availability of financial means.

To comply with these principles it is considered indispensable that supply gaps as well as functional deficiencies are identified and remedied, as far as possible by approaches based on prior investigations and research. In the Ministry's view the most urgent problems to be dealt with in such a long-term strategic planning for change in the health care system and the underlying trends are:

1. The steep increase in costs and the burden to the economy this represents. (There are limits to the extent to which insured individuals and enterprises can be expected to pay for the rising expenditure of the social health insurance institutions.)
2. The sub-optimal co-operation and distribution of competences in various sectors and institutions of the health care system. (Shortcomings in the distribution of tasks and in co-operation tend to lead to medically unjustified overlaps.)
3. Organisational deficiencies and irrational work organisation in the health care services. (An inappropriate extension of the supply of medical services may engender a medically unjustified increase in health care demand.)
4. Inappropriate transfers of advances in medicine and technology to the health care system. (Medical-technological over-equipment and overstaffing of health care institutions induce a medically unjustified oversupply of health care services.)

The Austrian health authorities are paying increasing attention to the prevention, diagnosis and treatment of mental illnesses; they are aware of the difficulties and uncertainties, and the relative backwardness of scientific achievement in this field so far, and the close interaction between mental and physical components of many states of ill-health. They stress, moreover, the difficulties of distinguishing between minor transitory deviant reactions and illnesses calling for psychiatric treatment and serious crises calling for other aid. We agree with this prudent and balanced evaluation by the Austrian health authorities.

As regards the medical, vocational and social rehabilitation of the physically, mentally and socially handicapped, we have gained the impression that the many Austrian authorities and organisations concerned with this sector of health policy are developing a comprehensive and clear policy concept and designing the instruments to implement it. This field is so complex that we refrain from any comment before reviewing the subject in greater detail below.

The same qualifications apply to the development of a comprehensive and efficient policy for persons requiring permanent care to varying degrees, such as the mentally or physically handicapped or elderly people. Much is still in the making in this area, in particular as regards the borderlines and division of functions between the intra-mural and extra-mural health care systems on the one side, and other provisions for care on the other. The Ministry of Health certainly has an important role in this field, but so have the Ministry of Social Affairs, the competent social insurance institutions, the Länder governments, the communes and last but not least the voluntary agencies.

B. RECENT TRENDS IN HEALTH DEVELOPMENT AND THEIR DETERMINANTS

We shall limit ourselves, at this stage, to an overview of recent trends in respect of morbidity, mortality and life expectancy, trying as far as possible to take into account differentiations by socio-economic groups and regions and also the underlying determinants of the specific structures and trends of recent health development.

a) Demographic, mortality and life expectancy trends

The mortality rate in Austria is very high by international standards. It declined from 13.4 per 1,000 in 1970 to 12.3 in 1977, but rose again in 1978 to 12.6. According to the most recent Austrian estimates(38) it is expected to go on rising to 13.1 in 1981, to remain at this level until 1989 and then to decrease slowly to 12.5 around 2000. Mortality during the first years of life declined from 25.9 per 1,000 live births in 1970 to 15.0 in 1978 but is still higher than in any of the other developed countries. We must not lose sight of the significance of the age structure and its trends on the level of mortality. In 1970 persons aged 65 and over represented in Austria 14.2 per cent of the total population. Estimates show that the proportion for 1980 will rise to 15.5 per cent(39)(for both years Austria is among the top group of OECD countries) and will continue to increase at least until the middle of the eighties(38) even if allowance is made for possible compensating effects(40).

The main contributory factor to the rising share of the population aged 65 and over is the profile of the age pyramid, which has much to do with Austria's involvement in World War I and World War II. The share of the female population aged 15-64 in the total population of active age was 52.5 per cent in 1970 and is still 51.5 in 1980. For the population aged 65 and over the respective percentage was 62.1 in 1970 and 63.9 in 1980, and it is estimated that it will continue to rise to 65.7 by 1990. This reflects both the disequilibrium in the composition by sex among the present upper age brackets of the population of active age and the large and increasing differences in life expectancy as between males and females: at age 60 it was 15.6 years for males as compared with 18.8 for females in 1961, and 16.1 as compared with 20.1 in 1977. (At birth it was 66.5 as compared with 72.8 in 1961 and 68.5 as compared with 75.6 in 1977. Austrian males are thus, in terms of life expectancy at birth, still close to the bottom of the scale in the developed countries while females compare relatively well with their counterparts of most countries.)

There are significant differences in mortality rates and life expectancy as between various categories of population and different regions: a regular decline from the east to the west which cannot simply be explained by differences in the age structure; life expectancy is significantly lower than average for manual workers, farmers (in particular those combining farming with other activities), owners of small businesses, illegitimate children, widowers and young divorced males, which cannot be explained by differences in the access to and use of medical care services. We feel it is an alarming sign that life expectancy for males aged 20 years, 40 years, 60 years and 70 years has practically not increased from 1961 to 1977 - in Austria or elsewhere.

Even if allowance is made for the above-mentioned specific age and sex structure, Austria's position among the top group of countries is uncontested in respect of death from cirrhosis, accidents (in particular traffic accidents) and suicide. (More than 50 per cent of deaths of persons aged between 5 and 40 are due to accidents and suicides!) The differences both in the rates of mortality and in the spread of causes of death as between sexes, socio-economic groups and regions appear in many instances to be significant enough in our opinion to justify further research in depth on the cause-effect relationships with a view to identifying them and intensifying preventive action, including more effective public health education and counselling: the most significant increases (lung cancer,

cirrhosis, diabetes, heart infarctus, traffic accidents) are closely
related to social conditions and behavioural patterns(41).

b) <u>Morbidity trends</u>

In respect of data on morbidity the situation does not differ
much from that in other countries. Efforts to obtain better data
are being made by the Ministry of Health, by a Working Party for
Health Statistics at the Central Statistical Office, and by the social health insurance institutions. Moreover, the health examination
records of schoolchildren, working adolescents and military service
entrants are giving a clearer picture of trends in the morbidity profile of the Austrian population. There are also data which have
emerged from a special micro-census carried out in 1973 on a sample
of 90,000 Austrians. It covered both actual prevalence and incidence
over 12 months of illnesses strictly defined and other forms of physical or mental discomfort. The interviews were carried out by lay-
men, and in 48 per cent of the cases covered the answers were given
by a third person. Extreme caution must therefore be exercised in
drawing conclusions from the evaluations.

As far as current statistics are concerned one has to rely mainly on current reporting by hospitals and similar institutions, and
as far as wage earners and salaried employees are concerned, by the
social health insurance institutions. Unfortunately, the former
does not provide information by age and sex. There is in Austria
no current source on illnesses treated exclusively by extra-mural
care, but we hope that an initiative of the Ministry of Health in
this direction (current reporting by a selected number of practitioners in various Länder) will eventually provide useful information. We are strongly in favour of all endeavours aiming at improving current data on the occurrence of diseases both in the sense
of prevalence (number of cases of the disease there are at a given
time) and in the sense of incidence (number of new cases over a
particular period).

However, any purely quantitative analysis conceals many features
of today's morbidity panorama and their implications essential for
the shaping of preventive, curative and rehabilitative health policies. We present, therefore, in what follows a summary qualitative
appraisal of the four most preoccupying groups of illnesses in
Austria and the problems they pose.

In the first group, the <u>cardio-vascular diseases</u>, coronary ail-
ments (of which heart infarctus is one form) are the cause of more
than 60 per cent of all cases of death due to heart sicknesses, and
account for more than half of hospitalised heart cases. Heart infarctus, cerebral haemorrhage, sclerosis of the arteries and obstruc-
tion of the peripheral arteries are the most frequent forms of

arteriosclerosis. Arteriosclerosis is at present the most widely spread single major illness. There are two reasons why an efficient primary and secondary prevention against cardio-vascular illnesses has hitherto proved impossible:

1. Medical science still needs to know more about the causal pathogenic process of arteriosclerosis and high blood pressure. Risk factors such as high blood pressure, increased level of cholesterol, smoking, diabetes affect individuals differently and the real interactions are not yet sufficiently clarified. The effects of other factors such as mental or social stress and lack of physical activities must also be taken into account.

2. Public health education, counselling and information about the health risks connected with wrong diet, smoking, environmental factors, lack of physical activity, etc. have so far had little success.

The second group, <u>malignant neoplasms (cancer)</u>, are the second most frequent cause of death in Austria (20 per cent). Three factors are responsible for the increased incidence of malignant neoplasms:

1. Increase of cancerogenic influences from the environment.
2. Higher life expectancy (the incidence of cancer increases with age).
3. Changes in the age pyramid which have led to the growth in relative numbers of age groups most exposed to cancer risk (see pages 107 and 108).

<u>Mental illnesses</u>, the third group of major illnesses in Austria, present even greater difficulties, in particular in the case of personality disorders and neuroses. Established knowledge about the origin of the illness and the possibilities of therapy is still too limited. Moreover, compared with other disciplines of medicine, psychiatry has only recently acquired successful methods of treatment such as psychopharmaceutical treatment and various methods of psychotherapy. Many mental disturbances are in fact the consequence, an accompanying symptom or a partial cause of physical illnesses. The interaction between the mental and physical components of an illness plays a particularly important role in child psychiatry, alcoholism or drug addition, serious arteriosclerosis, geriatric psychiatry and in the field of psychosomatic medicine. As far as elderly people are concerned, the fact that the mental ailment is probably combined with physical disabilities, serious cardio-vascular

diseases or other physical sicknesses poses a serious problem. More-over, aspects related to the personality structure and environmen-tal factors such as social isolation become important. Also, healthy persons subject to extreme psychic stress may develop long-lasting or permanent mental disturbances or, in the case of an endogenic psychosis, suffer a relapse.

The fourth group, the so-called "rheumatic" illnesses, have be-come one of the major health problems of the Austrian population. ("Rheumatism" is an umbrella term for a wide variety of quite dif-ferent sicknesses.) Persons suffering from a "rheumatic" disease live, as a rule, as long as they would without this illness, but the quality of their life is often much impaired. Most of these ill-nesses are incurable and engender high costs in terms of social bene-fits, medical treatment and cures so that they acquire, on the cost side, an even greater importance. Rheumatoid arthritis is widespread and is the most frequent single cause of severe articular disability.

We shall now highlight a few trends derived from health insur-ance figures:

1. The average duration of absence through illness of wage earners and salaried employees decreased steadily from 1961 to 1976 from 20.1 to 16.9 days (20.4 to 16.8 for males and 19.7 to 17.1 for females)(42). No major group of illnesses showed an increase over this period.

2. The number of cases of sickness per 1,000 wage earners and salaried employees increased during this period from 765 to 908, but the increase in the case of males was significantly larger (from 783 to 965 as compared with 732 to 819 for females).

3. The average number of days of absence from work through illness fluctuated around 4 per cent of all employed throughout the period 1961 to 1976. (In this respect Austria is among the countries with rates close to average.)

4. The number of days of hospital care per 1,000 wage and salary earners and their insured family members declined over the period 1961-1976 from 2,336 to 2,220 while the corresponding figures per 1,000 insured rose slightly from 2,473 to 2,540.

This picture is complemented by the trend in recognised work accidents (excluding accidents on the way to and from the work place): 215.5 per 1,000 wage and salary earners in 1961 and 190.2 in 1976 (a figure which is still higher than that achieved in some other countries). Fatal accidents at the work place show, however,

a sharper downward trend(43). (We have noted that for females the
number of accidents at home is still greater than for those at work,
which leads us to the observation that in all countries increasing
attention should be paid to the causes of morbidity among housewives
and ways of countering them.)

Figures on physically and mentally disabled persons quoted in
Austria vary greatly according to the criteria used. It seems that
the figure for the disabled other than by reasons of age could be
set somewhere between 7 and 10 per cent of the population. In spite
of the reasons put forward in Austria (as in other countries)
suggesting a trend towards an increase(44) we have found no evidence
for this. The number of invalidity pension holders, at any rate,
does not support such a hypothesis: it declined steadily from
268,000 in 1966 to 236,000 in 1977(45), which appears to us to be
an indicator of a successful rehabilitation policy pursued by the
social insurance institutions.

It has not surprised us at that all available data on morbidity
which permitted some judgement on the distribution of morbidity by
sex, socio-economic groups, urban and rural areas, etc. point to
significant differences. Generally speaking, males are more at risk
then females, manual workers, farmers and owners of small business
more than other socio-economic groups, and children of farmers or
from rural areas more than those living in urban areas. The differences are particularly significant in regard to early invalidity.

C. PREVENTIVE AND PROTECTIVE HEALTH POLICIES

a) Environment protection

We share the federal government's concern about a situation in
which health-relevant environmental regulations are spread over a
great many of different laws of the Federation and the Länder the
implementation of which is assigned to a considerable number of federal ministries, Land authorities and communes. In the seventies
the government prepared the draft of an overall environmental protection frame law (protection of the biosphere through the fixing
of uniform limits; "environment alarm" systems; arrangements for
measurements; environmental inventories; procedures for the determination of compatibility of projects with environmental standards).
In view of the delicate problems of changes in the distribution of
competences raised by this draft bill, it is still under discussion.
While some Länder have in the meantime adopted laws in some specific
fields of protection, the Ministry of Health still has no more than
overall co-ordinating responsibility at the federal government level,
assisted by an interministerial committee, a consultative council,

in which the social partners are also represented, and a scientific advisory committee which prepares directives.

Whatever form of comprehensive legislation is ultimately adopted, the basic prerequisite for all regulations is the determination by experts of permissible limits and the availability of technical equipment for measuring infringements of the law(s). A good deal of preparatory work for the implementation of a general law has already been done by the Ministry of Health and some Länder and communes, e.g. setting up a basis for the environment inventory; study on the handling of garbage; measurement of water and air pollution.

b) Hygiene in and around the home

Various housing indicators show that housing standards in Austria are still below those of many comparable countries. We found it, for example, an alarming sign for the state of hygiene in and around the home that according to a recent investigation by the Institute of Urban Research about 350,000 of the 1,100,000 apartments of 18 large and medium-sized towns (of which 270,000 in Vienna) required in 1978 extensive maintenance and adaptation work to remain inhabitable(46). We understand, therefore, that the Ministry of Health is keen to contribute to an alleviation of the related physiological and mental hygiene problems by a law on hygiene in and around the home and regret that lack of clarity about competences is delaying the legislative procedure.

c) Work hygiene and industrial medical care and supervision

We consider that the work environment and working conditions as a whole (including conditions of daily transport) are of importance for health policy, but we have no basis for an overall assessment of the Austrian situation. We have met with many positive developments: an extensive framework of provisions for the protection of wage and salary earners (for which the Ministry of Social Affairs is competent at the federal government level); obligatory periodic consultations on related matters between the labour inspector, management of the works council, and the works doctor; periodic reductions of real working time (except for employees with household responsibilities or with a second gainful activity, e.g. farming); decreasing incidence of early invalidity and work accidents, and finally, improvement of the health situation of adolescent workers revealed by the periodic examinations (financed since 1973 by the social insurance institutions).

There are, however, a number of negative aspects to which we should like to draw the attention. The most important is the fact that, as far as industrial medical care and supervision are concerned,

Austria is still a long way behind other countries. The labour in-
spectorate has only five doctors and, what is worse, there are less
than ten full-time works doctors in the whole of Austria. Only establishments with 750 employees or more are obliged by law to have
works doctors under contract. It is hardly surprising that works
doctors play practically no role in the improvement of working conditions or in job (re)- design, and are not able to be involved in
scientific enquiries into the influence of work on the health of
different groups of workers, to say nothing of periodical medical
checkups of all employees or the role works doctors could play in
health education. From what we have learnt we have also gained the
impression that the special training in industrial medicine and hygiene for works doctors does not meet the rising requirements. We
therefore support plans to make works doctors obligatory for establishments with much smaller work forces than the present 750 employees, to have all works doctors employed by an independent body
on a full-time basis, to create centres for industrial medicine and
hygiene for smaller establishments, to provide for the involvement
of works doctors in changes in work places, to introduce a study
course for specialists in "industrial medicine and social medicine",
and to make periodic medical examinations obligatory for all employees.

d) Social prevention in the broadest sense

We should voice our support for Peter Fleissner when he points
out in a recent study(47) that "mortality has far less to do with
the achievements in the health field than with the social and economic conditions in which the people of a country live". It is true
that the improvement of the health situation was not in the past the
prime goal of many specific economic and social policies, but to the
extent that health has been allocated increased importance as a major
component of wellbeing, it has come to the fore, in Austria too, as
one of their principal sub-goals. We consider this to be one of the
essential features of the Austrian government's understanding of an
integrated social policy.

When we learn that psychogenic and socio-psychogenic factors
have played an important role in the rise of what is in Austria
termed the "new poverty" (see Parts III and V), we are reminded of
the Austrian government's commitment to the positive notion of health
which puts mental and social wellbeing on the same footing as physical wellbeing. This implies that the factors in life environment in
general which can upset people's mental balance and social wellbeing
are taken as seriously as those that affect their physical balance.

e) Health impairment in transport

We mention in this context traffic accidents which, even when not fatal, often lead to long convalescence and rehabilitation (with all the social and human costs involved) or to serious and permanent disability, and the vehicle exhaust emissions and disturbing noise levels. Like other countries, Austria has been following three lines of policy:

1. Improvement of the public rail and road networks aimed, among other things, at diminishing risks in road traffic and stimulating people to switch from private to public transport.
2. The setting of limits for vehicle exhaust emissions and noise.
3. Traffic education for school children and campaigns for influencing traffic behaviour, in particular of adolescent and young males, among whom the incidence of accidents (often fatal) is disproportionately high.

We appreciate that the Ministry of Health has taken the initiative as regards actions under the second group and sponsored a study of the traffic behaviour of young people. In face of a very high traffic accident rate, it might prove necessary to take drastic measures (e.g. stricter traffic controls and heavier penalties, in particular for driving under the influence of alcohol).

f) Health counselling and health education in schools and for the public in general

We have noted that the Austrian health authorities regard it as their duty to help citizens face up to their responsibilities for their own health as well as for that of their families and fellow citizens, and we have gained the impression that they are also fully aware of the need to adapt the methods and content of health counselling and education to the new morbidity and mortality patterns. As the average education level of the Austrians is high, and health awareness is said to have generally increased (without however producing any apparent improvements in health-relevant behaviour), we consider the task ahead of the Austrian health authorities to be particularly difficult. And yet the list of actions taken is a long one: cost-free prophylactic health examinations for the early detection of certain illnesses and general health consultation are offered to the entire adult population. The vaccination campaigns, in particular the one against poliomyelitis, have been highly successful and served as international examples. The provisions for reduction of infant mortality were combined with general health counselling to the mothers concerned and have led to a rise in the use of counselling services for mothers and families. The propagation of health examination at pre-school age has met with a positive response from parents. Improvements in school health examinations and school health education certainly make pupils and parents more health conscious. The health examinations of working adolescents include an important element of health education. There have been widely distributed brochures (to schools and parents) and a radio campaign on appropriate nutrition, and a brochure to help stop smoking. Every year there is an anti-alcohol campaign lasting one week. The Federal Institute for Health has carried out a series of studies which have served as a basis for anti-smoking measures.

Yet eating, drinking and smoking habits, behaviour in transport and other health-relevant behavioural patterns are changing too slowly. The Ministry is determined to intensify its measures along the above mentioned and other lines, and to do even more to mobilise the other public authorities, the social insurance institutions, the organisations of the social partners and certain state-owned enterprises. We believe that a comprehensive programme is the right avenue to follow but we are convinced, at least as far as smoking and drinking are concerned, that more prohibitions (e.g. prohibition of smoking in public buildings, as practised in some countries) and more severe penalties (e.g. in traffic) will have to complement information, persuasion, dissuasion and counselling.

The competent Austrian authorities might even consider whether any further intensification in schools of health education beyond the present level (health as a general principle to be integrated into each subject; special information materials put at the disposal of teachers) might not imply the gradual introduction of health protection as a subject (at least in the upper classes of secondary schools) and whether the generalisation of health education started under adult education schemes in some Länder should not be promoted. Moreover, the health education component of all medical examinations could be enforced and made more effective (which would call for a firm commitment by the Chambers of doctors and the conditioning of the doctors themselves for this task). Obligatory periodic health examinations of all employees could prove most efficient in this context since the family is still the basic unit for health education. Finally, we suggest that methods of health education, counselling and information should be based more on psychological and sociological research findings and on a proper assessment of bodily, mental and social health problems, and should also be more specifically addressed to the various groups. We welcome the fact that the Federal Institute for Health, one of whose main activities is health education, has strengthened its co-operation with its international counterparts, in particular the German Federal Centre for Public Health Education, since the science of health counselling and education is still in its infancy.

g) Consumer protection

In 1979 a new comprehensive law for the protection of consumers came into effect. Health is only one protection aspect in this law, which applies not only to food products but also to other consumer goods. There is an inventory of food products which has been established by experts and is kept up-to-date (Codex Alimentarium Austriacus). The risks of infection and poisoning by food or of injury by other products are thus being further reduced. We also welcome the agreements the Ministry of Health has reached with the Austrian tobacco monopoly and the beverage industry on self-restraint in marketing practices.

h) Medical prophylaxis

The Austrian government is going ahead with its aim of building up a system of continuous medical examinations for the early detection of illnesses and maintenance of health throughout life. Highest priority has been given to the reduction of infant mortality, and we can confirm that the introduction of "Mother/Child Passbooks" (Mutter-Kind-Pass), providing for a number of pre- and peri-natal preventive checkups at fixed dates combined with extensive health counselling and information, has become an example for appropriate preventive health care (mothers complying with these rules receive double the amount of the birth allowance). This scheme has done much to reduce infant mortality and disablement. It has certainly also been instrumental in persuading mothers to send their children later on to the cost-free pre-school medical examinations. Nevertheless, infant mortality is still very high and further measures to reduce it will have to be considered.

As for the regular medical examinations carried out in schools, the Ministry of Education and Arts and the Ministry of Health have co-operated with the aim of unifying the forms and procedures for the regular checkups. The government is considering a school health law which would provide, among other things, for full-time school doctors (at present the examinations are to a large extent carried out by established practitioners). This would be in line with our general considerations on preventive health care.

The regular medical examinations of adolescent employees and apprentices cover a large percentage of the non-school portion of the respective age cohorts (15-18). From information put at our disposal we gather that these examinations are fully meeting their purpose (better health among adolescents in employment; participation rate increased from 65 per cent in the mid-1960s to around 90 per cent at present; detection and early treatment of illnesses). We referred above to the potential preventive care role of periodic

medical examinations for all employees. A number of enterprises
have adopted this practice, and many public authorities have also
made it a rule for their personnel. The results are reported to be
encouraging and are also said to be benefiting the employers.

We have, however, reservations in regard to the Austrian approach
to cost-free population-wide examinations for the early detection of
the most prevalent chronic diseases, which has so far had little
success. In the pilot provinces Vienna and Carinthia the programme
providing, inter alia, for direct invitations, was limited to women
over 30 and men over 45. The programme was later on extended to the
whole of Austria and to all persons aged 19 and over. Participation
in Vienna and Carinthia varied considerably according to socio-
professional groups (76 per cent of middle and top managers but only
17 per cent of farmers and 16 per cent of unskilled workers). In
Voralberg, however, where a special model has been developed, the
results are reported to be most encouraging.

A study carried out under the auspices of the German Commission
for Economic and Social Change(48) stipulates for the early detection
of certain illnesses three conditions, namely:

1. It must be possible to provide effective treatment
   for the disease.
2. The early stage of the disease must be clearly recognisable.
3. Enough doctors and facilities must be available to
   enable the examination findings to be more closely
   diagnosed and the subsequent treatment to be provided.

We would like to add two further conditions:

4. Early detection must not have harmful effects on the
   mental state of the person concerned.
5. Early detection must be directed towards diseases
   which constitute significantly higher risks among
   certain groups of the population.

As far as we can judge the scheme for the country as a whole
does not meet all these conditions and we have gained the impression
that neither the Ministry of Health nor the social insurance institutions nor the doctors are happy about a number of its aspects.
Instead of a renewed initiative along the same lines (but under improved organisational and psychological conditions) the possibilities
should therefore be studied of directing the examinations more than
hitherto towards sex, age groups, work risks, living habits, special
risk groups such as socio-economically deprived groups, etc. In the
early detection of cardio-vascular diseases, inter alia by means of
regular blood pressure tests, examinations could be confined to

persons over 40 years of age. Early detection examinations for lung
cancer could for example be limited to the over-50 age group and
possibly heavy smokers. (We have been told that steps in this direction are already being prepared in Austria). On the other hand we
should like to recommend regular examination of women from the age
of 25 onwards, with special emphasis on the early recognition of
cervical cancer which can generally be successfully treated. Also
examinations for the early detection of breast cancer (mammography)
might be considered. We are well aware of the fact that the position we take here is not uncontested among doctors. We feel, however, that the Austrian health authorities would be well advised to
investigate the reasons why an increasing number of countries have
taken steps in this direction.

D. CURATIVE HEALTH POLICIES

First, we would like to stress that there is no clear dividing
line between preventive, curative and rehabilitative health care.
We are glad that the Austrian government takes this broad view of
health care and considers these three approaches to care as being
closely interdependent. As for curative health care we are pleased
to note that adaptation to the real needs of the patients has become
the guiding principle of the Austrian government's reform strategy
and measures, and we recognise that it is difficult to counteract,
by action affecting both demand and supply structures and levels,
forces which favour alignment of effective demand to already existing or emerging supply patterns and capacities - both in the intra-
mural and extra-mural systems.

a) Health care demand

The extension of social health insurance to 98 per cent of the
population has no doubt been an efficient instrument for influencing
health care demand. Equally important have been efforts towards a
reduction of the fragmentation in social health insurance and in the
provisions concerning medical services and supplies which entail,
inter alia, a wide variation in demand by socio-economic groups:
average expenses for medical services to civil servants and their
family members, for instance, were in 1976 still 74 per cent higher
than those for insured farmers. The fact that blue- and white-collar
workers have since 1974 similar entitlement to continued full pay in
case of illness has certainly also favourably affected the demand
pattern and level. The growing volume of private health insurance
may have worked in the opposite direction. In 1962 revenues of
private health and accident insurance companies accounted for 11.5

per cent of all revenues of public and private health and accident
insurance institutions, but in 1976 this had already risen to 15.1
per cent. In 1970 only 12 per cent of unskilled workers, but 48 per
cent of middle and top managers and civil servants held an insurance
policy. The share of private health expenditure in final private
consumption rose from 2.53 per cent in 1964 to 3.68 per cent in 1977.
(This includes contributions of the insured to the costs of medical
care, which vary from one social health insurance scheme to the
other.)

We cannot judge the compound effect of these developments on the
level and structure of aggregate demand. Total demand for extra-
mural services is supposed to have increased slightly over the past
decade. It is estimated in Austria that one in every two inhabitants now consults a general practitioner at least once a year and
one in three a specialist and a dentist. Cases of treatment in
hospitals have, however, increased significantly. In 1957 138 inhabitants per 1,000 were admitted, in 1977 179 (a 30 per cent increase), a ratio which is high by international standards. We realise that part of this increase is due to demand factors such as
rising levels of employment and real incomes, increasing gainful
activity of women, extension of social health insurance and decreasing availability of family members or neighbours for health care at
home. We have been told that the differences between socio-economic
groups in respect of hospitalisation ratios have almost disappeared.
The remaining differences in the quality of hospital care, and indeed of medical care as a whole, have as much to do with the supply
structure as with differing oonditions for cost coverage by social
and private insurance and with prevailing differences in the ability
to use to the full the opportunities offered by the insurance and
care systems. We consider, therefore, that a uniform rate of cost-
sharing for individual medical services, as is proposed in Austria
by some circles, would widen the differences in the quality of care,
and that public health expenditure could only be significantly re-
strained in the medium term if this rate were raised to such a level
that those with the greatest need of care would be forced to reduce
their consumption still further. Considerations of this kind under-
lie the reservations many countries have about trying to solve financing problems in this way.

b) Supply of extra-mural care

We agree with the Ministry of Health that an integrated development of the primary, secondary and tertiary health care functions(49)
implies that appropriate weight is given to each of these functions,
that a judicious division of roles is achieved between the intra-
mural and extra-mural systems and that the medical care function is

adequately combined with the paramedical function and services related to medical care. We recognise the authorities' and health insurance institutions' efforts to improve the supply of primary care by established general practitioners, in particular in rural areas and in certain urban quarters. We have noted that a wide range of incentives and disincentives is already used or under consideration (e.g. regional differentiations in the pay of services, cost-free facilities and other aids, equal pay level and status for general practitioners and specialists) and that the training of general practitioners after study is being brought more in keeping with today's requirements. Before taking a stand on this issue of concern to many countries we would like to present an analysis of the data put at our disposal.

There were 12,703 doctors in Austria in 1957, 12,722 in 1967 and 16,905 in 1978(50). With one doctor per 552, 570 and 443 inhabitants respectively in those three years, Austria was better provided than any of the other OECD countries. Established general practitioners totalled 4,963 in 1957, but only 4,145 in 1978, i.e. one per 1,432 and 1,809 inhabitants respectively. (In 1978 some 80 per cent of the established general practitioners had contracts with the larger social insurance institutions in which three-quarters of the population are insured.) Taking 1952 as 100, the index figure for established general practitioners was 99 in 1967, 93 in 1972 and 96 in 1978. During the same period the index figure for established specialists rose steadily to 269, or 5,188 in absolute terms, of whom only about 60 per cent had contracts with the big social insurance institutions. However, while the distribution among the Länder of general practitioners holding these contracts is fairly even (in 1978 one per 2,799 inhabitants in Vorarlberg as compared with one per 2,065 in Vienna) the differences as regards the distribution of established specialists are startling: 4,613 inhabitants per specialist in Burgenland, between 3,496 and 3,223 in Lower and Upper Austria and Styria, between 2,987 and 2,283 in Carinthia, Tyrol and Salzburg, and 1,491 in Vienna. Such structural imbalances in supply must lead to over-consumption in some Länder and to under-consumption in others. (To reinforce the point: the number of doctors in hospitals and similar institutions increased from 4,670 in 1967 to 8,274 in 1976, exclusively due to a doubling of doctors in training and an increase in specialists by two-thirds.)

We are not surprised that many established general practitioners are overburdened, all the more so as two-thirds of them say they have one or more ancillary activities. Extra-mural and intra-mural out-patient care arrangements have so far brought partial relief, but they are unlikely to extend very fast in the immediate future. The same may be true of schemes for mobile nurses, which help delay

or even avoid hospitalisation, if the payment for care is not satisfactorily settled by all social insurance funds. The primary care
framework might be further strengthened step-by-step by social
centres (nurses, social and social-medical workers, consulting doctor) and extended provisions for the care of sick old people in
their homes and in the medical care departments of old people's
homes. However, all these measures can only be complementary to
the work of the established general practitioner, not a substitute
for it.

We would not like to be misinterpreted. We, too, consider it
as inevitable that the continuing advances in medicine and medical
technology should push up the numbers of specialists and paramedical
technicians in both intra-mural and extra-mural systems. However,
we believe that the primary need of a sick person is not instruments
and new techniques but a friendly person who will listen to him,
give him an expert examination and then talk it over again with him
and devote time to him. We learnt that what happens in practice is
still often the opposite: doctors with too little time are tempted
to make a rapid diagnosis in the face of more and more patients with
unspecific or trivial symptoms, and to prescribe a medicine since
many patients seem to feel they are not properly treated if they do
not obtain a prescription.

c) Supply of intra-mural care

As in other countries, the emphasis in health policy had for a
long time been placed on institutional treatment and adaptation of
the intra-mural system to the new requirements. However, the expansion in the number of beds was slowed down in Austria at an early
stage. Indeed, there were 10.8 beds per 1,000 inhabitants already
in 1961 and 11.3 in 1977(42). (Austria is thus no longer in the top
group of OECD countries in this respect.) Apart from the two extreme cases - the Burgenland (less than six beds per 1,000 inhabitants) which is partly served by Vienna, and Styria (12.6 beds) -
supply by the Länder varied between 9.8 and 11.7. Yet the number
of hospitals and similar institutions (in terms of beds nearly 80
per cent under public ownership)(51) declined only slowly over the
last decade and is still above 300, with great contrasts in size:
Graz (Styria) has the largest hospital in Europe, while half of
Austria's general hospitals have less than 200 beds. Moreover,
there is still a backlog in regard to beds for the treatment of
longer-lasting illnesses, for the chronically sick and for old people
needing institutional medical care.

We mention in this context the amendment to the federal framework
law on hospitals and similar institutions (Krankenanstaltengesetz)

passed in 1974, which provides for a restructuring of the entire institutional system according to the principles of regionalisation, rationalisation and reorganisation. (The government programme has accorded priority to the development of long-term care and special care departments and institutions.)

The Länder have in the meantime passed the implementing laws and started to carry out the reform on the basis of a series of periodically revised development plans for the institutions providing the two categories of care (acute illnesses and long-term and special care) which are consolidated in the national hospital development plans. The target for 1980 was 12.5 beds per 1,000 inhabitants, of which 7.5 for the care of acute illnesses, but this target has not been reached. We have the feeling that the Austrian health authorities pose themselves the question whether this target is not too high.

Hospitals have been given statutory responsibilities for additional functions such as pre-institutional diagnosis, out-patient care and after-care. Hospitals as basic health centres are also supposed to assume counselling functions and play a key role in prophylactic examinations. In our opinion such an evolution would increase the already existing overlap between the intra-mural and extra-mural systems, since pre-diagnosis, after-care, out-patient care centres, joint practices, etc. are concomitantly promoted in the extra-mural system. Hence, we have the feeling that, as in other countries, co-operation and the division of functions between the intra-mural and extra-mural systems still pose many problems difficult to solve in the short or medium term.

d) Care of the mentally and psychologically sick and the elderly

Co-ordination between intra- and extra-mural systems is particularly difficult in the case of care for the mentally and psychologically sick which is, moreover, not well integrated into the somatic care system(52). There are many Austrian initiatives aimed at reducing care in "closed" institutions, such as a country-wide network of counselling and care centres serviced by specialist personnel (including social workers), "open" institutions, group therapy, homes for the mentally ill where they can do some work. We welcome this development since the often unnecessary abrupt change in life-style through the hospitalisation of behaviourally disturbed people can lead to such deterioration in their conditions that the term "hospital syndrome" is justified. Where hospitalisation proves unavoidable, decentralisation in special departments of hospitals as now promoted in Austria is the best solution. Great progress towards improved psychiatric care could, moreover, be achieved by overcoming the reluctance of established practitioners to refer patients to psychiatrists, and the widespread hesitation among the population to seek psychiatric aid. We have, therefore, not been surprised to learn that there is, on the average, only one established psychiatrist per 25,000 inhabitants and only one per 80,000 insured.

The fact that people can expect to live longer also confronts the health care system with a greater number of problems. Thus, geriatric hospitals must work in systematic co-operation with general hospitals if they are to be able to provide the chronic sick and older patients with optimal care and offer them the possibility of rehabilitation. As regards out-patient treatment, a broad network of advisory centres for old people could supply counselling services and assistance in social and socio-medical problems. Austria might well be obliged to go further in this direction, since the numbers of very old and of single old women are increasing and the establishment of old people's homes and medical care departments in such institutions is lagging behind needs. People must, therefore, not only be encouraged, but also enabled to remain independent and continue to live in their own homes. We do not need to elaborate on the serious, seemingly intractable social problem of the rising number of mentally disturbed old people and of providing accommodation for them.

E. POLICIES FOR HEALTH PERSONNEL, RESEARCH AND PLANNING

There are two closely interrelated conditions which we consider as the main prerequisites for the materialisation of the reforms initiated under the Austrian government's concept of health policy; these are medical and para-medical personnel in the right numbers at the right places and with the right mix of qualifications and attitudes, and adequate research and planning.

a) Further training for doctors

Doctors are ascribed the key role in reformed health care systems, but governments all over the world come up against doctors' associations which protest as soon as reforms are conceived which they consider to be contrary to their interests. The Austrian government, too, may have to face the fact that doctors quite frequently treat the health needs of the population as being of only minor importance. We have, therefore, serious doubts that the Austrian concept of a comprehensive health policy can be advanced rapidly enough with the present stock of doctors. In this respect the government's leeway for effective action is small indeed. One possibility could be balanced programmes for periodic attendances at refresher and further training courses for practising doctors, to be made compulsory at a later stage. Health economics, the interplay between physical, psychogenic and socio-psychogenic factors, social epidemiology, industrial and social medicine, social and medical prevention and rehabilitation should have a central place in such programmes.

b) The training of doctors

We understand that the Austrian health authorities are concerned about shortcomings in the post-university training of doctors (in 1978 21 per cent of all doctors were attending such courses; their average age was 31). The training of a general practitioner takes in reality on average six years, and of a specialist more than ten years, while the legally prescribed duration is only 3 years and 6 years respectively. Many of the hospitals licensed for training are too small, but at the same time there is a scarcity of training places. Requirements of industrial and social medicine, social prevention, prophylactic medicine, psychosomatic medicine, and rehabilitation, not to speak of health economics, are not adequately taken into account. Many trainees are insufficiently prepared for the conditions they will meet as established practitioners after completion of training. The training facilities for dentists(53), psychiatrists, pediatrists and for familiarisation with industrial and social medicine are too limited. Provisions for the control of the quality and breadth of training are inadequate.

The Austrian health authorities expect that the corrective measures now being considered, under preparation or already introduced will bear fruit in the medium term: assignment of trainee general practitioners to out-patient care in hospitals during the final stage of their training; designation of "training hospitals" and stipulation that the training curricula must include practical work in designated "training practices"; review of the conditions for training in hospitals; intensification of training in subjects of increasing importance for diagnosis and therapy of illnesses falling within the present spectrum of morbidity; steps to overcome acute shortages in training places for certain specialisms, e.g. dentists; reduction of posts for specialists in hospitals and limitation of the contractual employment of specialists by the social insurance institutions. Our plea for more established general practitioners is not inconsistent with our recommendation that action should be taken to cope with the new morbidity panorama by opening up facilities for training in corresponding specialisms, e.g. cardiology, rheumatology, cancerology and industrial and social medicine. Other countries have taken such action with satisfactory results, but we fully appreciate how difficult this would be in the Austrian context.

c) University studies

We understand the caution with which the Austrian government is proceeding in trying to adapt the study of medicine at university to the requirements of an up-to-date health policy. Reform of the curricula, for example, takes a very long time. We are therefore glad to learn of the decision to set up a chair for social medicine at Vienna University, and appreciate the difficulties that had to be overcome before social medicine could become an examination subject in the third cycle of studies. Only recently a chair for geriatrics at Vienna University was rejected by the competent university self-governing bodies. We consider this state of affairs to be a serious constraint on the road to a comprehensive health policy. How can this be achieved if the institution responsible for providing the key health personnel with their basic qualifications and imparting to them the spirit, ethics and traditions of their profession has seemingly not assimilated this concept? Judging from several Austrian reports the main motivation for the majority of students of medicine and of doctors in training seems still to be to spend a relatively extended period in hospitals as well-paid trainees with a view to settling down afterwards either as established specialists or as specialists in an institution. Employment in a public health administration function with the manifold tasks touched on in this part of our report seems to be even less sought than establishment as a general practitioner. This is said to be not only a matter of payment but also of social prestige and of "freedom" in a "liberal" profession. Strangely enough, many of the tasks of the public health administration hitherto developed in Austria are still fulfilled, under contract, as second or third activities by established practitioners. And - as in many other countries - it is quite common that a doctor employed with a full-time salary by an institution is also an established practitioner.

d) Role and status of doctors; doctor-patient relationship

We would like to recommend to the Austrian health authorities that they initiate a series of inquiries into behavioural patterns and attitudes of doctors and into patterns of doctor-patient relationships. Several of the points made in this report provide evidence of the crucial role doctors play in the health system. We know that this is a very delicate subject for any government to touch on, but we fail to see how the role and status of doctors can be altered without precise knowledge of the factors determining them, and we cannot imagine that the Austrian concept of a comprehensive health policy can be realised without fundamental changes in the doctors' social role and status and in their relationship to patients.

e) Other health personnel

Concerning para-medical personnel we have noted that numbers of technical medical personnel more than doubled between 1967 and 1976, while the number of nurses increased by only about 40 per cent(54). The overwhelming majority of this personnel is employed in institutions. Auxiliaries with little or no training nearly trebled over the same period, making up in part for shortages in respect of nurses. This growth has slowed down since the mid-1970s when the policies for the improved training of nurses adopted in the early 1970s became fully effective (for example: lowering of the age of entry into nursing schools to 15; building up of a dense network of nursing schools; accommodation facilities; improvement of training, partly by lengthening the training time; introduction of special courses for rehabilitation, socio-medical nursing, etc.). In 1977 there were nearly three times as many students at the nursing schools than in 1967. If this trend continues an increasing proportion of the graduates would become available for the various extra-mural functions referred to in Section D. The Ministry of Health might therefore (together with the authorities running the schools) consider arrangements for courses in socio-medical nursing and related subjects, open to both students and graduated nurses who want to turn to these new tasks.

We would like to mention here the so-called "Hospitessen" in the hospitals of Vorarlberg. They help the patients to maintain their contacts with the world outside the institutions and assist them in other matters such as dealings with social insurance institutions, preparation of after-care arrangements, etc. We were told that other Länder are considering following Vorarlberg in this experiment. It is true that social workers would be best qualified for this task (some bigger hospitals already draw on their aid). However, the function is important as such. The competent authorities should therefore examine ways in which other people could be attracted and trained for it (possibly by offering them employment on a part-time basis).

f) "Traditional medicine"

We should like to say something about another problem which does not refer specifically to Austria. Is it still considered compatible with people's right to choose that they are always obliged to go to university-trained doctors and their para-medical assistants? Or does not the right to choose also include the right to turn for help to someone in whom one has confidence, even when he or she is not a qualified doctor? We are thinking in this context of homeopathologists, acupuncturists, and so on. If the answer is "yes", then would this also mean for example that their fees should be reimbursed under sickness insurance schemes? We put these problems in the form of questions only, but we believe that the question of whether a doctor's monopoly is the best guarantee for the provision of health care is a matter for thorough investigation. It goes without saying that we do not have in mind a return to the earlier "quack" cures, but help by "unqualified" people the quality of which is controlled by stringent legislation, which would also have to guarantee that, in cases when it was indispensable, treatment by a qualified doctor was not hindered or unduly delayed. In many countries and in the World Health Organisation increasing interest is being shown in what English-speaking countries call "traditional medicine".

g) Research and planning

Health planning(55) will be but one of the functions in a field which we would like to call "health science". We have noted that the Austrian health authorities' conception of "social medicine" is also very broad without abandoning the rigorous principles of the respective scientific disciplines encompassed by their definition. Over the last 15 years a lot of pioneering work has been done in Austria in this broad area by research institutions and individuals. Important contributions have been made by the Federal Institute of Health set up in 1973 at the instigation of the Ministry of Health. It is charged with surveys and action-oriented research over the whole area of health, as conceived in this report, with a view to providing a basis for policy making, policy evaluation and health planning. It has moreover been entrusted with the training and further training of health personnel and with health information and education. Of no less importance for the advancement of health-related studies seems to be the working association (Arbeitsgemein-schaft) for institutionalised co-operation on health questions in which the ministries, organisations, institutions and research institutes concerned are represented. In this context we mention also the recent setting up of the Federal Institute for Demography and for Work Science. The relevance of extensive and co-ordinated work in these fields has become evident in many instances in this part and in Part III.

F. REHABILITATION POLICIES

a) Rehabilitation in the Austrian context

A federal government initiative towards better integration in the field of rehabilitation was taken in the 1970s when complete physical, mental and social wellbeing and social integration were adopted as the ultimate goals of both health and rehabilitation policies. This would have implied for rehabilitation a broad framework for integration and co-ordination along many different lines and at many different levels. However, at this time rehabilitation in Austria was still in its early stages in terms of numbers and groups of handicapped covered, diversity of programmes and measures, co-ordination between organisations and institutions involved and unification of legislation. Hence, priority programmes and measures, and fields and levels for co-ordination and integration, were first designed at federal level under the auspices of the Ministry of Social Affairs, which had the widest legislative and executive competences and disposed of machinery for implementation, namely the Public Employment Service (Arbeitsmarktverwaltung) and the social insurance institutions and their related programmes. The employment and economic utility aspects were therefore bound to be at the outset more in the forefront of the concept that emerged than might otherwise have been the case if the initiative could have come from the Ministry of Health, all the more so since the first steps were taken in a period characterised by serious manpower shortages.

Some agents still had to be won over to a broader approach to rehabilitation. Many doctors, for example, tended to neglect integration as an objective, except in cases where medical rehabilitation measures were imposed by regulations under social insurance schemes. Others failed completely to consider rehabilitation phases and measures according to the potentialities of the individual concerned, or to recognise the importance of ensuring smooth transition between the various stages of rehabilitation. Education agencies, for example, care mainly about special schooling arrangements for handicapped children, and many private organisations focused on benevolence and social aid, part of which in the form of work therapy. The Land governments competent for the rehabilitation of people not provided for by federal legislation (e.g. victims of non-work accidents, persons disabled since birth) and for social integration approached their task with varying degrees of enthusiasm so that their regulations and programmes for rehabilitation are far from being uniform.

b) Objectives and principles of rehabilitation

   We have encountered in Austria most of the objectives and principles which should guide an integrated rehabilitation policy: inclusion of people whose psychogenic or social problems have led (or
are likely to lead) to (economic and/or social) disintegration; rehabilitation conceived as one process in which medical, vocational
and social rehabilitation follow on from each other; priority to
integration in normal work contexts and only subsidiarily in sheltered workshops or in institutions for work therapy (with possibilities of moving from work therapy to sheltered work and from there to
normal, possibly subsidised, work places); concomitant preparatory
steps for medical and vocational rehabilitation at an early stage;
equality between the disabled and the healthy, and between people
suffering from the same type and degree of handicap; rehabilitation
as help for self-aid; involvement of the social environment such as
family, neighbours, key persons and colleagues at the work place;
qualified personnel for counselling for rehabilitation, and for
medical, vocational and social after-care; early identification of
candidates for rehabilitation.

c) Data base and recording

   There are a number of procedures for identifying candidates for
rehabilitation measures, but too many cases are completely overlooked
or not ascertained in time. The "Concept for Rehabilitation" presented in 1977 by the Ministry of Social Affairs urges that provisions be made for comparable statistics on the handicapped, with
breakdowns by medical and employment criteria. We should like to
add that a current recording system should complement quantification
by groups of handicaps. Rehabilitation measures required could thus
be defined individually with a view to providing a basis for timely
action by the competent agencies. In our view the design and implementation of a comprehensive rehabilitation policy depends on appropriate statistics and identification and referral procedures which
do not exist at present in Austria.

d) Counselling, social workers and after-care

   We have gained the impression that the key role of counselling
and social work in rehabilitation is recognised in Austria. We were
told of some advanced experiments such as team counselling (doctor,
psychologist, social workers) followed by specialised after-care and
therapy in one Land, and mobile counselling services by one federal
administration, but we also learned of overlaps and a scarcity of
qualified counsellors. The importance now accorded to rehabilitation

and the great number of disabled cases potentially eligible for rehabilitation would, to our mind, justify the introduction of a course of study in rehabilitation in post-secondary schools for social work as well as courses in rehabilitation for social workers already in jobs. An adequate policy for counselling and for social work accompanying rehabilitation and after-care such as is now being developed in Austria can help to avoid many inadequate measures and failures and overcome the serious bottleneck in the integration of cases with problems of a psychogenic or socio-psychogenic nature such as alcoholics and drug addicts before, during and after treatment.

e) Sheltered workshops

The almost complete lack of sheltered workshops and the programme for rectifying this is being referred to under Part V. Here we limit ourselves to noting for the record that plans for these workshops have already been prepared by nearly all Länder.

f) Vocational rehabilitation

We regret that we cannot review here in detail the diversified, flexible and effective rehabilitation regulations and measures under the direction of the Ministry of Social Affairs (carried out mainly by the Public Employment Service) which focus on vocational rehabilitation. (The Länder also have regulations and programmes for integration in employment, but their responsibility includes "social integration" too, even where this does not imply any direct gains to the economy.) The success of the recently amended law for the preferential employment of the handicapped (providing for quotas and penalties), the measures for creating sheltered or subsidised jobs, and the team-work and integration plans for more difficult cases developed at Land or county level have much impressed us, as has the close co-operation on general rehabilitation questions between the Land Employment Offices (Landesarbeitsämter), the social insurance institutions, the Land authorities and other agencies concerned, institutionalised by joint rehabilitation committees set up in the Land Employment Offices and based on a network of bilateral and multilateral agreements. These teams, committees and agreements are important assets for a gradual unification at the operational level of rehabilitation services rendered to persons with similar disabilities.

Austria has only a few vocational rehabilitation centres, one of which was recently established in Upper Austria with 240 places. (Most of the centres recorded under the label "vocational rehabilitation" seem to be institutions for work therapy only.) Requirements for up-to-date vocational rehabilitation include a minimum size, and work conditions similar to those prevailing in industry. Therefore a small number of additional centres for larger regions might be appropriate for Austria in the medium term. In the longer term consideration might be given to following other countries and extending sheltered workshops in such a way that they could be combined with vocational rehabilitation centres. Moreover, the efforts of the school and Land authorities to build up specialised schools for physically and mentally handicapped children should be complemented as soon as possible by provisions for a specialised vocational rehabilitation centre for young people.

g) Medical rehabilitation

Medical rehabilitation is characterised in Austria by the importance attached to the after-care facilities, and to provisions and rehabilitation schemes under the various insurance institutions which have been continuously extended and are becoming more aligned as regards right and procedures. The decline in work accidents might perhaps lead the Austrian government to consider an extension of entitlement to rehabilitation to victims of other types of accidents, including those occurring in homes. Under the invalidity pension schemes the first consideration has to be given to rehabilitation possibilities, and the health insurance schemes increasingly finance preventive cures, after-care and rehabilitation, but we could not ascertain the extent to which there is equality of treatment and entitlement irrespective of the activity status, e.g. for non-working females or elderly people for whom medical rehabilitation would be a prerequisite for social reintegration. We have the feeling that a great deal more concerted action between the health insurance schemes and the Länder is still needed to solve this important problem satisfactorily. Another weak point seems to be the referral of patients to rehabilitation by established doctors and by hospitals. As curative care and medical (and vocational) rehabilitation have to be co-ordinated at an early stage, we recommend - further to our plea for a greater awareness by doctors of rehabilitation needs - the early involvement of social workers acquainted with rehabilitation matters and of vocational rehabilitation counsellors.

h) Social integration

We believe that under the constitutional conditions of Austria a higher degree of unification of objectives, entitlements, services, etc., aiming at social integration, including provisions for the social integration of persons who will never (or no longer) make any useful contribution through the labour market, could best be achieved

132

at Land level. The success of efforts towards the full integration
of the handicapped into society depends not least on the extent to
which the families concerned, the neighbourhood, the community, the
social workers and the personnel of enterprises can be mobilised,
and prevailing prejudices against physically, mentally and socially
handicapped people attenuated. It depends also on adaptations to
the needs of disabled in housing, urban transport, town planning,
etc. Favourable conditions for initiatives in all these directions
and for their co-ordination can only be created within each Land.

i) Further developments towards co-ordination and integration

    We feel that in the Austrian context there is no alternative to
the pragmatic method of improving co-ordination and integration already being used. The medium- and long-term target of the federal
authorities is the improvement of co-ordination and co-operation between the various institutions for medical and vocational rehabilitation (including sheltered workshops and institutions for work
therapy), since there are still serious problems standing in the way
of co-operation between these institutions and the setting up of
new centres or the extension of existing ones. We agree with the
federal authorities(56) that a federal co-ordination body will sooner or later prove indispensable for this purpose. However, we consider it reasonable to expect that it will be at Land level that
co-ordination and co-operation will first extend over most aspects
of rehabilitation.

G. EFFECTIVENESS AND ECONOMIC EFFICIENCY IN HEALTH CARE

    We have considered the social objectives of Austrian health poli-
cy in the preceding sections mainly from the points of view of shaping of health care according to needs and reducing inequalities. In
Austria, too, however, it is now generally recognised that the marginal utility of increasing resources for health care in terms of
the improved health of all population groups has tended to decrease
through the interplay of a variety of reasons.

a) Effectiveness

    We agree with the Austrian Ministry of Health that the utility
of measures in health care cannot be measured in economic terms
alone and that the effectiveness of health care does not depend
solely on the state of development of medical science. Organisational structures such as the division of functions and the co-
operation between the health care sectors and the institutions and

vocational groups involved are also important determinants, as are incentives, disincentives and monitoring mechanisms. We share also the Ministry's judgement that the effectiveness of health care is demonstrated by the promptness and thoroughness with which causes of illnesses and health risks are identified and combated, by the extent to which diseases are diagnosed and treated at an early stage, by the rate of successful integration of the physically, mentally and socially handicapped in employment and society and, finally, by the adequacy of measures for people requiring permanent care. We also support the view that effectiveness depends to a great extent on priority being given to the sectors and tasks with the best input/ output ratio in health terms, which necessitates in-depth investigations into the structure of health care going beyond the generation and analysis of data on morbidity, mortality, life expectancy or on the quantity, organisation and equipment of health care institutions.

We do not know to what extent the Austrian health authorities are aware of the difficulties encountered by other countries in their endeavours to develop applicable methods and procedures for the assessment and evaluation of medical technology, including medical practices. The problems involved have turned out to go far beyond the creation of a satisfactory methodological and data basis and include such questions as the involvement of doctors and of producers of medical equipment or supplies, etc. We recommend, therefore, to the Austrian authorities a study of selected foreign experiences. This is an area of health policy making to which the countries participating in the activity of the OECD Manpower and Social Affairs Committee on "Health Care and Health Insurance Systems and Policies" have decided to devote part of the resources.

As an interim solution the Austrian authorities might consider the application of less sophisticated methods. Many statistical, research and planning activities hinted at in this part of the report provide constitutive elements for such an approach. We are thinking of work on aspects and causes of differing exposures to health risks, the under- and over-consumption of medical care and the statistical and analytical work preceding the elaboration of concepts, plans, programmes and projects, sponsored on the understanding that it would contribute to the increased effectiveness of health care as defined above (page 105).

b) Economic efficiency

There is also in Austria a tendency in some circles toward cost-benefit approaches for which there is only limited scope in the health field. We agree, however, with the Ministry of Health that for the assessment of the economic efficiency of health care as a whole, or of certain of its sectors, institutions and measures, it has become indispensable to identify the costs with a view to making their cost effectiveness measurable or at least permitting some judgement on the basis of input and output evaluations. Such evaluations should, to our mind, mainly serve as a basis for decisions between possible alternative actions at the micro- and intermediate levels of the health care system proper, and for demonstrating the macroeconomic soundness in the medium and long term of the (re)allocation of resources to other health care areas such as preventive and protective policies and rehabilitation.

c) Public health expenditure

In Austria, too, the recent disproportionate cost push, in particular in the institutional sector, and the increase in total claims under the social health insurance schemes (the latter entailed no general increase of the contribution rates and only a relatively insignificant raising of the ceiling for contributions) has brought the economic efficiency of health care to the forefront of public concern. However, this seems to have been due to other factors such as increases in other social insurance levies and the increasing size of hospital deficits to be covered out of local, regional and national budgets during a period of continuous fiscal constraints rather than to the increase in public health expenditure as such. The share of public health spending (including social insurance expenditures) in total public spending had only risen from 9.0 per cent in 1967 to 10.0 per cent in 1976(57). As far as we know, there is no evidence that there has been a dramatic growth in the share of health expenditure in total public spending from 1977 to 1979.

The principal question with which the health authorities are faced is, in our opinion, of a different nature. Expenditure for curative health care might have to be curbed in order to free personnel and financial resources and even premises for use in areas of health care which are to be regarded, even from the economic point of view, as being in the long run of greater importance (e.g. environment protection, social prevention, medical prophylaxis and rehabilitation). We consider it is unrealistic to expect to obtain from the powers who decide on the public finances agreement to substantial increases in financial and personnel resources for these areas of health care on top of the formidable amounts at present allocated to curative, preventive and rehabilitative health care. Returns on outlays under the headings "preventive and rehabilitative care" can only be discounted from relatively distant dates in the future, and there is as yet hardly any reliable basis for assessing them in macro-economic terms. (Given the prevailing distribution of competences and budgetary practices, such shifts of resources would imply, moreover, shifts to budget items at present, and perhaps also in the future, not accounted for under the heading of "public health expenditure.")

d) Outlays for hospital care

The net effects of factors making for an increase of outlays for hospital care and of countervailing factors and measures resulted in Austria in smaller growth rates for hospital care than in most other OECD countries. Trends in admission rates and in the age and morbidity structure have been almost entirely offset by a decrease in the average hospital stay from 24.1 days in 1961 to 19.6 in 1977. The main reasons for increased costs were a steep rise in personnel costs (increase in numbers of medical and para-medical personnel; shorter working hours; higher salaries of nursing personnel; progress in medicine and medical technology with the ensuing more than proportional growth in technical medical personnel) while other items, in particular investment costs, decreased in relative importance. It must be remembered in this context that the cost containment measures considered or under implementation include reductions in the length of stay in hospital (e.g. out-patient diagnoses and after-care; day- and night-clinics; substantially shorter hospitalisation periods in cases of light surgery), better management coming closer to business management practices (e.g. more competition in tenders on material inputs; better utilisation of heavy technology; "production line" rationalisation; elimination of overlaps; gradual introduction of a uniform costing and accounting system), and a shift from intra-mural to extra-mural care (e.g. the recently introduced leave with pay for care of family members).

Most important for the long term are the overall structural reforms in the hospital framework based on integrated hospital development planning, and the Fund for Co-operation among Hospitals (Krankenanstaltenzusammenarbeitsfonds) created at federal level on the basis of a State Treaty between the federal Länder and the Federation. This Fund, operated at the Ministry of Health with the representation of all hospital owners and financed by contributions from the federal budget, the budgets of the Länder and the budgets of the social health insurance institutions (according to differentiated but fixed ratios) could become the major instrument for a uniform hospital financing concept and a medium-term financing policy oriented on needs and effectiveness. No doubt the influence of the Federation on the development of the hospital system is gradually growing, but the social insurance institutions on the one side, the Länder and the communes on the other, still have more to say on matters of management. To a foreign observer it appears desirable that the social insurance institutions should use their influence more than hitherto with a view to ensuring an improvement in the effectiveness and economic efficiency of hospitals. The Länder for their part (except Carinthia) will have to rectify the somewhat anomalous situation which permits the head doctors of hospitals or heads of hospital departments to dispose of "special services" and other hospital facilities for their "private" patients, and to gain in this way considerable extra income. As we have read in a number of studies on the Austrian system, this tends to lead to medical over-consumption in the "special service" and under-consumption in the "general service".

e) Outlays for medical and para-medical services

Outlays for medical services outside hospitals have also grown less in Austria than in the majority of OECD countries. This might change if the envisaged shift of emphasis to extra-mural care, in particular primary care, and to new forms of care motivated by both social and economic reasons should materialise, unless other measures under consideration keep cost increases within narrow boundaries or offset them: stricter controls by social insurance institutions to restrain excessive consumption (medicines, overlaps in laboratory analysis, etc.), reform of the remuneration system to established doctors with a view to adjusting the type and intensity of care to needs without discrimination between members of different insurance schemes; increasing the cost-consciousness of patients in regard to public expenditure for their treatment; introduction of the first features of a "health passport" to rationalise co-operation between established doctors and between extra- and intra-mural care, and to reduce overlaps in diagnoses and examinations. As so much emphasis is now being laid in Austria on a reform of primary care we should like to commend to the attention of the Austrian health authorities decentralised experimental problem-oriented care projects and a greater involvement of the community for instance in the care of people suffering from hypertension, diabetes, cancer and fracture of the hip. In our view the reforms of primary care can only achieve the results hoped for if the population is involved and if the care takes account of all the problems of the patients, not only their medical problems.

f) Structure and trends of health outlays

We have tried to compare the structure and trends of Austrian health outlays and financing with those of other countries. However, the data available are incomplete and sometimes divergent. This gives rise to the question whether Austria could follow other OECD countries and develop a system of national health accounts. First steps could be a study of the approaches so far developed and an inventory of the data available or to be made available on the basis of existing statistics. We are convinced that such "satellite accounts" of national accounting will become indispensable in future for monitoring health policy.

In Austria total public and private health expenditure(58) amounted to 5.9 per cent of GNP in 1967 and to 6.4 per cent in 1973(59). Then it rose more rapidly to 7.8 per cent in 1975. Recent information suggests that the rise continued until 1979, though at somewhat lower yearly rates. The level of expenditure is close to the average for OECD countries(60); its growth considerably below average. Over this period the ratio of public health expenditure to private health outlays fluctuated around 70 to 30. In contrast to the trend in many other countries there has been no shift from private to public outlays. About 70 per cent of the latter were covered both in 1967 and in 1976 out of social health insurance funds(59).

The share of expenditure on hospital care in total private health spending rose from 32 per cent in 1967 to 40 per cent in 1976. No comparable figures are available for the development of public outlays for hospital care. According to estimates their share in total public health spending has risen from about 35 per cent in 1967 to 40 per cent in 1976. Austria would thus appear to be the country with the lowest growth of public hospital expenditure relative to trend GDP growth. As regards its share in total public health expenditure Austria ranks lowest but one of OECD countries, but it is second highest as regards public expenditure on medical and para-medical services, slightly above the average as regards medical supplies, and very high in the scale as regards other expenditures. But as regards the relative growth of public expenditure on medical and para-medical services and medical supplies Austria is considerably below the average.

g) Provisions for co-ordination and integration

Throughout this part of our report we have come across problems of "vertical" and "horizontal" as well as "internal" and "external" co-ordination and integration. We have given a number of examples of the Austrian government's growing awareness of the part played by appropriate co-ordination and integration provisions and mechanisms in the effectiveness and efficiency of health policy, and have also indicated the constitutional and institutional conditions for co-ordination and integration. We believe that further progress in the achievement of the objectives of health policy depends to a

considerable extent on the manner in which all the Austrian bodies
concerned solve existing and future co-ordination and integration
problems.

In regard to health policy the Austrian authorities and organisations might soon find themselves in a situation similar to the one
they were in around 1970 in regard to regional development policies
and programmes (see Part III). We therefore ask the Austrian authorities concerned whether the time has not come to study the
feasibility of a more developed common framework for shaping policies,
institutions, programmes and measures within the broad range they
have delineated for health policy. One possible solution might be
a permanent joint body for health policy, based on a series of agreements on the distribution of responsibilities, operational objectives,
principles of financing, priority areas, procedure. and bodies for
study, approaches for the elaboration of mutually binding programmes,
terms of reference for working parties to be established, etc. The
Länder, the communes, the social insurance institutions, the chambers
of doctors, the social partnership organisations and organisations
representing the client population could all be brought in in accordance with the Austrian tradition. The concretisation in some detail
of the concept for a comprehensive health policy could be the first
task to be tackled under such a scheme. The elaboration of a national health development plan, a long-term plan for health personnel
(supply and demand) and more detailed programmes (including time
horizons and financing implications) in priority areas agreed upon
could follow. Given the constitutional distribution of competences
and the necessity of bringing policy and programme development and
implementation closer to real needs - which would also comply with
the new emphasis on the development of primary health care - complementary institutional, planning and programming arrangements at
Land and local area level might also be considered.

A move in this direction is, in our opinion, one of the most important preconditions for substantial progress towards the realisation of the Austrian concept of a comprehensive health policy.

H. CONCLUSIONS

The structure for health policy formation and public health administration has proved adequate for coping with past problems.
However, more competences will have to be vested in the Ministry of
Health and Environment Protection so that the broad Austrian approach
to health problems can be further developed and materialised. This
applies in particular to its preventive aspects. Redistribution of
competences and improved co-ordination and co-operation between the

agents involved are as important as intensified research into and
corrections of identified supply gaps and functional deficiencies
in health care. The guiding principles for the structural reform
of health care within the framework adopted in Austria, the priority
targets chosen and the methods now being developed have emerged from
a comprehensive health policy concept, but much remains to be done
in ascertaining trends in health development and their determinants,
in promoting the various fields of preventive health policy, in reforming curative health and health personnel policies, and in developing rehabilitation policies.

a) Health situation

Austria's health situation is similar to that in other developed
countries. A number of specific features call for substantially improved statistics and intensified multi-disciplinary research into
cause-effect relationships. This applies particularly to demographic factors, the interaction between psychogenic (and socio-psychogenic)
and somatic symptoms, the reasons for the high suicide rate, the
differences in prevalence and incidence of many illnesses and in
mortality as between the various regions and socio-economic population groups, the extent and structure of disablement and, finally,
the changes in the morbidity and mortality patterns.

b) Preventive health policies

Great efforts towards effective environment protection have been
made by the Austrian authorities, and it would seem desirable that
they should soon lead to a unified system of control of soil, water
and air pollution. Action against exposure to noise detrimental to
health is particularly important, because noise is also increasingly
found to be the cause of mental instabilities. A law on hygiene in
and around the home could support strengthened housing and urban renewal policies in the solution of the serious problems of both physiological and mental hygiene still prevailing in many of the larger
towns, and especially in Vienna. As regards work hygiene and industrial medical care and supervision, the many positive developments
are far outweighed by negative aspects such as the striking deficiencies in the network for industrial medical care and supervision.
Remedial programmes under consideration in this area should be given
top priority. The broad range of policies aimed both at higher
living standards with reduced inequalities and at providing a greater degree of social security also aim at improvements in the health
field. The present campaign against the "new poverty", in the evolution of which psychogenic and socio-psychogenic factors play a
prominent part, is in line with this tradition. Health counselling,

information and education are given high priority in Austrian preventive health policy. Since the campaigns against detrimental eating, drinking and smoking habits, traffic behaviour and other behavioural factors of increasing relevance for morbidity and mortality have so far had little success, it is recommended that future action be based more on psychological and sociological research findings and directed more specifically to particular target groups. Appropriate targeting according to risk groups should also be the guiding principle in a reformed programme for prophylactic health examinations, since the scheme for population-wide examinations for the early detection of certain diseases has so far met with little response. In contrast to this, the incentives offered and the methods developed for pre- and perinatal checkups have so far proved successful and have largely contributed to lowering infant mortality, but as this is now stagnating new measures will have to be designed.

c) Curative health policies

The objective of an integrated development of primary, secondary and tertiary health care has led to a structural reform of the hospital network based on the principles of regionalisation, rationalisation and reorganisation, to efforts towards better co-operation and division of work between the extra-mural and intra-mural systems and to first steps towards an overall reshaping of primary care. There is, however, still much to be done to even out regional imbalances of supply, to eliminate the simultaneous existence of over- and under-consumption, and to establish a sound relationship between primary, secondary and tertiary care, and between intra-mural and extra-mural care. The target of strengthening the latter will only be met if primary care provisions (with the general practitioner playing a central role) are developed at the expense of the secondary care system, if conditions are created for more care of the sick at home instead of in institutions, and if nurses and other para-medical personnel can take over some functions from doctors. Moreover, a network of socio-medical nurses, of health counselling offices and of social centres might prove to be an indispensable complement, in particular for the care of the aged. This would in turn call for the integration of related social services of different agencies at the local area level. A revision of the payment of services of doctors by the social insurance systems designed to make them more effective is a further precondition. Finally, help by "unqualified" personnel such as homeopathologists and acupuncturists controlled by legislation must be reconsidered.

The integration of care for the mentally and psychologically sick into the health care system has been advancing too slowly, and there is still too much segregation between intra-mural and extra-mural care in this field of medicine. Initiatives directed towards the care of people outside "closed" institutions, closer co-operation between psychiatrists and other doctors, and the establishment of more psychiatrists should be encouraged.

d) Policies for health personnel

Progress in reforming the post-university training of doctors to bring it into line with new requirements has been limited, in spite of the many initiatives by the authorities concerned. Changes in this area need to be speeded up by appropriate new measures, including adaptation of the training curricula and arrangements and better control of effectiveness. In this context the problem of further training and refresher training for practising doctors calls for solutions going far beyond the present voluntary arrangements. As regards the faculties of medicine, comparison of the health policy lines adopted with the structure and orientation of university studies suggests the need for even greater changes.

e) Planning and research

The Austrian health authorities have embarked upon an all-embracing approach to the planning of the structural adaptation of the institutional network to real needs which is continually improved. It will have to be complemented by adequate planning for health personnel, including an indication of the policies needed for the implementation of the plans. Due account should be taken of prevailing attitudinal patterns, doctor-patient relationships and other barriers to more rapid change. Finally, these planning activities should be conceived of as belonging to an evolving new discipline to be called "health science", which should go much beyond the borderlines of "social medicine" as traditionally drawn. It would have to embrace all problems connected with social and medical prevention and medical, vocational and social rehabilitation, and include permanent care, health economics, public health administration and the management of health institutions.

f) Rehabilitation policies

In the area of rehabilitation, in which Austria has made little progress compared with some other countries, the recent initiatives concentrating on vocational rehabilitation (including sheltered workshops) and on co-ordination of activities in this field are examples of an appropriate approach. However, there is scope for considerable improvement in the co-ordination between the quite advanced

system for medical rehabilitation and the schemes for vocational rehabilitation, and between the latter and social integration. The
same applies to co-operation between the medical care system and the
rehabilitation system as a whole. The objectives and concepts evolving in Austria are to be welcomed, but there are still many gaps to
be bridged, such as the lack of specialised vocational rehabilitation
facilities for disabled young people, medical and social rehabilitation of persons who are not going to return to the labour market,
e.g. the elderly, and arrangements for the overall integration of
all aspects of rehabilitation and of all agencies, institutions and
programmes engaged in it (including those for counselling). Given
the constitutional conditions, the main impact of such an integrative
approach should be focused at the level of the Land.

g) Increasing effectiveness and economic efficiency

Financial constraints have led, in Austria as in other countries,
to increasing concern with the effectiveness and economic efficiency
of health care in the broad approach underlying the Austrian concept
of health policy. A number of steps have been taken with a view to
increasing effectiveness and economic efficiency. Austria should
draw as much as possible on the experience of other countries which
are more advanced in the assessment and evaluation of alternative
measures, procedures, structures and technologies (including medical
practices). The strengthened position of the federal budget in
health care financing and the creation of the Fund for Co-operation
among Hospitals should entail a greater emphasis on performance param-
eters in the allocation of funds and should give an impetus to the
development of a national framework for medium-term financing and
national health accounting. Austria should, on the other hand, experiment with problem-oriented health care projects, both within
the hospital system and at the primary care level, with a view to
stimulating the joint involvement of patients, health personnel,
social workers and the community. This would help to improve the
macro-economic records of the Austrian health care system, which
already compare well in almost every respect with those of other
countries.

h) Improved co-ordination and integration

One of the essential preconditions for the realisation of a comprehensive health policy as it has been conceived in Austria is improved co-ordination and integration at all levels and among all the
functions concerned. This objective, important for the effectiveness and economic efficiency of health policy and health-related

policies, is being pursued in Austria in a pragmatic manner from various angles. Further substantial progress will depend, however, to a large extent on the elaboration of a comprehensive national health development plan embracing all relevant areas and including policies, institutions, action programmes and measures coming under the competence of many different authorities or organisations. A solution similar to that found at the beginning of the 1970s for an integrated approach to regional development might provide a framework for this task which would appear appropriate to the Austrian conditions.

Part V

REFORM PRIORITIES AND PROBLEMS FOR THE FUTURE

In this concluding part of the report we discuss specific problems the solutions to which are essential elements of an integrated social policy oriented towards the realisation of the "concept of a humane and just society". We make suggestions concerning further steps to be taken along a road already being followed, and about whose ultimate goal a broad consensus exists. In the final section we present some admittedly very speculative reflections about the possibilities the "Austrian model" can offer for coping with the demands of a society less oriented towards growth, and ask whether elements of the undoubtedly successful Austrian model could be applicable to other countries.

A. THE CAMPAIGN AGAINST POVERTY

The existence of "poverty", whether in the literal, traditional sense, or in a more relative sense, must be regarded as a shortcoming in a society which has given priority to equality of opportunity, the well-being of all its citizens and social integration. In her report, Fischer-Kowalski describes existing inequalities in Austria in a number of social fields such as incomes, education, health, housing, the labour market, etc.(21), but she does not tell us whether the efforts to achieve equality have led to a greater reduction in inequalities in Austria than in other comparable countries.

There is no doubt that "poverty", as the extreme expression for social inequality, is still to be found to some extent in Austria. In 1971 Federal Chancellor Kreisky spoke of 450,000 "poor people", among whom he included recipients of supplementary allowances, widows receiving supplementary pensions from the War Victims' Benefit Schemes, and people on permanent relief. These groups must in the meantime have declined in numbers, and the social assistance provided for them has been so improved that they now all come above the lower limits and some of them above the upper limit of the poverty line (the rather arbitrary definition of which is shown by the reference,

145

in the study on Poverty in Vienna, to "minimum adequacy" and "minimum comfort"(61).

Even though poverty in the form of physical need and serious deprivation has declined, a number of studies show that there are still many cases of poverty in the form of an inadequate standard of living such as bad housing conditions, no money to spare for holidays or cultural activities, lack of durable consumer goods, i.e. poverty as a relative concept. The extent of poverty estimated according to objective criteria corresponds more or less to the numbers of people who subjectively think of themselves as poor or disadvantaged. According to a survey by the Institute for Empirical Social Research (IFES), quoted in the federal government's Report on Poverty, some years ago 3 per cent of Austrians thought of themselves as poor, 15 to 20 per cent as socially disadvantaged(62). Answers to a questionnaire put to social workers by the Institute showed that one-third of all poverty cases consisted of persons who did not take full advantage of public assistance possibilities open to them, that in half of all cases poverty could not be remedied by the assistance provided, and that a considerable proportion of existing poverty is unknown to the authorities(63). In about half the cases of perceivable poverty it was possible to diagnose insufficient diet, substandard housing, damage to health and social isolation. These, in other words, were cases of "cumulative deprivation".

A study of "Poverty in the welfare society" by the Styrian Land government, based on a sample of 3,700 households and interviews of 800 households, shows that poverty both as a reality and as a subjective awareness still exists in these lowest income groups(64): 16 per cent of these households had a weighted per caput net income of less than A.Sch.2,500 per month, almost half of them had no bath or shower, only 12 per cent could afford a holiday away from home; 25 per cent of the households interviewed classified themselves as "poor" or "very hard pressed".

Poverty in the sense of low incomes, bad housing and transport conditions, and cultural isolation is also to be found among hill farmers, even though conditions for this group are by no means uniform(65).

The Austrian government is very much aware of this problem and has laid down the strategies for the anti-poverty campaign in its Report on Poverty already referred to above. It puts the main emphasis on its comprehensive package of measures on the fight against unemployment and poverty among the elderly, and also on a vigorous development of family policies, but stresses that preventive measures are often more important than financial assistance, especially in the fields of employment and health policies. "Primary prevention to forestall the emergence of poverty can therefore be attempted only in the framework of a social policy for society as a whole, which aims at a just distribution of incomes and opportunities for education and employment throughout the whole population; it is not simply a question of caring for the poor"(62). Poor co-ordination is referred to as a problem, and co-operation between Bund, Länder, communes and voluntary organisations is regarded as an indispensable condition for an effective anti-poverty campaign. On the occasion of an enquiry into poverty held by the federal government in January 1978, Helga Nowotny stressed the integrative nature of the problem: one must get away from the traditional anti-poverty strategies and aim not only at material assistance but at the social integration of those concerned, and at mobilising their ability to help themselves. Similar views are expressed in the findings of three working groups of experts who worked out a comprehensive list of measures as part of the "Anti-poverty Campaign" programme: co-ordination between the various welfare authorities and organisations must be improved.

The campaign of the Austrian government against the poverty still remaining in the welfare state - a poverty which is increasingly non-economic in nature and therefore difficult to identify conceptually and statistically - is progressive and exemplary. Indeed, the examiners feel that their task is to present Austria as an example to other countries in these fields, rather than making recommendations to the Austrians concerning actions in which they have already advanced a long way. The Austrian concept of poverty not only as a failure of the social security system but as a result of social conditions which can only be remedied in the main by integrated social policy measures, seems to us to be an important starting point for current and future action(36). But we feel that that action would be even more effective if the government could get a clear overview of poverty and the social processes which give rise to it and are frequently cumulative in effect. Consideration might be given to initiating a thorough, Federation-wide survey of the incidence and components of poverty on a sample basis (on the lines, say, of the Swedish survey of low income groups). This could be the starting point for a series of successive social indicators which could be used to assess the effectiveness of measures taken.

B. SHELTERED WORKSHOPS

One of the chief problems of social integration, that is to say of the fight against poverty in the sense of unemployment and social isolation, is the integration of the handicapped into working life and hence into social life. According to a survey of the whole of the federal area in autumn 1978, about 2,800 persons were considered as requiring employment in sheltered workshops; of these 900 had

had no previous occupational experience and the remainder were unemployed(66). These figures are surprisingly low compared, say, with surveys in Sweden, which showed almost ten times that number of handicapped. Very strict criteria must be being applied in Austria, presumably. The decisive factor in identifying this group should, however, be the extent to which those considered to be handicapped are absorbed or not by the labour market. According to other figures, obviously based on quite different criteria, the number of physically handicapped alone in Austria is far greater (in the hundreds of thousands), and this ignores the large number of mentally handicapped(56). These different figures are in fact extreme figures of limited operational use.

Nevertheless, the number of sheltered workshops and those employed in them is low and that means the unsatisfied demand is high, even though the employment of handicapped persons in private industry is supposed to be given priority. An increase in these institutions, which at present employ only 150 persons, is therefore urgently necessary.

As far back as 1977 the Ministry of Social Affairs' "Konzept" of rehabilitation referred to above had adopted as one of its tasks the development of sheltered workshops in co-ordinated form. In the meantime, a joint working party has been set up for this purpose by the Bund, the Länder and Social Security. That this task can only be dealt with in progressive stages is understandable, as is the decision to make a start with persons whose working capacity is approximately 50 per cent. In the longer term a reduction of this limit should be possible, so that persons with very low working efficiency rates can be prescribed employment therapy.

The proposal in the "Konzept" for the formation of a federal central association for dealing with co-ordination and rationalisation questions, while Land associations are responsible for the workshops to be created, is a constructive solution for a difficult problem where both local conditions and the general requirements of economic management must be taken into account.

These efforts to integrate a seriously disadvantaged group should in our opinion be pursued as a matter of urgent priority to which significant resources should be devoted. This is after all a field in which considerable backwardness has to be made good in a social system which is very advanced in other respects. Objections to the increased costs entailed would be less strong if a cost-benefit study based on macro-economic criteria were to be made of sheltered workshops. The cost of subsidies should be compared with savings in unemployment benefits, invalidity pensions, care costs and so on. From this point of view consideration should be given to the idea of limiting subsidies to a certain amount per workplace.

C. AN ACTIVE LABOUR MARKET POLICY

The development of protected workshops dealt with in the previous section is an acute problem requiring an almost immediate solution, and its urgency is clearly recognised in Austria. On the other hand, any increase in expenditure on employment policy measures beyond the present level of about A.Sch.1 billion in a situation of low unemployment like the present may seem to be unjustified. Nevertheless we regard an increased effort in this respect as desirable in the long run, and would like to justify that view as follows.

In the first place it would seem that public opinion in Austria concentrates too much on the low unemployment figures and thereby overlooks the fact that Austrian participation rates - although they have, unlike those of many West European countries, risen even in the recession years - are lower than those of a number of industrially advanced countries in Western Europe. According to OECD statistics for 1975 the percentage of the population between the ages of 15 and 64 in civilian employment was 65.3 per cent in Austria, compared with 78.5 per cent in Sweden, 76.8 per cent in Denmark, 73.5 per cent in England and 69.2 per cent in Norway(8). A further analysis can only be done on the basis of continuous "labour force surveys", with samplings of sufficient size to permit detailed breakdowns by age, sex, training, region, etc. In particular the very large group not in civilian employment (35 per cent of all those of working age, compared with 20-25 per cent in the North-Western European countries) would have to be examined to see whether the grounds for not working were personal, social or institutional in character, i.e. whether it is a question of forms of concealed unemployment, or whether statistical explanations can be found for this phenomenon. Civilian employment rates for men of only 89 per cent for the 50-60 age group and 35 per cent for 60-65 age group (1976)(67) can indicate a kind of "discouraged unemployment"(68). If it should prove that there is concealed unemployment or underemployment - which would be quite compatible with the picture of lower overt unemployment - then a considerable extension of employment policy measures directed towards certain groups is required.

A second justification for such an extension could also be the need to prepare in advance employment policy measures which can cope with difficulties which can be expected to arise on the Austrian labour market. In G. Biffl's prospective study of the Austrian labour market up to 1991, already referred to, it is estimated that in the ten years up to 1986 almost 400,000 new jobs will have to be created, partly because of the larger cohorts coming on to the labour market each year, partly because of higher participation rates for women, and finally also because of the further shift of self-employed out

of agriculture and forestry. Only if there is an annual GNP growth
rate of 4 to 4½ per cent, a shortening of working hours in line with
the past trend, and a standstill as regards employment of foreign
labour will it be possible to avoid an increase in unemployment. A
number of Austrian authors consider these growth preconditions to be
far too optimistic. Thus Ewald Walterskirchen for example describes
a scenario of a growth crisis which would lead to a five-year stag-
nation of the Austrian economy. Even supposing there were to be a
steep reduction in the number of foreign workers, an increase in
concealed unemployment and an extension of the public sector, he
calculates that this would still leave unemployment at about
300,000(69). A prospective study by the Institut für Höhere Studien
gives a less gloomy picture of future labour market conditions in
Austria.

Labour market policy should however not be regarded merely as a
quantitative task. Austria is in the middle of a structural transformation process of the kind described by Fourastié: the tertiary
sector developing at the expense not only of the primary sector but
also of a declining secondary sector(70). The majority of industries
in Austria are already showing stagnating employment figures. Austria
stands on the threshold of post-industrial society, a development
which, as experience shows, leads to serious labour market problems.
Even within the industry sector structural problems are arising
which the hoarding of labour in the recession has concealed and pent
up. Many imbalances are also to be feared in the adjustment between
the training system and the labour market. Finally, increased numbers of handicapped will require integration into working life,
which will mean a stepping up of advisory and rehabilitation measures.

Even though the labour market position in Austria provides no
grounds for concern at present, anticipatory action in the form of
medium- and long-term planning should in our view be taken to ensure that these changes can take place without endangering full employment.

To do this the structural changes in the economy from employment
policy points of view should be analysed, the goals of employment
policy formulated, care being taken to ensure that the measures required to achieve those goals are co-ordinated.

D. REGIONAL POLICY

Regional policy is in the main employment policy in its regional aspects. In spite of its small size, Austria has regional policy
problems: a certain economic decline from East to West, problems
of mountain farmers, of the areas bordering on Eastern European

countries, and of parts of the country encountering structural difficulties.

A look at the wide variations in unemployment rates is already
enough to reveal regional problems:

Table 2

UNEMPLOYMENT BY LÄNDER
(Average in per cent, 1978)

Vienna	1.4	Salzburg	1.7
Lower Austria	2.0	Carinthia	5.2
Upper Austria	1.8	Tyrol	2.5
Styria	2.7	Vorarlberg	0.5
Burgenland	3.2	Austria	2.1

In a report to the OECD the Austrian government gave as goal for
its regional policy approximately equal employment opportunities and
living standards, and as instruments for achieving this focused programmes for economic, social and physical development within the
framework of a national development policy.

Regional policy is dealt with in detail in Part III as an example of social policy integration. The programme for the Aichfeld-
Murboden region is a concrete example of co-operation between Bund,
Land and communes to create new jobs in an area with declining industrial employment. Further development of regional efforts in the
coming years is undoubtedly of the greatest importance for social
policy integration. But in a period of stagnating or even declining
industrial employment, regional policy has increasingly difficult
tasks to perform, since it traditionally makes use of industry policy measures. It is therefore worthwhile considering how the shaping
of the public sector (administrations, public utility enterprises,
and to some extent social institutions too) should proceed, in its
regional policy aspects as well. The necessary groundwork should be
done, primarily through the commissioning of research tasks, for
assessing the efficiency of the measures applied according to macro-
economic cost-benefit criteria.

E. INTEGRATION OF FOREIGN WORKERS

The vigorous growth of the Austrian economy and the consequent
exhaustion of the potential indigenous labour force supply in the
1960s led to considerable immigration of foreign labour, which by
1973 reached its peak level of 8.7 per cent of the total labour
force. The figure is approximately the same as the foreign labour
element in a number of Western European countries and causes Austria
the same kind of problems.

For the overwhelming majority of foreign workers market-related motives were decisive in causing them to leave their home country and work in Austria: in the countries of origin (mainly Yugoslavia and Turkey) there was a surplus of rural unqualified labour, in Austria a need for labour, especially in seasonal industries like building and tourism which were not sufficiently attractive for Austrians. The textile and rubber products industries also have high percentages of foreign workers(71). There is clear evidence that foreign workers are concentrated in seasonal enterprises and unqualified jobs. Only 10 per cent of the foreign workers can be considered as skilled workers compared to over 20 per cent for Austrian workers.

There is no doubt that the 170,000 foreign workers and their families still working in Austria represent a problem for social integration, even though the majority come from areas with historical connections with the host country. Foreign workers enjoy essentially the same labour law and social insurance rights as Austrians, but work permits not linked to a specific workplace are only granted after eight years; when jobs are scarce indigenous workers have priority; and foreigners have only passive voting rights in works' council and chamber of labour elections. But the real integration problem which we are concerned with here lies at quite a different level.

"Integration" in this context is not to be understood as a uniform concept, but rather as a frequently lengthy process which occurs in stages. An analysis of foreign workers' problems in Austria divides integration into four stages(72):

Stage 1: adaptation to the work field,
Stage 2: development of an Austrian life-style,
Stage 3: incorporation into an Austrian contact system, and
Stage 4: complete assimilation.

The first stage, which is also aimed at by foreign workers intending to return home (at the time of emigration the overwhelming majority), seems to be achieved in most cases. The Austrians are usually indifferent or even favourably disposed to foreign workers as colleagues at work, since they do not represent any threat to their own jobs - rather indeed an improvement of their own promotion prospects. The second stage of integration is also probably often achieved, although immigrants' housing conditions remain inferior to those of Austrians for a long time: 60 per cent of the Austrians questioned consider that the foreign workers should live in special quarters, only 5 per cent felt it was pleasant to have a foreigner as neighbour. School attendance of foreign workers' children is often unsatisfactory: one-third of Yugoslav children stay away from school. The higher integration stages are still more difficult to achieve: the contact system is built up only with difficulty and after overcoming prejudices. Two-thirds of Austrians do not want their children to marry foreign workers; 90 per cent of Austrians are against the complete integration of foreign workers.

The problems of insufficient integration of foreign workers are therefore both material and caused by attitudes and prejudices. Ernst Gehmacher was demanding as far back as 1971 a "clear and long-term concept for foreign workers"(73) as a basis for the rational application of measures. He argued that it was necessary to have some idea of what the order of size of the foreign labour contingent would be over longer periods, what regions foreign workers were to be settled in and how far they should be integrated. He spoke in this connection of "integration strategies", "rotation strategies", or combinations of both.

On the basis of the material available to the group of examiners it seems clear that a concept of this kind does not exist, and that views as to the approach to adopt differ widely. In government statements and in the Austrian Socialist Party programme the question is ignored. The Austrian People's Party is in favour of assimilation of foreign workers, the FPÖ (the Austrian Liberal Party) takes the opposite view. The recommendations of the Advisory Council for Economic and Social Policy Questions (Beirat für Wirtschafts- und Sozialfragen) of 1976, expressing the joint views of the social partners, are in the main of a social policy nature and evidently aim at a certain integration of the foreign workers, especially in the fields of housing and education. Views also differ in the enterprises which employ foreign workers: one-third in favour, two-thirds against integration.

While we fully understand that Austrian policy in regard to foreign worker integration tends rather to be pragmatic in character, it is our view that Austria needs to gain a clearer conception of the foreign worker question which can be used as a basis for suitable strategies. These, however formulated, will require a long series of measures. A first task would be to obtain better statistics about the position as regards foreign workers, to examine their role in the economy and to analyse their social situation. It seems to us that Austria, with its comparatively favourable labour market situation and the relatively uniform composition of the foreign labour force (almost 80 per cent from one neighbouring country), is in an exceptionally good position to find solutions to the foreign labour problem through planned and co-ordinated measures which would be good both for Austrian society and for the foreign workers themselves. The fact that, up until the mid-1980s, for demographic reasons (an increase in the domestic labour force from 1975 to 1985 of 225,000 persons is to be expected), for structural reasons (shift

of the self-employed out of agriculture) and, not least, in view of
the probability of slower economic growth, any increase in immigration into Austria is highly unlikely does not significantly alle-
viate the problem. Indeed, the problem of integrating the foreign
workers who remain and are therefore willing to integrate could become more acute as a question for integrated social policy in Austria.

In this connection it is worth noting that Germany, with a foreign resident population of over four million and the concomitant
integration problems, has set up a co-ordination group in the Federal Ministry for Labour and Social Affairs in which employers, trade
unions, associations, the Bundesanstalt für Arbeit and the parliamentary political parties are represented. The recommendations put
forward by this working group include intensive pre-vocational
courses for foreign children without school-leaving certificates,
intensive language courses for young people, more intensive occupational and social counselling for foreigners, easier conditions
for naturalisation and improved information of the German population
about the problems of foreigners.

F. EQUALITY OF WOMEN

It can already be inferred from the participation rates for
both sexes that the question of the low overall participation rate
compared with other countries - which can be due to social factors
or labour market conditions but also to some extent to a different
set of priorities - is in Austria as in many other countries mainly
a women's question, even though the problem of sex-specific participation rates is partially concealed by regional structural problems and qualification differences. The Austrian figure of 48 per
cent (1975) for gainfully employed women in the working age groups
is far below the corresponding figures for the Scandinavian countries, although it must be borne in mind that in Austria this figure includes part-time employment ranging from 14 to 36 hours per
week, whereas the Scandinavian participation rates include women
employed part-time for lower totals of hours per week(74). Women's
participation rates in Austria, especially those for married women,
have however increased in recent years. Gudrun Biffl, in her analysis of the Austrian labour market, expresses the view that poor
working prospects always mean a certain discouragement of secondary
breadwinners (i.e. women). In particular she expects the unfavourable working prospects to produce a declining "willingness to go
out to work" among women over 55 up to the mid-1980s.

In a report by the Advisory Council for Economic and Social
Policy Questions on the employment of women it is stated that

women's earnings are about two-thirds those of men, which reveals a tendency to pay less for typical women's jobs(75). But even with equal qualifications women have considerably less possibilities of promotion in their careers. The findings of the report on women are confirmed in current publications of the Ministry for Labour and Social Affairs on women's problems in occupational and social life in the series Schriftenreihe zur sozialen und beruflichen Stellung der Frau (since 1972).

In 1975 the federal government presented a comprehensive report on the situation of women in Austria, which deals inter alia with women in employment, and the education and health situations of women(76). The report shows that progress has been made, but gives a lengthy catalogue of fields in which the situation is far from satisfactory. Women's educational levels are much lower than those of men. In professional life the majority of women are in jobs requiring lower qualifications, which means that they are in the lower paid occupations and junior positions. They are often unskilled, rarely skilled workers. The average wages of women are, as already mentioned, much lower than those of men, and for the period 1968 to 1973 the report can find no significant improvements to mention. The principles concerning equal pay in the ILO Convention 100 "have definitely not been satisfactorily incorporated into collective bargaining practices or in the job classification practices of enterprises"(77). In a new survey by the Austrian Economic Research Institute it is stated that in the period 1960 to 1977 women's wages have caught up somewhat, but that women's wages are still about two-thirds of men's wages(78). The different hours worked could have had something to do with this.

The Austrian government pays much attention to the question of women, which can be considered to be one of the most comprehensive and difficult social policy problems of the welfare society. The first goal, that of formal equality of rights for women, can be considered to have been achieved in Austria. But the government sets itself a higher goal, namely, in the simple but eloquent words of the Report on Women, "the transition from formal equality of rights to actual equality of status for women in society"(79). The Report on Women is a good basis for such efforts, and suggests a number of measures, particularly in the chapter on "Women in Professional Life". The Council's Report of 1974 concludes with a list of detailed recommendations, giving the views of the social partners and covering all the social fields relevant for the "actual equality of status" of women: education, social legislation, working life, creation of infrastructural institutions which can provide women with a genuine choice between looking after children and going out to work.

In 1966 a special Division for Women's Questions was set up in the Ministry for Social Affairs with the principal task of improving the status of women in professional life, and in 1979 in the same Ministry, on the basis of the Law on Equality of Treatment, a Commission was set up to deal with discrimination both in individual cases and in general rules and regulations. In view of the importance it attaches to the women's question, the Austrian government must take the required action as regards staffing and other aspects. Precise recommendations by our group would seem superfluous, since a large number of such recommendations are contained in the Austrian literature already quoted. But we should like to mention that experience in Sweden has shown that initiatives to persuade the social partners to conclude agreements to promote the equality of women in professional life are very worthwhile.

G. REFLECTIONS ON THE LONG-TERM OPERATIONAL EFFECTIVENESS OF THE AUSTRIAN MODEL

What are the characteristic features of the "Austrian model"? First, we have the picture of a "mixed economy" with a high degree of nationalisation in credit management and large-scale industry, a relatively strong consumer co-operative movement, but also a still important private industrial sector with a strong admixture of affiliates of multinational enterprises. This pluralism, but at the same time the lack both of real planned-economy machinery and of private high financial and large-scale industrial power centres, typifies the Austrian form of the market economy, which is however also subject to the modifying influence of the social partnership system.

This system, although mentioned as the second feature here, constitutes the real core of the model, and is the institutionalised device - by no means to be considered as a temporary expedient - whereby the powerful social partners, themselves intimately interconnected with the legally constituted self-governing organs of both sides of industry, settle their conflicts by negotiation and top-level discussion round the table. To do this requires a willingness to compromise and to consider the points of view of the other partners to the negotiation, and a moderation in pressing one's own claims which is not to be found anywhere else - at least not as a system which has been operating for decades and is therefore not thought of as a temporary solution for use in an emergency.

The third feature of the model is the interconnection between the social partners and the political parties, and hence a high degree of political concordance which is not only applied to the institutions of the mixed economy but also embraces important social

156

goals like full employment and greater equality. A pragmatic form
of socialism, a liberalism rich in tradition, and the Christian-
social doctrine are the foundations for a broad concordance which
wishes to preserve the existing system, avoid damaging confrontations,
and reform society in such gradual stages that no essential interests
are infringed.

Finally, the fourth feature of the Austrian model is a very high
degree of centralisation. Not only are the organisations and Chambers of trade, industry and labour strictly centralised, even the
forms of social partnership decision-taking are centralistic. Since
moreover social partnership and the political parties are extensively linked through the multiple posts held by individual leaders
(Personalunion), it must be said that in Austria, for all its pluralism and whole-hearted respect for representative democracy, the
decision-making process is extremely highly centralised. Since this
process can only succeed by finding a balance between strong and
opposed interests the risk of any misuse is limited.

Summing it up in a few key words, therefore, the main features
of the "Austrian model", a welfare society which exists in a state
of harmonious balance and constant development relatively untroubled
by political confrontations and labour market conflicts, seem to us
to be as follows:

1. A "mixed economy" in which a pluralism of forms of
   enterprise exists but the basic elements of the market
   economy are preserved.
2. Social partnership - a system for solving conflicts by
   negotiation.
3. Close interconnections between the social partners and
   the political parties, which guarantees a high degree
   of concordance concerning the essential goals of social
   policy; and
4. A high degree of centralisation in decision-making.

By definition alone the concept of harmonious "balance" implies
a weakness: balance is not necessarily a stable state, but one in
which the interplay of forces constantly changes in response to
changes in the relationships between those forces. Even among
qualified observers of the Austrian scene, opinions differ as to
whether the system as a whole is flexible enough to make it possible
to cope successfully with the demands that can be expected to be
made upon it, or whether it does not rather seem threatened by them.
We certainly shall not presume to claim to be able to give a considered opinion on a question of such vital importance for Austrian
social policy, but we would like to conclude our report with a few
general remarks on the subject. These will focus on three points:

- Are structural changes of such an intensity and order of
  magnitude to be expected that the social system will be
  subjected to strong tensions?
- Does the tendency towards a higher quality of life also
  imply increased demands for participation in decision-
  making at various levels?
- Is the stability of the system threatened by slower economic growth over the longer term?

a) Tensions in the social system

   The successful way in which Austria has so far withstood the international crisis could lead one to close one's eyes to the fact
that the economic and hence social changes which have to some extent
been postponed during the crisis years must now in future come about.
We have already mentioned above that agriculture and forestry seem
to be overmanned by comparison with other countries, and that a further not inconsiderable migration to other economic sectors is to
be expected. Within industry itself structural transformations from
basic products to processing industries have to be faced which, on
employment grounds, could not be fully carried out. The pressure to
be internationally competitive, rendered even more acute by Austrian
exchange rate policy, will certainly become increasingly urgent and
require even greater economic dynamism. The circumstance that Austria is to such an extent a country of small and medium-sized enterprises is often regarded as favourable for the ability of the Austrian
economy to survive the crisis. But the advantage of size in international competition could also come to apply to Austrian industry
and lead to a wave of mergers, transfers and closures.
   The need for efficiency, competitivity and mobility to some extent runs counter to goals which have high priority in the welfare
state: job security, social protection, humanisation of the world
of labour, and environment. These partially contradictory aims of
a competitive society and a welfare society are naturally not something specific to Austria. The question which may be asked is simply
whether, in the not unlikely case of a heightening of the tensions
between economic and social goals, the Austrian system is flexible
enough to overcome these partially conflict-loaded tendencies. Is
the truce-like consensus on questions concerning established group
interests and distribution an obstacle preventing the necessary
shifts and rearrangements from taking place? Is the form of decision-
making sometimes referred to over-critically as "a consensus of
élites" adequate for the solution of tasks which could prove much
more difficult than those it has successfully dealt with hitherto?
   Austrian authors have frequently pointed out that the social
partnership system, the close interlocking of the social partners

and the political parties, and the resulting highly centralised forms of decision-making must be based on the trust and approval of the population. As long as full employment and social security are provided, this approval should be forthcoming. But if large-scale shifts and social changes occur, this basis of trust could crumble away. In our concluding discussion in Vienna in January 1979, reference was made from the university side to the increase in "destabilized groups", migration from the rural areas, the self-employed undergoing a process of social demotion, white-collar workers finding their jobs threatened for the first time, industrial workers in stagnating industries or having their occupational self-confidence sapped by automation, groups of foreign workers insufficiently integrated socially. The common factor for these otherwise heterogeneous groups is that they see themselves as marginal to the welfare system and as not fully represented in the social partnership system. These phenomena, so far not distinctly developed, merit close attention. The interviews we had, and the discussion initiated by university representatives, gave us the impression that people in Austria are very much aware of the dangers of such a development.

b) Participation in decision-making processes

This brings us to the second question: does the centralistic decision-making system, whose roots are in "reform from above" and in the traditional professional civil service, need greater participation by the population going beyond high electoral participation and the large memberships of the political parties and interest group organisations? In many Western democracies the great improvement in popular education has created an awareness of democracy which is not satisfied with the mere act of voting at intervals of several years. In the world of work particularly, the growing desire by workers to share in decision-making has led to trade union efforts to propagate co-determination. Austria is one of the few countries in which co-determination at higher than enterprise level seems to have taken priority over co-determination at enterprise level. If this is to be interpreted as expressing a tendency towards centralism, then the proponents of anti-centralism might attach greater importance to co-determination at enterprise level.

But demands for greater participation and decentralisation are also being made in political life. The nuclear power referendum is indicative of forces which do not consider representative democracy as the only form of democracy, but make their appeal directly to the people. Citizen initiatives are occurring in various areas of social life(80). The desire to participate in decision-making ("Mitbestimmenwollen") can be considered as an expression of a rising quality of life, and ought to be integrated to a greater extent into the

Austrian system, which traditionally allows it too little room. This issue constitutes "an acid test for the bureaucratic administrative system" (Eva Kreisky).

c) The stability of the system in a period of slower economic growth

A final question which also preoccupies Austrian authors is connected with the fact that social partnership, like the "Austrian model" as a whole, has as a pre-condition continuing economic growth. Kienzl considers that Austria has for a long time been a typical production and consumption society (Leistungs- und Konsumgesellschaft) and predicts a slowdown in growth(81). In a study on growth alternatives the authors start with an assumption of slower growth, mainly caused by external influences, and examine the consequences for, inter alia, consumption, production, environment and their political aspects(82).

As to the effects of a long-lasting slowdown in growth on the social partnership system as the core of the Austrian model, opinions differ. Pelinka thinks that since social partnership is based on constant distribution formulae, it can only survive in a growing economy, and sees the whole system as threatened by the loss of growth(83). Klose believes that a crisis for the system is hardly likely to develop from a cyclical slowdown of limited duration, but considers that well co-ordinated strategies would be necessary for a lengthy period of stagnation(84).

There are therefore quite as good grounds for arguing that a stabilizing system like the Austrian one will be undermined by a slowdown in growth because it depends so much on growth, as for arguing on the contrary that a tradition-rich and proven consensus system is well suited to survive a growth crisis. The only point on which agreement is likely is that the Austrian system must be adapted to the conditions which could emerge under slower growth. Since the conflict potential is increasing, disputes over distribution are becoming tougher. This, according to Matzner, would increase the danger of putting greater influence in the hands of the bureaucratic machine. That would have to be prevented by "strengthening the active democratic legitimation of existing institutions"(85). We join Matzner in thinking that Austria is probably one of the few countries in which, because of historical experience and decades of practice of co-operation between the large social groups, important attitudinal and institutional points of contact for overcoming growth crises already exist.

The concluding question, which we shall deal with only briefly, concerns the possibilities of making use of Austrian experience for other countries.

We identified the essential preconditions for the Austrian integration model as: a large non-private sector in the economy (in particular nationalised industries), a predominance of small and medium-sized enterprises, and social partnership as a stabilizing and conflict-solving system. It would of course not be possible for another country to take over these preconditions, but it is nevertheless possible to learn from Austrian experience.

The nationalised industries are the almost accidental result of a historical development, and the consensus on these is therefore something specific to Austria. An extension of the state industry sector could only be brought about in other democracies after a political struggle which would destroy consensus as a constructive factor.

What can be learned from Austrian experience is that a state industry sector, no matter how it emerged historically, can fulfil the twofold aim of economic efficiency and operation in the general interest of the economy as a whole, that it can maintain its innovatory power and thus constitute a dynamic element in the economy as a whole. It is clear that, through its employment and price policies, the state sector helped to overcome the last crisis without sacrificing competitivity. The Austrian nationalised industries seem to us to provide proof that state enterprises can be managed in ways which are efficient and nevertheless in accordance with the interests of the economy as a whole.

The favourable assessment of the role played by small- and medium-sized enterprises in overcoming cyclical fluctuations and in adjusting the economy to structural changes provides no clues for policies in other countries. Austria is now in a stage of industrial structure which a number of other countries have already passed through. The trend towards larger enterprises is a feature of industrial development which, under conditions of increasing internationalisation, is a neeessary precondition for small countries engaging in a large amount of foreign trade if they wish to be competitive in world markets.

But the position is quite different as regards the core of the Austrian model, social partnership. Here, too, there can be no question of transposing historically determined institutions to other countries. Both the social truce and the "Chambers" system are specific to Austria. But having made full allowance for the special preconditions for this system, the trouble-free settlement of differences, the moderation and readiness to compromise of the social partners provide an inspiring example for a world full of unsuccessful attempts to find viable models for an incomes policy. Even for sceptics in this field, Austria offers an experience which can be useful in the constant striving to reconcile the economic policy interests of the economy as a whole with the autonomy of the associations representing group interests. The Austrian combination of self-governing organs (chambers) and voluntary group-interest associations is an optimal solution which other countries ought to think seriously about, even though they cannot imitate it.

Within this institutional framework efforts at integration are in progress which for all their pragmatism are inspired by an acute awareness of still existing inequalities and an unshakeable determination to carry out reforms. The fight against poverty, the efforts to achieve equality of status for women in working and social life, the regional policy measures, are all examples of well-aimed, co-ordinated work at various levels of administration to ensure close co-operation between the authorities, the chambers and the autonomous associations. With this, Austria provides an example of a society which is in many respects successfully integrated, and a welfare state which is by international standards very advanced.

NOTES AND REFERENCES

Part I

MAIN CONDITIONS FOR SOCIAL POLICY INTEGRATION

1. Voigtländer H., "Von der wirtschaftspolitischen Entscheidungs-
   findung", in: Pfaff-Voigtländer, Sozialpolitik im Wandel - Von
   der selektiven zur integrierten Sozialpolitik, Verlag Die Neue
   Gesellschaft, Bonn, 1978.

2. Reithofer H., Die ausgleichende Gesellschaft - Strategien der
   Zukunftsbewältigung, Europaverlag, Vienna-Munich-Zurich, 1978.

3. Pfaff M., "Grundlagen einer integrierten Sozialpolitik", in:
   Pfaff-Voigtländer, op.cit.

4. Pfaff M.-Voigtländer H., "Soziale Sicherheit zwischen Anspruch
   und Wirklichkeit", in: Pfaff-Voigtländer, op.cit.

5. Stadler K.R. - Weidenholzer J., "Faktoren und strukturelle Be-
   dingungen der Gesellschaftspolitik in Österreich seit der
   Gründung der Republik", unpublished manuscript, Johannes Keppler
   Universität Linz, Linz, 1978.

6. Kostelka P. - Unkart R., "Vom Stellenwert des Föderalismus in
   Österreich", in: Fischer H., Das politische System Österreichs,
   Europaverlag, Vienna, Munich, Zurich, 1974.

7. See Annex I: Pelinka A., "Austria's Political System".

8. OECD, Labour Force Statistics 1964-1975, Paris, 1977.

9. Kramer J. - Scheer G., "Zur Arbeits- und Lebenssituation der
   Bauern in Österreich", in: Armut in Österreich, Leykam Verlag,
   Graz, 1977.

10. Beirat für Wirtschafts- und Sozialfragen, Vorschläge zur Indu-
    striepolitik, Verlag Carl Ueberreiter, Vienna, 1970.

11. Drennig M., "Vermögensverteilung in Österreich, ihre politische
    Relevanz", in: H. Fischer, op.cit. note 6.

12. Lacina R., "Verstaatlichung in Österreich", in: Wirtschaft und
    Politik, Festschrift für Fritz Klenner, Europaverlag, Vienna-
    Munich-Zurich, 1975.

13. Grünwald O., "Investitionen und Finanzierung in der verstaat-
    lichten Industrie", unpublished manuscript, Bund Sozialistischer
    Akademiker, Vienna, 1974.

163

14. Grünwald O., "Verstaatlichte Industrie im Strukturwandel", in: Gemeinwirtschaft 1/1977, Verlag für Jugend und Volk, Vienna-Munich, 1977.

15. Pfaff M., "Politische Erfordernisse für eine integrierte Sozialpolitik", in: Pfaff-Voigtländer, op.cit. note 1.

16. Popper K.R., The Open Society and its Enemies, Vol. II: "The High Tide of Prophecy", Routledge, Kegan & Paul, London, 1958.

17. Popper K.R., The Poverty of Historicism, Routledge, Kegan & Paul, London, 1960.

18. Österreichischer Gewerkschaftsbund (ÖGB), Chancengleichheit durch Sozialpolitik, Bericht des 4. Arbeitskreises zum 8. Bundeskongress des ÖGB, Verlag des ÖGB, Vienna, 1975.

19. Bundeskammer der gewerblichen Wirtschaft, Grundsatzprogramm der Handelskammerorganisationen, Vienna, 1978.

Part II

SOCIAL PARTNERSHIP IN AUSTRIA

20. Sozialistische Partei Österreichs (SPÖ), Das neue Parteiprogramm der SPÖ - Beschlossen am 20. Mai 1978, Politik und Dokumentation No. 9, 12. Jahrgang, Vienna, 1978.

21. Fischer-Kowalski M. - Bucek J., Ungleichheit in Österreich - Ein Sozialbericht, Verlag Jugend und Volk, Vienna-Munich, 1979.

22. Lachs Th., Wirtschaftspartnerschaft in Österreich, Europaverlag, Vienna-Munich-Zurich, 1976.

23. Ohlinger Th., in: "Gesellschaftspolitische Reformansätze", verbatim record of meeting held in Vienna on 18 January 1979, unpublished manuscript, Federal Chancellery, 1979.

24. Pelinka A., in: "Gesellschaftspolitische Reformansätze", ibid.

25. Location of nuclear power plant, the putting into operation of which was turned down by a plebiscite.

Part III

CO-ORDINATION AND INTEGRATION OF VARIOUS AREAS WITH SPECIAL EMPHASIS ON REDISTRIBUTIVE ASPECTS

26. There have been several studies recently on the theme of income redistribution in Austria:

   - Suppanz H. - Wagner M., Die Einkommensverteilung in Österreich, Forschungsbericht Nr. 143, Institute for Advanced Studies, Vienna, 1979;

- Walterskirchen E., "Die Entwicklung der Lohnunterschiede in Österreich", Monatsberichte 1/1979, Österreichisches Institut für Wirtschaftsforschung, Vienna, 1979;

- Bundesministerium für soziale Verwaltung, Bericht über die soziale Lage - Sozialbericht- Tätigkeitsbericht (annual social reports), Vienna;

- Statistisches Zentralamt, "Schichtenspezifischer Lohn- und Einkommensvergleich in Österreich", Statistische Nachrichten 10/1978, Vienna, 1978;

- Kitzmantel E., Steuern, wer sie zahlt und wer sie trägt, Bundesministerium für Finanzen, Vienna, 1979;

- Chaloupek G., Die Verteilung der persönlichen Einkommen in Österreich, I. "Die hohen Einkommen", Wirtschaft und Gesellschaft 1/1977; II. "Die Arbeitsverdienste", Wirtschaft und Gesellschaft 2/1978; III. "Haushaltseinkommen und soziale Stellung", Wirtschaft und Gesellschaft 3/1980, Wirtschaftsverlag Anton Orac, Vienna.

27. Geldner N., Die soziale Sicherheit im Wirtschaftsverlauf, Schriftenreihe des Forschungsinstituts für soziale Sicherheit beim Hauptverband der Sozialversicherungsträger, No. 3, Vienna, 1976.

28. Bundesministerium für soziale Verwaltung, Bericht über die soziale Lage 1976-1977, Vienna, 1978. These percentages refer exclusively to pensions properly so-called, without taking into account supplementary allowances paid by the federal authorities. If these supplementary allowances are taken into account in the total of pensions paid, the federal budget's contribution as a proportion of the total are respectively: a surplus of 5 per cent compared to total payments to white-collar workers; deficits met out of the federal budget of 37.3 per cent for blue-collar workers, 35.6 per cent for railway workers, 71.3 per cent for miners, 74.3 per cent for non-wage non-farm workers, and 81.1 per cent for farmers (figures calculated by the Ministry for Social Affairs).

29. Source: Ministry of Finance, but the Ministry for Social Affairs gives a figure of 22.5 billion (including the supplementary allowances charged against the federal budget. The amount announced by the Ministry of Finance (24 billion) includes the whole of chapter 16 of the Budget (social insurance schemes) including all contributions by the Federation to sickness-accident insurance on the pensioners' account.

30. Source: Ministry of Finance. According to the Ministry for Social Affairs, A.Sch. 6.2 billion.

31. In July 1978 20.3 per cent were earning wages higher than the ceiling which was then at A.Sch. 12,600. Put more precisely, this was the case for 13.2 per cent of blue-collar workers and 31.3 per cent of white-collar workers.

32. 6.3 per cent for wage earners who benefit from the Law on the Continued Payment of Wages (Entgeltfortzahlungsgesetz) and for farm workers; 7.5 per cent for other insured wage earners.

33. To this must be added a contribution of 0.1 per cent paid by the employers for insuring their employees against losses of wages due to the insolvency of their employers.

34. See in particular:

    - Manpower Policies and Problems in Austria, OECD, Paris, 1967;

    - Reviews of National Policies for Education: Austria, OECD, Paris, 1970;

    - Reviews of National Policies for Education: Austria - Higher Education and Research, OECD, Paris, 1976;

    - Reviews of National Policies for Education: Austria - School Policy, OECD, Paris, 1979;

    - Policies for Apprenticeship, OECD, Paris, 1979.

35. Steindl J., "Emigration, Ersatzbedarf und Nachwuchs an Akademikern bis 1981", in: Arbeitsmarkt der Achtzigerjahre, Bundesministerium für soziale Verwaltung, Vienna, 1976.

36. Bundesministerium für soziale Verwaltung, Kampf gegen die Armut in Österreich - Massnahmen, Probleme, Konzepte, Vienna, 1979.

Part IV

TOWARDS A COMPREHENSIVE HEALTH POLICY

37. Teleky L., Vorlesungen über soziale Medizin, Gustav Fischer Verlag, Jena, 1914.

38. Österreichisches Statistisches Zentralamt, "Bevölkerungsprognosen für Österreich 1978-2010", Statistische Nachrichten 6/1979, Vienna, 1979.

39. OECD, Demographic Trends - 1950-1990, Paris, 1979.

40. Natality for immigrants has for example cushioned the fall in the birthrate. This declined, nevertheless, from 15.2 in 1970 (in 1963 it was still at 18.7) to 11.4 in 1978 when the mortality rate was 12.6. This ranked Austria among the countries with the largest rate of net population decline.

41. Popper L., Regionale Unterschiede der Sterblichkeit in Österreich, Österreichisches Bundesinstitut für Gesundheitswesen, Vienna, 1976, and Krebserkrankungen in Industrieländern am Beispiel Österreichs, Österreichisches Bundesinstitut für Gesundheitswesen, Vienna, 1977.

42. These and the following figures on Austria have been taken from Indikatoren zur gesellschaftlichen Entwicklung, 2. Ausgabe, Beiträge zur Österreichischen Statistik, Heft 523, Österreichisches Statistisches Zentralamt, Vienna, 1979.

43. Total accidents on the way from and to the work place account for a third of fatal work accidents.

44. See for instance: Bundesministerium für Gesundheit und Umweltschutz, Österreichischer Krankenanstaltenplan, Teil B., Langzeit- und Sonderversorung, Entwurf, Vienna, 1975.

45. Kammer für Arbeiter und Angestellte für Wien, Wirtschafts- und Sozialstatistisches Handbuch 1972, Vienna, 1973; and Wirtschafts- und Sozialstatistisches Handbuch 1978, Vienna, 1979.

46. Weber P. and Knoth E., Sanierungsbedarf in Städten, Schriftenreihe des Instituts für Stadtforschung Nr. 64, Verlag Jugend und Volk, Vienna, Munich, 1980. (The study reveals that in 1971 the number was not much bigger than 350,000).

47. Fleissner P., "Erkrankungen und Sterblichkeit in Österreich unter Berücksichtigung sozialer Schichten", unpublished manuscript, Institut für sozio-ökonomische Entwicklungsforschung der Österreichischen Akademie der Wissenschaften, Vienna, 1978.

48. Rosenberg P., Möglichkeiten der Reform des Gesundheitswesens in der Bundesrepublik Deutschland, Otto Schwartz Verlag, Göttingen, 1975.

49. Primary care consists of basic preventive and curative services provided for outside hospitals; secondary care of hospital services in the basic medical specialisms (e.g. internal medicine, surgery, pediatrics, gynecology) and tertiary care of medical services by sub-specialisms (e.g. neuro-surgery, endocrinology, child psychiatry).

50. Österreichisches Bundesinstitut für Gesundheitswesen, Ärztliche Versorgung in Österreich, im Auftrag des Bundesministeriums für Gesundheit und Umweltschutz, Vienna, 1979.

51. 55 per cent owned by the Länder, 14 per cent by the communes, 3 per cent by counties or associations of communes and 7 per cent by social insurance institutions.

52. No country-wide surveys have been made of the extent of the need for psychiatric care, only estimates. One expert has put it at 15 per cent of the population. But all such figures should in our opinion be treated with the utmost caution.

53. In 1959 Austria had 1,166 university-trained dentists with at least two years training in selected dental clinics, but 2,475 dentist-technicians who had received a special vocational training (they are all entitled to provide normal dental treatment with some exceptions). In 1949 a law was passed putting an end to the training of further dentist-technicians. The result: in 1977 there were 1,733 dental doctors and only 1,354 dentist-technicians. In other words, the number of inhabitants per dentist of one or other category was 2,433 in 1977 as against 1,753 in 1959.

54. Pelikan J.M., Laburda A.S., Laburda E., Analyse der gesundheitlichen Versorgung in Österreich, Institute for Advanced Studies, Vienna, 1979.

55. See Section D (c), passage concerning planning for the intra-mural system. Planning for health personnel is in Austria, as in many other countries, still at an early stage of development.

56. Bundesministerium für soziale Verwaltung, <u>Konzept zur Eingliederung Behinderter</u>, Vienna, 1977.

57. The federal budget contributed in 1967 2.8 per cent and in 1976 4.1 per cent to the total public health expenditure, but the Federation's share rose more sharply from 1977 to 1979.

58. Including investment and part of expenditure for preventive measures and for medical rehabilitation.

59. Schönböck W., "Ausgabenentwicklung und Kostenfaktoren im Gesundheitswesen Österreichs", unpublished manuscript, a study sponsored by the Federal Ministry for Health and Environment Protection, Vienna, 1978.

60. OECD, <u>Public Expenditure on Health, Studies on Resource Allocation</u>, Paris, 1977.

Part V

REFORM PRIORITIES AND REFORM PROBLEMS FOR THE FUTURE

61. Kammer für Arbeiter und Angestellte für Wien, <u>Armut in Wien</u>, Verlag des Österreichischen Gewerkschaftsbundes, Vienna, 1974. (According to these criteria 5 per cent of the Viennese population were considered as very poor, 14 per cent as poor).

62. Bundesministerium für soziale Verwaltung, <u>Kampf gegen die Armut-Tätigkeit der Bundesregierung</u>, Vienna, 1977.

63. Hoffman-Zenta-Hexel, <u>Arm sein in Österreich</u>, European Centre for Social Welfare Training and Research sponsored by the United Nations, Vienna, 1979.

64. Amt der steirischen Landesregierung, <u>Armut in der Wohlstandsgesellschaft</u>, Graz, 1979.

65. Tausch W.,"Vergessene Österreicher: die Bergbauern", in: <u>Armut in Österreich</u>, Leykam Verlag, Graz, 1977.

66. Arbeitsgruppe Geschützte Werkstätten, summary record of inquiries made in Bregenz, Vienna and Innsbruck, unpublished manuscript, Bundesministerium für soziale Verwaltung, Vienna, 1978.

67. Biffl G., "Der österreichische Arbeitsmarkt bis 1991", <u>Monatsberichte 2/1978</u>, Österreichisches Institut für Wirtschaftsforschung, Vienna, 1978.

68. Biffl G., "During the recession older workers were increasingly compelled to retire", <u>op.cit.</u>

69. Walterskirchen E., "Der Arbeitsmarkt in der Krise", in: <u>Wachstumskrisen in Österreich</u>, Volume II, Braumüller Verlag, Vienna, 1979.

70. Fourastié J., <u>Le Grand Espoir du XXe siècle</u>, Presses Universitaires de France, Paris, 1952; Gallimard, Paris, 1963.

71. The percentages of foreign workers in 1979 were: construction 11.7 per cent, tourism 17.1 per cent, textiles 19.7 per cent, and rubber and synthetic products 21.4 per cent. (Source: Bundesministerium für soziale Verwaltung, Arbeitsmarktvorausschau 1980, Vienna, 1980.)

72. Arbeitskreis für ökonomische und soziologische Studien, Gastarbeiter, Wirtschaftsfaktor und soziale Herausforderung, Wirtschaftsverlag Anton Orac, Vienna, 1973.

73. Gehmacher E., "Die soziale Problematik der Gastarbeiter", in: Gastarbeiter in Österreich, Europaverlag, Vienna-Munich-Zurich, 1972.

74. The comparative figures are taken from OECD statistics. In Austrian publications, evidently based on different statistical methods, the figures are considerably higher.

75. Beirat für Wirtschafts- und Sozialfragen, Frauenbeschäftigung in Österreich, Verlag Carl Ueberreiter, Vienna, 1974.

76. Bundeskanzleramt, Bericht über die Situation der Frau in Österreich, Vienna, 1975.

77. Bundeskanzleramt, "Die Frau im Beruf", in: Bericht über die Situation der Frau in Österreich, Vienna, 1975.

78. Walterskirchen E., "Die Entwicklung der Lohnunterschiede in Österreich", Monatsberichte 1/1979, Österreichisches Institut für Wirtschaftsforschung, Vienna, 1979.

79. Bundeskanzleramt, "Zusammenfassende Darstellung", in: Bericht über die Situation der Frau in Österreich, Vienna, 1975.

80. Kreisky E., Alternative Strategien der Organisation staatlichen Handelns, Institute for Advanced Studies, Fachverlag für Wirtschaft und Technik, Vienna, 1979.

81. Kienzl H., Gesellschaft am Wendepunkt, Verlag des Österreichischen Gewerkschaftsbundes, Vienna, 1975.

82. Arbeitskreis für ökonomische und soziologische Studien, Wachstumsalternativen, Wirtschaftsverlag Anton Orac, Vienna, 1979.

83. Pelinka A., "Die Sozialpartnerschaft als spezifische Komponente des österreichischen Systems der Integration sozial- und wirtschaftspolitischer Entscheidungen", unpublished manuscript, Innsbruck, 1978.

84. Klose A., "Sozialpartnerschaft in Stagnationsphasen", in: Wachstum in Österreich?, Volume II, Studienreihe Konfliktforschung, Braumüller Verlag, Vienna, 1979.

85. Matzner E., Wohlfahrtsstaat und Wirtschaftskrise, Rowohlt Verlag, Hamburg, 1978.

OPENING STATEMENT

by

the Secretary of State DDr. A. Nussbaumer
at the Special Review Meeting
of the Manpower and Social Affairs Committee
(Vienna, 7 October 1980)

The federal Austrian government attaches great importance to the two-day review of Austria under the OECD research programme on Integrated Social Policy, since it believes that a successfully integrated social policy is a most important factor in bringing about social and economic equilibrium in a modern state and that constant efforts are necessary to improve the integration of social policy.

In this respect this two-day Review Meeting, which is really the closing phase of a much longer examination process, can be expected to be most instructive. Reviews of this kind, especially an international confrontation of social policies in several countries as the OECD has arranged, are very important because comparison with other countries' experience is always conducive to a better appreciation of conditions in one's own country. This review exercise will give us a better insight into developments in Austria; it is true here as elsewhere that we sometimes do not see our own work, the institutions we have created or even our general environment in true perspective, so that an examination by "outsiders", who are not necessarily unappreciative of the system's finer points because they are not part of it, takes on particular significance. Important findings for Austria are to be expected, even from the statements of outsiders, and the examiners are still outsiders even if they have been concerned with the case study of Austria for months or possibly years. These findings will be of great significance for understanding the structure of the Austrian social system and also for the further development of social policy in Austria and in the other countries concerned by the Review of Integrated Social Policies.

In attempting to summarize the Austrian position on integrated social policy, it must be stated at the outset that the leading political forces in the Republic have together conceived Austria as a welfare state. It is difficult to define welfare state or "Sozialstaat" precisely. Reference is therefore made to the definition given in the Handwörterbuch der Wirtschaftswissenschaften (Dictionary of the Social Sciences), Volume Seven, according to which a welfare state is a state which, in assessing, assuring and altering economic and economically-determined conditions in the society, strives towards the objectives of guaranteeing a decent existence for all, reducing differences in wealth and removing or controlling relationships of dependence. This definition has been chosen deliberately not from Austrian concepts but from a standard reference work published in Germany. In a welfare state then, society should not be directed from the centre, but neither should it be entirely left to an unregulated interplay of forces.

The basic concepts of social freedom and social equality appear particularly important for a welfare state. It may be said in connection with the establishment of a welfare state, that right from the definition of objectives there must be a very considerable readiness to compromise, both between principles and then also between the social groups involved.

Since 1945, the whole of Austrian policy has been oriented towards creating a welfare state. Its basic pattern was, and still is, to unite different tendencies, sometimes even regarded as mutually antagonistic - for example linking the interests of employers and employees, linking traditional Christian Socialist and Social Democratic ideas.

The social science term "integrated social policy" denotes this basic attitude of political and social integration, an idea that was tacitly accepted and has consequently not been explicitly defined. Integrated social policy is thus best defined as the path to be taken and the goal to be aimed at if it is desired to bring different economic interests and different political and ideological goals in a state into lasting harmony. Integration in this context can be described as the degree to which a system's individual components are linked to one another. Integrated social policy in Austria is thus poised between autonomy on the one hand and central concentration of the components on the other. Moreover, this is clear from the fact that not only is the autonomy of individual social partners recognised, but also that Austria is a federal state, which means that integration between centralist and federalist elements is involved.

Too much emphasis on any one of the different principles of organisation could endanger or even upset the equilibrium. Integrated social policy in Austria is the outcome of various moves and experiments over the years, a process of trial and error. A distinguishing feature of the "Austrian" type of policy is the parallel nature of social policy decision centres. Policy-making balance is achieved in Austria in two ways: first, through the decisions taken in Parliament in the framework of the Constitution - here both through the political parties and through the give-and-take of Nationalrat and Bundesrat, the representatives of the State and of the Länder; second, outside the framework of the Constitution, through the major bodies representing different interests and their informal cooperation in a "Joint Commission". These bodies also play a part in connection with proposed legislation through their right to be heard and also to some extent in the application of legislation and in subsequent judicial procedures.

This institutionally-guaranteed representation of the citizens and the strong associations looking after their interests, also explain why the direct democratic instruments are less markedly apparent than in Switzerland, for example, although the referendum and the plebiscite are provided for. Such direct methods are used, however, but only in the case of those problems where it is felt that a solution cannot be found either in Parliament or through the normal regulating mechanisms of the bodies representing social interests, or issues where individual groups believe that their ideas and aims are not represented adequately by such bodies. This has been the case in Austria in the past, for example, in questions of environmental policy.

After these introductory remarks on the essentials of the Austrian social system, we now come to the findings of the Examiners' Report itself. The report contains both positive and negative comments on Austrian social policy. On the negative side, for example, it is pointed out that the statistical basis is not always adequately developed and that social awareness, i.e. awareness of problems to do with social conditions, is not always sufficiently developed, so that for example a social dimension of sickness and health is not always sufficiently taken into account. In addition it is stated that economic innovation is neglected, that no "social policy response" is given to socially conditioned crisis situations and that wealth and income redistribution is not taken into consideration. Housing policy is also said to show uneven social effects through which certain non-organised and thus more vulnerable groups such as the handicapped, foreign workers etc. are disadvantaged. Further measures were also recommended therefore. These are probably the most important criticisms and they will therefore be commented on in detail from the Austrian standpoint during the Review.

The examiners also pointed out some areas of successful social policy integration, notably in regional planning and the campaign against poverty. The fact that Austrian policy does the maximum to guarantee full employment was also recognised. The Austrian government's premise is that full employment policy is one of the most important weapons in the fight against poverty, as no one is poorer than the person who cannot find work, at least where people of working age are concerned. The second weapon in the fight against poverty is naturally the policy of assistance to the elderly; here the aim is to provide adequate pensions and prevent poverty arising from social or personal mishaps by developing good social assistance and health care systems. The examiners also consider Austrian family policy to be successful and the result of a comprehensive social policy.

It can also be said that the policy intentions of the Austrian federal government, as contained in the Declarations of Intent of the federal government, for example, coincide on many points with

the comments and suggestions of the examiners appointed by the OECD.
A few examples:

As early as 1970 the federal government pledged to implement a
policy of reforms with the aim of improving people's welfare and to
support all attempts to make our society more democratic. The federal government also considers it an important task to make the
right to work a reality so that all citizens are given the opportunity to work. The federal government is also aware of the shortcomings in the existing economic system. In this connection the
Austrian view is that the nationalised sector has special importance
and responsibility, though nationalised industries are not to be regarded as a special group here, but rather as that sector of industry
for which the State, as owner, has particular responsibility. Austria
also attaches great importance to a goal-oriented policy for industry
which attempts, through structural change and encouragement of investment, to ensure the long-term competitiveness of industry and
hence to maintain stable jobs. This type of industrial policy is
one and the same for both the nationalised and private sectors. It
should be added that because of the size structure of Austrian industry, considerable attention is paid to small and medium businesses, probably more than is the case in other countries with an
advanced industrial structure. It is only natural that special measures are sometimes taken to help small- and medium-sized business
when this is not the case in other countries, since because of the
size structure of Austrian industry and the restricted space available, particularly in the Alpine areas, these businesses often make
a very significant contribution to employment and welfare in certain
regions. This explains the strong emphasis on regional policy measures in Austria.

The federal government has also contributed to the rapid modernisation of the country's infrastructure through increasing public
investment, the transport and educational infrastructures being regarded as particularly important. It is planned to maintain the
high level of public investment while making special efforts to ensure fairness of distribution. It may be added, incidentally, that
this public investment has placed a considerable burden on the
federal budget and the budgets of the Länder and communes in recent
years, but it has helped greatly to keep overall investment in
Austria at a level which is extraordinarily high for a market economy, even during the period of economic setbacks since 1974. This
high rate of investment, together with the incomes generated by it,
has been a major factor in maintaining the high level of employment
found in Austria, in all parts of the country.

The federal government is also endeavouring to give people better opportunities as regards education, work and leisure activities

through improving the public transport system. This is a particularly vital requirement in Austria, since precisely because of the country's topographical structure opportunities for education and work are not evenly distributed; and leisure opportunities are most unevenly distributed among the different regions, whereas every citizen has the same right to leisure and recreation - further justification for very extensive efforts to achieve regional integration.

The federal government also sees one of its main tasks as ensuring equal access to the law for all, irrespective of wealth, education and social position. Here too, substantial progress has been achieved in recent years. Furthermore, in implementing a modern education policy the government is endeavouring to make Austrian schools both up-to-date and more human and to improve equality of opportunity between regions. The federal government is also aware of the fact that the largest families are those of farmers and especially unskilled workers, where the average income is lowest, and that there is therefore a connection between relative poverty and large families.

Finally the federal government also advocates the implementation of a contingency plan for doctors that should help to remove regional differences in medical care. It intends to continue the campaign against poverty, especially in the case of handicapped persons, by creating assured jobs and setting up sheltered workshops on modern lines in greater number than hitherto. The government declares its intention to place manual and non-manual workers on an equal footing with regard to labour law. This goal was resolutely pursued in recent years by the late Social Affairs Minister, Gerhard Weissenberg, and he was able to bring his efforts close to conclusion. The federal government has also promised to go further in removing regional inequalities through co-operative regional planning. Thus, many of the objectives advocated by the examiners and pursued by the Austrian federal government are well on the way to achievement.

In this respect, the Examiners' Report on Integrated Social Policy in Austria is an interesting review of achievements to date, and at the same time a cause for critical reflection. In that connection one remark stands out in particular: "Without an overall social strategy it will be difficult to achieve greater social equality". This statement of the examiners finds its counterpart in the government's Declaration of Intent of 19 June 1979: "Every social system requires a constant effort to improve it and this also applies to the present system. The aim here is to achieve the highest degree of social equality through economic progress and stability." A final reference to the 1979 government Declaration of Intent should serve to confirm the large measure of agreement between the Examiners'

Report and the government's policy. "The federal government will continue to see that the principle of social justice is taken into account in the provision of public services".

I hope that I was able, in this brief attempt at a summary account of the situation, to show our generally positive attitude.

<u>CONCLUSIONS OF THE SPECIAL   REVIEW MEETING</u>
<u>OF THE MANPOWER AND SOCIAL AFFAIRS COMMITTEE</u>

(Vienna, 7-8 October 1980)

INTRODUCTION

The Special Review Meeting on Integrated Social Policy in Austria which the Committee held in Vienna in October 1980 showed how a country has striven to reconcile an improved utilisation of economic measures with emerging patterns of social aspirations and needs of the population. All Member countries endeavour to integrate the economic with the social dimension in the shaping and implementation of policies and programmes. The overall framework for managing this process has been widening everywhere. The evaluation of a country's approaches and experiences - in the present case Austria - needs, therefore, to be set against a broad background and in the context of its basic characteristics. These, as distilled from the Examiners' Report, the annexes thereto and the statements by the Austrian Delegation at the Special Review Meeting, are therefore described hereafter.

BACKGROUND AND CONTEXT OF INTEGRATED SOCIAL POLICY

The notion of social policy in the sense of a concept for the shaping of the entire social and economic system, in other words an "integrated policy for society as a whole" (Gesellschaftspolitik), has been alive in all ideological camps of Austria for a long time. The Federal State Constitution, which dates back to the 1920s, and the Rechtsstaat (legal state) principle impose on the central, regional and local powers a continuous search for joint frameworks to meet changing policy requirements. The federal Länder are relatively small and homogeneous and the Constitution provides for a fair measure of communal autonomy. This government system enforces a continuous process of consensus finding and co-ordination. It is matched by a system of chambers(*) with self-government and mandatory powers which embrace nearly all socio-economic groups by compulsory membership and a network of strong voluntary associations organised on socio-economic, denominational and other principles. Chambers and associations are interwoven in manifold ways with the formal government system. They are involved in most areas of policy-making and in many areas of implementation.

---

*) For an explanation of the term "chamber", see Examiners' Report, Part I, Section D(c) and Annex I, "The associations system".

The main features of the economic structure of Austria are a high degree of diversification, important roles played by small and medium-sized business and small farming, and a large public enterprise sector.

A special type of advanced welfare state has evolved in the context of these structures. It has emerged from a judicious mix of direct and indirect state intervention, including some pragmatic planning approaches, and the free play of market forces. It provides for a social security system which was already highly developed in the years following the First World War, and which has so far never stood in the way of economic expansion and the achievement and maintenance of full employment. Hitherto, a fair measure of built-in flexibility has enabled the Austrian welfare state to develop patterns of a more differentiated development of the social security system as well as entirely new ways of meeting social needs. Whether this will prove sufficient to meet future needs is uncertain. The fact that a broad consensus on the basic objectives of this welfare state prevails might help overcome barriers to necessary adaptations. These basic objectives are: full employment, "appropriate" rates of economic growth, "socially-oriented efficiency" of the economy, taking into account social considerations in income distribution and life opportunities, and a gradual shift towards non-economic interests in life. There is also a broad consensus on many of the operational goals to be derived from them. These joint basic objectives and operational goals are denominators for policy-making and implementation in practice. They are not inconsistent with the continuance of fundamental differences in political philosophies and long-term programmes.

Austria is a small country of 7.5 million inhabitants. Regional and local identities and loyalties are highly developed and reflected in the power system. People involved in policy making and implementations know each other well, and informal processes are at least as important in decision-making as formal ones.

INTEGRATION PROCESSES IN AUSTRIA

Austria thus enjoys a set of interrelated institutional and political conditions which further the emergence of integrated policies and measures. The growing needs of integration are met without a comprehensive systematising concept. All-embracing rationally structured machinery for centralised policy development and implementation and review appear to be incompatible with this system. But the view of the examiners that further frameworks for overall co-ordination, integration and review will have to be developed is shared by many

Austrian policy-makers. Nevertheless, the preconditions for coping
with the challenges of the eighties through strategies supported by
all socially relevant forces still appear to be better in Austria
than in many other countries. Looked at from outside, Austria's performance in the past is attributable to no small extent to the efficient and pragmatic interaction between the main elements of the political, economic and social systems on the basis of implicit rather
than explicit general goal concepts. These general goal concepts
stemming from a fundamental consensus are viewed as mutually consistent and supportive, and conceived to meet simultaneously economic
and social ends. As a consequence the customary distinction between
economic and social policies is of little relevance in the Austrian
context. This is certainly, at least in part, due to the fact that
Austria has achieved relatively high economic growth rates and that
consequently incompatibilities between economic constraints and social objectives have not come to the surface as much as in many other
countries.

There are institutional frameworks for keeping the appropriate
balance between national, regional and local government powers, and
mechanisms for settling divergences between interests of socio-
economic groups. The two systems are complementary and interlinked.
It has so far proved possible to adapt them to permit integration of
policy-making and policy implementation in specific policy areas at
the economically and socially most desirable levels and the reconciliation of economic and social objectives. Comprehensive schemes
for interrelated policies have thus emerged, like those for maintaining full employment, structural and regional development, public
infrastructure expansion, building up adequate networks for transport,
education, training, health care, the fight against hidden poverty,
and rehabilitation. As is the case elsewhere, there is no systematic
frame of reference for an integrative review and monitoring of distribution and redistribution of income, wealth and non-material interests in life, and the effects of various policies on the distribution of well-being.

Policy reform in Austria, perhaps more than in many other countries, depends on public opinion. This is characteristic of the consensus-oriented Austrian system. Complex processes and structures
of decision-making ensure the involvement of the various population
groups and their identification with policy reform, which contributes
to the high degree of cohesion in society. Nevertheless, disengage-
ment and withdrawal, and resistance against certain policies and
measures are tending to grow among a number of population groups in
Austria too. Although, compared with many other countries, Austria's
population is quite homogeneous, social disintegration is now affecting a greater proportion of it than in the sixties and calls for additional emphasis on co-ordination and integration. More comprehensive

approaches have been launched to reform public finance, streamline the social security system, improve the distribution of well-being, and reshape the schemes for housing, health care, rehabilitation of the handicapped, the fight against poverty, and the social integration of the aged, women and immigrants. But this has intensified existing conflicts of interest, and also created new ones.

FULL EMPLOYMENT AND ECONOMIC GROWTH

Austria's record in the 1970s and up to 1980 includes:
i) a steady and significant rise in the numbers of wage and salary earners;
ii) increased labour force participation in the population of active age;
iii) unemployment rates which are very low by international standards;
iv) a sustained high level of investment as a proportion of GNP;
v) reasonably high rates of overall productivity increase compared with the average for OECD Europe;
vi) inflation rates well below the average of OECD Europe;
vii) GDP growth rates well above the average of OECD Europe.

A number of factors have contributed to this record:

i) voluntary restraint in the process of wages and prices formation leaving scope for continuous real wage increases and a high level of fixed capital formation;
ii) continuous adaptation of the qualification structure of the labour force to new requirements (this applies particularly to the young, among whom the unemployment rate is very low);
iii) the adaptability of Austrian enterprises;
iv) structural and regional changes entailing reconversions without large lay-offs;
v) a buoyant labour demand from the service sector (public and private);
vi) vigorous use of public deficit spending as an instrument to maintain full employment, balanced by monetary instruments to restrain prices;
vii) a small defence budget as a proportion of GNP;
viii) continuing reduction of working time to one of the lowest levels in the world;
ix) the entitlement of more people to early retirement according to rules laid down in the sixties, and new provisions for early retirement for social and health reasons;

x) stringent regulations for unemployment benefits and assistance which compel the unemployed to seek for new jobs or (re)training;

xi) highly diversified and selective labour market programmes;

xii) reduction, by about one fifth, of the number of immigrant employees.

All these policies and measures involved concerted action by government and the organisations of the social partners. They also facilitated the financing of the extensive social security system and permitted a number of substantial improvements for disadvantaged groups and the elimination of discriminatory provisions. They depend, in part, on general agreement that unemployment must be prevented if this is possible at a reasonable price, and the conviction that it is easier to prevent unemployment from rising than to reduce it once it is established, to say nothing of the economic and human losses incurred during protracted periods of high unemployment. It must be noted, however, that delays in indispensable structural adaptations inherent in such a policy have made it more difficult to devise policies for the future aimed at both full employment and sustained economic growth at reasonably high levels.

In Austria full employment and economic growth are of prime importance to the social system as a whole. They create a frame of reference for the integration of a broad range of policies and measures. As a result of full employment, specific employment policies and direct and indirect employment subsidisation play only a supplementary role. However, some of the major conditions for this policy no longer prevail in Austria to the same extent as in the seventies. For instance, it would be difficult to expand public expenditure without unduly increasing public indebtedness, to reduce working time further without entailing real income losses, to decrease the number of foreign workers or substantially to extend employment in the service sector. As the international growth prospects for the eighties remain gloomy, a different policy mix and new instruments are being prepared in Austria. Government and social partners appear to be confident that with these they will again be able to keep unemployment at a low level and restore growth rates above the average for OECD Europe. They trust that the social partnership will prove once more in periods of adversity its integrative and conflict-resolving power, as it did in many critical periods in the sixties and seventies, such as during the final phase of the Great Coalition Government and in face of the 1967 and 1973/1974 recessions. The determination to solve problems jointly, the consensus on major policy priorities and the public's fear of social strife seem to be as strong as ever.

SOCIAL PARTNERSHIP

The social partnership system as described and analysed in the
Examiners' Report and in the Austrian statements appears both as an
integral and as an integrating component of the Austrian decision-
making system. It complements, in a variety of ways, the government
system with which it has multiple links. It is not only a mechanism
for peaceful wages and prices formation, but a system for pluralistic participation in power and responsibility in virtually all areas
of social policy in the broadest sense. Its strength is derived from
a broad consensus on the basic objectives of policy, an agreed assessment of economic and social interrelationships, the preparedness of
all groups involved to forego "victories" over others by unrestrained
use of power, and the efficiency of centralised decision-making procedures matched by a great flexibility in the institutional networks
and in the areas and methods of co-operation. Social partnership as
it has evolved after World War II is perceived by the vast majority
of the population as the most significant and specifically Austrian
response to the universal concern for social peace and for conflict-
resolving approaches which meet this concern. As social partnership
has been successful so far over more than three decades, in particular during politically and economically critical periods, the majority of the people credit it at least as much as the government for the
judicious management of economic and social affairs.

The functioning of social partnership is dependent on the acceptance of stability in the long run of the per-capita shares of labour
and capital in the national income. This is of vital importance in
the Austrian consensus. However, in the past conditions have been
particularly favourable. Economic growth rates and the employment
situation have remained satisfactory and provided room for a continuous rise in the income share of economically and socially weak
groups of active and retired employees and self-employed, without
entailing real income losses for the other groups.

Within the limits set by social partnership, there has always
been ample scope for the initiation of, or participation in, policy
innovation, although the number of areas or problems not suitable
for settlement primarily by social partnership, such as regional development, public health, education, housing, transport, energy,
integration of immigrants, is tending to grow with a corresponding
shift in the balance of power in favour of the government. However,
the social partnership system has in the past given evidence of its
capacity not only to work during critical phases, but also to adapt
its policy stance and its structure to changing conditions and requirements. There is no guarantee that this capacity will remain
unimpaired, should the determinants of economic and social development alter more radically and the crisis be more lasting than is at

present expected in Austria. Neither complacency nor excessive pessimism concerning the economic and social outlook appears justified, but a vigorous unbiased endeavour to reappraise social partnership in the light of likely future conditions, and a readiness to apply joint solutions, are required.

DISTRIBUTION AND REDISTRIBUTION OF RESOURCES AND OPPORTUNITIES

The basic objectives on which there is general consensus include a minimum of equality in the distribution and redistribution of resources, a progressive increase of equality in the distribution of life opportunities and a gradual shift towards non-material interests in life. This sets a broad framework for the consideration of distribution and redistribution policies and measures, which becomes even wider if extended to closely related objectives such as a high level of employment and appropriate growth. Substantial progress towards greater policy transparency in this respect has been achieved over the past decade, but the knowledge gaps are still too big to permit more than qualitative conclusions. Nevertheless, it is safe to state that full employment has been a major vehicle for more distributive equality and that the stress on meeting economic efficiency criteria has a lot to do with the relatively modest reduction in inter-personal primary income differentials over the long run. It is also established that persons with low incomes (employees, self-employed, pensioners and welfare assistance receivers) and socially weak population groups (e.g. farmers) have been the main net beneficiaries of the income redistribution system. There is also some evidence that the socially-oriented policies for structural and regional development and for infrastructure and public service systems such as those for education, transport, health care, employment and personal social services have brought about greater net gains to the lower income groups than to the higher ones. Comprehensive policies and measures emerging with the gradual shift to non-material objectives such as full integration in society (the elderly; the physically, mentally and socially handicapped; the poor, and recently also immigrants), environment protection, agreeable environment for work, recreation and social activities and direct participation in decision-making on matters concerning the work place, neighbourhood, the local community and the region, aim explicitly at favouring lower income groups.

The picture becomes less clear if one looks only at the financial burden of this redistribution process. There has existed, for some time, an all-embracing social security system based on the principle of solidarity in which, in the final analysis, the active pay for

186

the retired, the healthy for the sick, the employed for the unemployed and single people and childless couples for families. But the compound social effect of the regulations and practices for the raising of direct and indirect taxes, of pay-roll levies and contributions to the social insurance system cannot be assessed. The relative burden of the lowest and most needy income groups seems to be smallest and, as in other countries, the middle income groups both put in and take out the largest share in the benefits and services financed collectively. In the welfare state of the Austrian type this is apparently not considered as a reason for replacing, to any noteworthy degree, by market forces a system of collectivisation which redistributes essentially among the same social group. But complementary or alternative forms of organisation, financing and delivery of social welfare benefits and services are under discussion or on trial.

It can be noted that in Austria "social" public expenditure in the narrow sense, already at a high level by 1970, has grown more slowly in the seventies than the average of OECD Europe. Moreover, projections of future financing are less gloomy due to past economic growth, full employment and increasing activity rates and anticipated demographic trends. Nevertheless, the pressures for more efficiency (e.g. in the health care system) are becoming stronger and might soon be paralleled by pressure for more social equality, including a narrowing of the differentials in primary income distribution and greater equality in the distribution of the burden and benefits of redistribution. More rigorous initiatives for making distribution and redistribution in all their ramifications as transparent as possible, and for assessing the redistributive impact of the broad range of policies and measures with redistributive effects in the broadest sense might become a political imperative sooner than appears to be expected in Austria.

REGIONAL, LOCAL AND INFRASTRUCTURE ASPECTS OF INTEGRATION

The Austrian variants of federalism, of a mixed economy and of the welfare state appear to favour the putting of general social policy objectives into practice. Schemes for concerted national, regional and local development and for balanced growth of public facilities play a key role within the frameworks of federalism, the mixed economy and the welfare state. The federal Constitution and the constitutions of the Länder leave scope for a de facto redistribution of competences between ministries, and between the federal State, the Länder and the communes. However, the need for gradually establishing, extending, differentiating and interlocking these

development schemes cannot be met only by such adjustments. All
agencies concerned have therefore to strive continuously for concertation in medium- and long-term planning and for co-ordination and
integration of operations. In the eighties, greater efforts than in
the past will be required in this respect in view of the increasing
difficulty of the problems to be coped with as a consequence of
changing overall economic conditions.

The appraisal by the examiners of the past national, regional
and local area development approaches and of government activities
in the fields of education, health care and transport, and the explanations given by the Austrian Delegation, have revealed a large
degree of "regionalisation" and "localisation" of national policies.
This seems to have facilitated the achievement of both the economic
and social goals underlying these policies, and the tailoring of
individual measures of all kinds to the specific regional and local
economic conditions and social needs. The small size of Austria
even permits in many cases specially adapted combinations of capital-
and labour-related measures for the promotion of structural adjustments according to the specific situations of individual enterprises
and establishments. Many public and private enterprises seem to
have become agents of an integrated structural and regional policy,
because of the importance of their own manpower policies for the
supply of adequately trained labour and for the stabilisation of labour demand during slack periods. Together with extensive programmes
for public infrastructure development focusing on the education and
transport networks, this strategy has contributed to keeping employment and investment levels high and slowing down the decline of the
economic and social viability of disadvantaged areas. This has diminished the under-utilisation of physical and human capital, over-
development in large conurbations (with the diseconomies and social
problems this entails) and inequalities in access to employment,
social amenities (in particular education and health care) and leisure. It has thus been possible to keep inter-regional and intra-
regional relocation low by international standards.

A number of indicators signal increasing difficulty in counter-
acting the tendencies towards growing regional disparities. Long-
term economic prospects for certain areas, branches and enterprises
are becoming particularly gloomy, and in view of continuous fiscal
constraints the scope for substantial direct or indirect public aid
to such areas, branches and enterprises is becoming even narrower
than in the seventies. Long-term considerations of the improvement
of the overall competitiveness of Austrian industry which is essential for the reduction of the growing structural current balance and
budget deficits might make it more necessary to channel public expenditure, tax concessions and other measures increasingly into the
promotion of research, innovation and competitive products. Although

it might prove possible to achieve a general consensus on this line
of policy, conflicts of interests might become more difficult to re-
solve than in the past, as the interests of employers, employees and
the Länder and communes concerned could be more vitally at stake.
Moreover, the extension of some sections of the public and private
service networks could soon reach the point where further extensive
investment is no longer justified such as in education and health
care. In others, such as transport, the competition between the
territorial authorities for priority in investment might become keen-
er. Tighter budget conditions for all territorial public authorities
will in any case increase the pressure for more social effectiveness
and economic efficiency in the use of resources, in particular by
better co-ordination and, where possible, increased integration
arrangements. They could also lead to the intensification of the
struggle now going on for a redistribution of the burden between the
various public authorities and agencies concerned, and of the benefits between social groups.

PUBLIC HEALTH

In Austria, as in other countries, the prime objective of health
policy has become that of aiding in the solution of all problems
which bear on the physical, mental or social well-being of the population. This extends the traditional field of health policy to prevention, health protection and rehabilitation. A great number of
different agencies are involved and the network of elements to be
interrelated in such an integrated health policy is complex. A
comprehensive concept for policy reform can in these circumstances
only be developed through a strategic long-term plan. Specific solutions must be sought simultaneously on many different fronts in a
variety of ways, with constant care for consistency within the overall frame of reference. The examiners have stressed what they consider to be desirable in their report and the Austrian Delegation,
whilst agreeing on most of the objectives to be aimed at, had specific reservations as to how far, and by what methods, they could be
achieved.
In view of the emerging morbidity and mortality patterns, a high
priority is assigned to the various areas of preventive and protective
health policies such as environment protection, work hygiene and industrial medical care and supervision, reduction of traffic accidents,
health counselling and health education, and medical prophylaxis. The
range of programmes and measures under implementation or consideration
is wide, and many public authorities and other agencies are involved.
The methods to be considered and the institutional options vary from

case to case. Thus, the co-ordination and integration difficulties to be surmounted are immense. Notwithstanding, Austria could draw on other Member countries' experiences and, vice versa, some Austrian achievements or projects revealed by the Review appear worthy of study by other countries.

The intensification of preventive and protective policies has become very expensive in the short run, whereas any cost-reducing effect can only be felt in the medium and long term. This enhances the need for cost containment in the curative system, whereas the cost rise has been steep, although recently slowing down. The fact that both over- and under-consumption of medical treatment by certain population groups and in certain geographical areas has to be combated on economic and on social grounds does not facilitate the task. The measures for doing this which are under way or envisaged follow the main lines of international trends, namely:

i) improving the supply and qualifications of health personnel and their distribution between regions, between extra- and intra-mural care, between categories of doctors and between different qualification levels;

ii) better co-ordination between intra-mural and extra-mural care, in particular as regards care for the mentally sick and aged;

iii) diminishing the role, whilst increasing the efficiency, of institutional care, and laying greater stress on new approaches to extra-mural care, in particular through building up a network of primary care units around general practitioners in which social services are integrated;

iv) selective cost control measures;

v) strengthening the position of patients in their relationship to doctors by the appointment of an Ombudsman.

In Austria's highly pluralistic and consensus-oriented political and social system, measures of this kind can only be developed and implemented jointly and stepwise - often only in a piecemeal way. An all-embracing federal scheme for the planning and management of the curative care system, based on a series of agreements committing the public authorities, organisations and agencies mainly involved, is not envisaged. One of the reasons for this is that a good deal of authority rests with the Länder. But the pressure for a more comprehensive framework for integration and co-ordination has grown over the past decade and led to a number of schemes, such as the federal framework for the planning, financing and rationalisation

of the intra-mural care system. The linking to a coherent whole of
various fields of curative care might be furthered through the
strengthened role of the regional and local authorities and agencies
in conceiving and implementing reforms.

From this point of view the Austrian experience in regard to co-
ordination and integration in the field of medical, vocational and
social rehabilitation is revealing. There are still considerable
gaps in certain areas of rehabilitation, such as sheltered workshops
and the harmonisation of entitlements irrespective of the cause of
disability (and hence of conditions for cost coverage). Co-ordination
in the establishment and use of institutions is another high priority
task. Harmonisation of federal and Land legislation and regulations,
joint elaboration of broad federal concepts for future policy and
measures, and the transfer to Land level of the main responsibility
for the development and use of instruments for integration, co-
ordination and collaboration, are the ways in which these gaps are
being closed.

SOCIAL INTEGRATION

There is a basic consensus in Austria on the need to focus on
the economically and socially disadvantaged in the distribution of
resources and life opportunities, on a gradual shift towards non-
material interests in life and - typical for a consensus-minded
society - on the maintenance of a maximum degree of cohesion and integration in this society. From these objectives stems an increasing general concern for the social and cultural integration or reintegration of individuals or families belonging to specific groups,
and the avoidance of any disintegrative tendencies. If this calls
for comprehensive approaches also entailing more differentiation
(i.e. positive discrimination) in policies and schemes designed for
the entire population, such as those for employment, education, transport, housing, social security, social assistance and social services,
health care and regional development, the Austrian population seems
to be prepared to support them. Wider frames of reference and
appropriate new settings for co-ordinated policy development and
implementation, which are compatible with the Austrian system of
distribution of responsibilities among a great many authorities and
organisations, are thus emerging.

By international standards, social and cultural integration of
young people has so far posed minor problems, since education, training and employment opportunities are largely in line with qualifications and aspirations, and are unlikely to diminish drastically as
the qualitative and quantitative equilibrium between supply and demand may be expected to persist even during a period of slow growth.

Some of the deficiencies still prevailing, such as the de facto separation of boys and girls in different streams in vocational education and training, and partly also in higher education, are long-term policy preoccupations. On quite another plane, there are symptoms of increasing differences in the value scales of the young and middle-aged, and of a growing withdrawal of adolescents and young people in regard to the "Austrian system". These should give rise to more intensive search for reasons and remedies.

The situation of the elderly also appears to be satisfactory by international standards. This is due to a number of factors, namely:

i) low unemployment among the 50-60 age group;

ii) efficient provisions to protect elderly people against dismissals;

iii) arrangements for facilitating the transition from active life to retirement;

iv) opportunities for early retirement on medical or social grounds;

v) pensions which are periodically adjusted to the development of real wages and salaries (with higher than average increases for the lowest pensions);

vi) periodically adjusted social assistance benefits which are gradually rising in real terms;

vii) special measures in the fields of housing, transport and communications;

viii) aids for housekeeping, special catering facilities and a wide range of other services and activities offered by communes, voluntary agencies and organisations for the aged, which meet with an encouraging response on the part of the aged.

A large proportion of the aged population is, moreover, integrated in a rural or small town social and cultural environment where, in contrast to bigger towns, medical care for the aged in their homes is less of a problem. However, the authorities of most of the Länder and bigger cities are now tackling the question of in-home medical care within comprehensive programmes for the aged and for the reform of health care.

The policy of raising lower incomes, including pensions and social assistance payments, by above-average rates, the numerous effective direct and indirect benefits provided for families with children, the all-embracing social insurance system, and sustained full employment in nearly all parts of Austria have substantially reduced poverty in the traditional sense. This has not weakened the awareness of the problem in Austria. The new forms of deprivation, characterised by an accumulation of disadvantages, handicaps or deficiencies were

therefore recognised early and approached systematically by concerted
action involving all welfare authorities and organisations concerned.
The final aim is a policy of primary prevention to forestall the
emergence of poverty in the framework of a policy for society as a
whole. The examiners and the Austrian Delegation have brought out
the main features of the existing approach - an integrative approach
par excellence which takes into account all aspects of the problem
and provides for the institutional machinery for action-oriented research, policy planning and adjustment of provisions in social insurance schemes and for model projects for adequate social services
and co-ordinated work in the field. These activities may also improve
the effectiveness of the concerted action for the rehabilitation of
physically, mentally and socially handicapped, many of whom belong
to the substratum of the deprived who find themselves outside society.

Another group particularly affected, the immigrants, has only recently been recognised by the public authorities as a target group
for a comprehensive policy for social integration. Mass immigration
is in Austria a comparatively new phenomenon and comes under the
joint control of Government, Labour and Management. However, throughout the seventies the share of foreign workers in the salaried labour
force never declined below 6 per cent, and the scope for future reductions in response to changing employment conditions is considered
to be limited. The proportion of foreign-speaking people among the
population has been on the increase and is likely to remain high to
the extent that immigrant workers intend and are permitted to settle
in Austria. The problems which have arisen are not much different
in nature from those of other European countries confronted with the
requirements of a large-scale integration of immigrants, but the conditions for the solution appear to be more favourable in Austria
since the vast majority of immigrants comes from a neighbouring country, Yugoslavia, which has traditional ties with Austria. Austria
seems therefore to be particularly suited to develop a strategy for
planned and co-ordinated measures for the successive stages of socio-
cultural integration. First steps in this direction have already
been initiated.

Austria is among the countries whose governments have stipulated
the goal of "transition from formal equality of rights to actual
equality of status for women in society" and who are developing step
by step a broad framework for an integrative approach to this end.
Taking the various aspects of the social and employment integration
problem into account, progress in this direction in Austria has much
accelerated over the seventies. Recent policy decisions, measures
and institutional provisions, and the growing sensitivity of public
opinion on this issue, might give even greater impetus to the process.
However, the further one advances along this road, the more difficult
the problems of co-ordination and integration seem to become, both
as regards substance and procedures.

Annex I

AUSTRIA'S POLITICAL SYSTEM
by

Professor Anton Pelinka,
Director of the Institute for Political Science
at the University of Innsbrück

CONTENTS

INTRODUCTION

The following study, being part of the Review of "Integrated Social Policy in Austria", is intended, in the context of that project, as an introduction to the political system of Austria. It is not a summary of the individual findings of the various parts of the project, but gives a general overview of the special features of the political scene in Austria.

This subject is approached from the political science point of view. Insofar as constitutional law or economic aspects are touched on, it is not claimed that these constitute a serious contribution to the sciences of constitutional law or economics.

The study is to be taken as a political science study, but not as an original contribution in the sense of a furthering of scientific knowledge, of that subject. It is a scientific compilation which, it is hoped, will facilitate the approach to and understanding of the research findings of the project as a whole.

1. THE POLITICAL SYSTEM

A. The Constitutional Structure

The bases of the Constitution

The Austrian constitutional system is based on the 1929 version of the Federal Constitutional Law of 1 October 1920. This Constitution was brought back into force by the Declaration of Independence of 27 April 1945 and the Constitutional Transitional Law of 1 May 1945.

From the point of view of content the Austrian Constitution is a compromise between the large parties (1920: Christlich-soziale Partei and the Sozialdemokratische Partei); from the standpoint of method it was strongly influenced by the legal positivism of Hans Kelsen. In consequence, unlike for example the Basic Law of the German Federal Republic, each particular part of the Austrian Constitution, as well as the Constitution as a whole, can be amended and indeed annulled by due process of law.

Power to change the Constitution lies in general with the Nationalrat (National Council), which can pass constitutional laws (including laws to change the Constitution) if certain conditions are met (quorum of 50 per cent present, approval by at least two-thirds of the deputies). Any change in the basic principles of the Constitution, to which by common consent the principles of democracy, the rule of law and the federal State belong, can however only be done by means of a nationwide referendum (Article 44, paragraph 2 B-VG).

The Austrian governmental system is of mixed type, combining elements of a parliamentarian system with elements of a presidential system, but in political practice the parliamentarian elements predominate. The Austrian governmental system is parliamentarian because the government must basically enjoy the confidence of a majority of the National Council; and it is also presidential because the government is appointed by the federal president and is also dissolved by him. Through a change in the Constitution in 1929 the governmental system - originally purely parliamentarian - was provided with a head of state with far-reaching powers. Since then the federal president has been elected directly by the people under an absolute majority system for a period of six years; re-election for one further term is possible.

The federal president possesses two main powers which go beyond the normal powers of a head of state in a parliamentarian system: he can dissolve the National Council (only once however on the same grounds); and he appoints (and dismisses) the Federal Chancellor and also, on the latter's proposal, the other members of the federal government. But the federal government also needs the support of a majority of the National Council, since the latter has the power to pass a vote of no confidence. It is possible, therefore, for a conflict to develop between the federal president and the National Council which could prevent the government from governing. This possibility is in practice avoided, however, in that the Federal President refrains from exercising his powers in this respect. All federal presidents so far have always appointed governments which had a majority behind them in the National Council, even when that majority was politically oriented differently from the federal president, as for example in 1966, when the federal president Franz Jonas (a socialist) appointed Josef Klaus - a member of the Austrian People's Party with an absolute parliamentary majority behind him, and a government consisting exclusively of Austrian People's Party members.

The federal government consists of the Federal Chancellor, the Vice Chancellor (until 1966 without a portfolio of his own), the federal ministers and the secretaries of State. Although the Austrian Constitution does not contain a "Chancellor principle" which lays it down that the Federal Chancellor shall lead the federal government, the Federal Chancellor has a definite superiority in ranking compared with the other members of the government. The extent of this superiority depends however on whether the Chancellor has to lead a coalition government (as was the case up until 1966), in which case he shares this superiority in ranking with the Vice Chancellor; or whether he leads a one-party government. Since 1966 a de facto "Chancellor principle" has developed in political practice, based on the Federal Chancellor's leadership of his own party.

The Legislature

The Austrian Parliament consists of two chambers, the National Council (Nationalrat) voted directly by the people, and the Federal Council (Bundesrat) which is made up of representatives of the individual federal states (Länder). Since the reform of the voting system in 1971, the Nationalrat has 183 members, the Bundesrat (on the basis of the population census of 1971) 58 members. The Nationalrat is elected for a period of four years. There are no such time limits on the Bundesrat, since, like the Senate in the United States, it continually partly renews itself, these partial renewals occurring after a State Diet election (Landtagswahl) or after a population census result requiring a change in the number of members in the Federal Council.

The Federal Constitutional Law, Article 26, paragraph 1, lays down that the Nationalrat shall be elected "on the basis of the equal, direct, secret and personal voting right of men and women...according to the principles of "proportional representation". Since 1971 the "principles of proportional representation" have taken the concrete form of each of the nine Länder constituting a voting constituency in which the voters vote for one of the party lists. The 183 seats are divided up between the Länder on a population basis. The whole of the federal area is also divided into two further voting constituency associations, in which the votes remaining after the seats have been allocated in the first round at the level of the nine Länder constituencies ("first counting procedure") are taken into account. In this "second counting procedure" at the level of the two constituency associations only those parties are taken into account which have already won at least one seat ("basic seat") in the first counting procedure at Land level.

Because of a preference vote system based on an Italian model, the list voting system used in the Austrian elections could have a certain personalisation effect which, however, in political practice has so far played no role at all. The lists submitted by the parties, with the candidates in the order of ranking decided by the parties, are the only recruiting instrument for the Nationalrat. In political reality, therefore, the two decisive characteristics of the Austrian voting system are proportional representation, and the list system which emphasizes the role of the parties in the State.

The Bundesrat (Federal Council) is elected by the Landtage (State Diets) of the nine Länder, the Constitution laying it down (Article 34, paragraph 2 B-VG) that the Land with the biggest number of citizens shall send 12 deputies to the Bundesrat, while the other Länder shall send as many deputies to the Bundesrat as the ratio of their citizen populations to the citizen population of the largest Land entitles them to. Each Land must however be represented by at least three deputies. On the basis of the population census of 1971, Vienna sends 12 deputies, Lower Austria 11, Upper Austria and Styria 9 each, Carinthia and Tyrol 4 each, Salzburg, Vorarlberg and Burgenland 3 each. Unlike the German Bundesrat, the Länder do not vote in blocks, the individual deputies voting even in the Bundesrat according to the party they belong to and in accordance with parliamentary party discipline.

In the distribution of parliamentary powers the Constitution gives a clear priority to the Nationalrat. In case of disagreement the Bundesrat possesses only exceptionally any genuine right of veto, and then only in questions which directly concern the Länder. In all other questions of the parliamentary decision process the Bundesrat possesses either merely delaying powers or no veto powers at all. Since the Bundesrat only receives bills for consideration after the

Nationalrat has considered them, the predominance of the directly
elected chamber is made clear by the wording of the Constitution.
This predominance is also reinforced by the fact that only the Nationalrat can pass a vote of no confidence in the federal government,
that is to say only the majority conditions in the Nationalrat have
any influence on the composition of the government.

The dominant position of the Nationalrat in legislation has admittedly, as has happened in other parliamentary systems in which the
political parties play a vital role, been progressively undermined.
The balance of power in the present decision-making process has
shifted towards the federal government, which - supported by an ex-
panding civil service apparatus - de facto prejudges issues before
they are considered by the Parliament. Most laws in Austria derive
from proposals by the government which are either not amended at all
by Parliament, or only amended in unessential ways. Only in except-
ional cases does the initiative actually stem from Parliament.

The dominant position of the Executive is made possible by the
actual parliamentary character and also by the pronounced political
party basis of the Austrian governmental system. Since the government and the parliamentary majority are politically identical, and
since the parliamentary parties in the Austrian Parliament are more
than usually disciplined and close-knit, government and Parliament
are closely interlinked with each other, the centre of decision being
located with the government.

The Executive

Austria's federalistic structure necessitates a division of the
administrative activity of the State between the Bund (Federation)
and the Länder. The Länder also administer certain affairs of the
federal administration, functioning in this case simply as subordinate authorities of the Bund ("indirect federal administration").
The lowest level of administration in Bund and Land matters is the
Bezirk (the county), each Bezirk administration being headed by an
appointed Bezirkshauptmann.

Alongside the executive authority, the legislative authority is
also divided between the Bund and the Länder - but not the judiciary
authority, which is exclusively a matter for the Bund. The Constitution lists limitatively the areas for which the Bund is responsible.
In comparison with other federal states (the United States), the
position of the Länder is not particularly strong, and this is brought
out even more clearly by the weak position of the Bundesrat.

The government system of the Länder is - with the exception of
Vienna and Vorarlberg - characterised by a proportional system: the
Länder constitutions lay it down that the parties represented in the
various Länder parliaments (Landtage) are to participate in the Länder

governments according to their respective strengths. The Länder parliaments are all single chamber systems. Each Land parliament has a Landeshauptmann as head of government.

The communes (Gemeinden), whose activity includes both their "own" activities (communal self-government) and a "delegated" area of activity (State administration), are organised according to the principle of the Einheitsgemeinde (uniform commune). Two types of Gemeinde are exceptions to this: the "Städte mit eigenem Statut" (towns with their own statutes) (in 1976 there were 14 of these - apart from Vienna) combine the characteristics of communes with those of Bezirken (counties). The city of Vienna represents a unique type: Vienna is a commune but also a Land. The Bürgermeister of Vienna is also Landeshauptmann, the Vienna Communal Council is at the same time a Landtag.

The Judiciary

Austrian law is organised on the basis of a "successive stages" structure. The foundation stage is the Federal Constitutional Law, on which - in the following order - other federal constitutional laws, simple federal laws and decrees and regulations are built up.

The judiciary is divided into two - the "ordinary" and the "extraordinary" judiciary. The ordinary judiciary has four elements: Bezirksgerichte (county courts), courts of first instance (Kreis- and Landesgerichte), courts of second instance (Oberlandesgerichte) and the Supreme Court (Oberster Gerichtshof). The extraordinary judiciary is entrusted to the Verfassungsgerichtshof (constitutional high court) and the Verwaltungsgerichtshof (administrative high court). The Supreme Court and High Courts sit in Vienna.

For the political system it is the Constitutional High Court which is most important. This court has very wide powers. Its members are appointed by the Federal President, partly on the proposal of the Nationalrat, and partly on the proposal of the Bundesrat. In practice a "tacit agreement" has grown up between the Austrian Socialist Party and the Austrian People's Party that membership of the Constitutional High Court shall be divided equally between judges with Socialist Party leanings and those with People's Party leanings.

B. The Socio-Political Infrastructure

The party system

Development of the party system

The lines of development of the Austrian party system show remarkable continuity and stability. The basic features of the party
system developed in the last years of the XIXth century and survived,
with only minor changes, the collapse of the constitutional monarchy,
the (first) democratic republic, the Austro-fascist dictatorship and
the period of national socialist occupation.

The chief feature of this stable and concentrated party system
is the presence of three "camps". These camps, politico-philosophical groupings, have thrown up parties with various names in the
course of a history which has now lasted almost one hundred years.
A common feature of the parties of the three camps throughout all
the historical periods has been personal and programmatic continuity,
and also continuity in their comparative strengths in relation to
each other.

The constant relative strengths of the parties to each other in
the past, and still at present, justifies the term "two-and-a-half"
party system, or a "limping" three-party system. The parties of the
two big camps - the socialist camp (today represented by the Sozialistische Partei Oesterreichs) and the Christian social-conservative
camp (today represented by the Oesterreichische Volkspartei) - have
alongside them the smaller party of the third, smaller, German-national camp (today represented by the Freiheitliche Partei Oesterreichs).
In spite of the continuity in the relative strengths of the parties
there is also a continuous tendency towards gradual change, namely
an increase in the concentration of the party system in favour of the
parties of the two big camps.

The continuity in the lines of development of the party system
is also underlined by the lack of success of fourth parties. The
Austrian Communist Party, the only party which was able for a short
time after 1945 to play a part in political life alongside the three
traditional camps, was never able, even during its best period, to
reach the threshold figure of 6 per cent. This continuity and concentration in the development of the party system has worked generally in favour of the parties of the two large camps, but also against
all parties which have attempted to operate outside the areas of the
three camps.

The socialist camp - the most important political, economic, social
and cultural organisation form of the Austrian workers' movement -
developed relatively late compared with similar movements in Western

and Central Europe. The main reason for this late development was the general delay in the development of capitalism in Austro-Hungary. It was not until 1888/89 that the Social Democratic Workers' Party of Austria was founded for the Austrian half of the Dual Monarchy. This party was a coalition of several movements covering a wide spectrum of ideologies, but all containing a definite marxist orientation. Working together with the trade unions, which were also developing at the same time, the Social Democratic Party succeeded in organising politically the vast majority of Austrian workers. By 1907, when general and equal voting rights for men were introduced in Austria, the social democrats were already the second largest party in the country. In 1911, after the last elections under the monarchy, the Social Democrats became the biggest party in the Reichstag (Parliament).

Between 1918 and 1920, at the beginning of the First Republic of the small rump state of Austria, the social democrats formed part of a coalition government. They then fell back into their former role of opposition, and finally in 1933 and 1934 were pushed by the authoritarian government step by step into illegality. After the short and bloody civil war of February 1934 the Social Democratic Party transformed itself into an underground organisation which played an important part in the resistance to Austro-fascism and subsequently against national socialism.

In 1945 the social democrats, in their newly founded Austrian Socialist Party, regained at once their old strength. But instead of being the "natural" opposition party they now assumed the new role of "natural" governing party. With the exception of the period from 1966 to 1970, the Austrian Socialist Party has always taken part in the government - up to 1966 as part of a "large coalition", and since 1970 as the sole governing party.

In spite of all the changes over these decades the social democrats have always retained the same essential features: in their social structure they represented as before the majority of Austrian workers; in their programmatic and practical orientation the Austrian Socialist Party is as before in theory partly marxist, in practice broadly devoted to finding solutions for present problems.

The party-political organisational forms of the Christian social-conservative camp developed in parallel with the organisation of social democracy. Out of the Christlichsozialer Verein founded in 1887 there gradually developed the Christlichsoziale Partei, which at first represented mainly the Catholic middle class but later also the Catholic farmers. With a programme of anti-capitalistic reformism and intermittent anti-semitic leanings, the Christian Social Party became in the last years of the monarchy the leading representative of a political catholicism interested in maintaining the Habsburg empire.

In the years of the First Republic the Christian Social Party was the party of government. In 1920, after the breakdown of the coalition with the Social Democrats, the Christian Social Party governed with the help of smaller parties of the German-national camp, and later with the support of the openly fascist Heimatschutz, against the social democrats. The Christian Social Party, which formally dissolved itself after the civil war in 1934, placed its reservoir of experienced members at the disposal of the authoritarian "Ständestaat" (corporate state). The leading positions in this Austro-fascist régime were occupied by former representatives of the Christian Social Party.

Between 1938 and 1945 the Christlichsozialen made common front with the Social Democrats - both persuasions oppressed, both persuasions finding increasing common ground during this oppression. This newly discovered common ground found expression in 1945, when, on 27 April, a few days before the end of the war, the "provisorische Staatsregierung" (provisional government) was proclaimed. Parallel with this came the foundation of the Austrian People's Party, which regarded itself as the successor organisation to the Christian Social Party, and whose organisational leadership was staffed almost entirely from former members of the Christian Social Party.

In contrast to the First Republic, the government coalition of the two large camps lasted this time more than twenty years. Only in 1966 was the Austrian People's Party able and willing to govern alone, only to be replaced in this role in 1970 by the Austrian Socialist Party.

Independently of all these changes in its role, the party of the Christian social conservative camp displayed a remarkable social and also programmatic continuity. As before, the Austrian People's Party is supported by the middle classes and the farmers, as before it is the essential representative of the activist section of Austrian Catholicism.

The development of the German-national (deutschnational) camp was different from that of the two large camps mainly because it was not until the Second Republic that this camp was able to concentrate into a single party. In the last years of the monarchy several movements came together covering a broad spectrum ranging from liberalism to aggressive German nationalism, in parties with various titles. The most important of these was the Alldeutsche Partei (All-German Party) which in the nationality quarrels of the dying monarchy represented a radical element which was both anti-semitic and anti-Slav.

Supported by the less explicitly catholic elements of the middle classes and the farmers, the German-national camp in the First Republic was organised in two parties - the Grossdeutschen Volkspartei (Greater German People's Party) and the Landbund. These two small

parties were at various times allies of the Christian Social Party.
At the end of the First Republic their existence was threatened by
the rising wave of national socialism and most of the leaders and
most of the membership of these two parties switched over to the
NSDAP (German National Socialist Workers' Party). From 1932 to 1945
national socialism was the dominating political expression of the
German-national camp.

Because of this structural link with the NSDAP it was impossible
to organise any German-national Party in the first years of the Second Republic. It was only in 1949 that the Verband der Unabhängigen
(Association of Independents) was able to take up once more the tradition of the Greater German People's Party and the Landbund. In
1955 the Verband changed its name to the Freiheitliche Partei Oesterreichs (FPÖ), and today the FPÖ is a party in transition between German nationalism and liberalism.

The Kommunistische Partei Oesterreichs (KPÖ) - the Austrian Communist Party - which split off from the Social Democrats in 1918,
was never able to play an important role in the First Republic. Unlike almost all the other European Communist parties, the KPÖ was
unable to win even one seat in the parliaments of the Bund and the
Länder. Especially active in resistance against Austro-fascism and
national socialism, the KPÖ ranks were swollen by influxes of dis-
appointed Social Democrats. In 1945 therefore the KPÖ expected that
it would be able to play a role similar to that of the two large
camps. In spite of its participation in the government between 1945
and 1947, the KPÖ could however not achieve its aim. Driven into
opposition in 1947, the KPÖ experienced a decline in membership which
led in 1959 to the loss of its last seat in the Nationalrat.

The Socialist Party of Austria (Sozialistische Partei Oesterreichs) (SPÖ)

The SPÖ is one of the most tightly organised and - to judge by
its success in elections - most successful of the democratic socialist parties. Programmatically and verbally always inclined more to
the left-oriented, partly openly marxist wing of the Socialist Inter-
nationale, in the ninety years of its existence the SPÖ has always
been able to keep the vast majority of the Austrian workers behind
it.

This solid, stable basis within the workers' movement provides
the SPÖ with a traditional electoral support of more than 40 per cent
of the Austrian electorate. Through a policy of winning over marginal groups (catholics, clerical workers, the liberal professions),
the SPÖ was able to increase its share of the electorate to over 50
per cent - a percentage which is by international standards all the
more remarkable in that the proportional voting system used in Austria

does not favour the large parties in any way and therefore does not exert any "suction effect".

Ever since the war, with the exception of the period 1966 to 1970, the SPÖ has always been in the government, and so has won a place for itself more than any other party as the "party of government". Its close organisational links with the tightly organised trade unions and the extremely co-operative style of "social partnership"(1) in Austria combined to make the SPÖ - in spite of significant remnants of Austro-marxist programmatics - a decisive factor in the existing political and social system.

The pattern of electoral support for the SPÖ shows a more than proportional representation of workers (in the narrower sense of the word). The farmers, and the self-employed in commerce, trade and industry, and the representatives of the liberal professions are all considerably under-represented. The clerical workers and civil servants group is more or less proportionally represented in the SPÖ electorate.

There is no perceptible bias in the distribution of the sexes among SPÖ supporters, the share of women voters for the SPÖ corresponding more or less to the share of women voters in the whole electorate. Neither is the age factor relevant in the long term, the only noteworthy phenomenon being that the share of young voters in the SPÖ is more than proportional whenever the SPÖ is flourishing. However, the voting structure of the SPÖ varies very much according to region. The SPÖ is in general stronger in large and medium-sized towns than in small towns or in the countryside. There is also a decline in relative support as one moves from east to west. As in the past, the SPÖ is particularly strong in Vienna and in other east-Austrian regions; this regional bias is however showing a general tendency to decline.

Besides the occupational factor, the most important structural characteristic of the Austrian electorate is the religious one. Because of the largely homogeneous Catholic structure of the Austrian population (89 per cent belong to the Roman Catholic Church) the significant structural feature in regard to religion is the distinction between "active" Catholics and all other confessional groupings, including the "non-active" Catholics. The SPÖ is definitely over-represented in the latter group but definitely under-represented among "active" Catholics.

Membership of the SPÖ has for more than a decade now fluctuated somewhere around 700,000, which means that about 30 per cent of the electorate which votes for the SPÖ are regular party members. As a directly structured party - membership can only be obtained through direct, individual entry into the party - the SPÖ with this degree of organised members is in a leading position among European Parties.

1) This expression, as the present text makes clear, has a special, precise, meaning in the Austrian context.

An important feature of the party is the principle of "Vertrauens-leute" (party activists). About 10 per cent of all members are trained in special training courses, which since 1973 have been main-ly organised by the Karl-Renner-Institut (the "University of the SPÖ). These 70,000 party officers constitute the communicating link between the party leaders and the party membership and also serve as a reservoir for recruiting leaders. Because of the changed conditions regarding communications the first of these two tasks has faded some-what into the background, the second task being today the real func-tion of the "Vertrauensleute".

The SPÖ is directly and centralistically organised. Neither the party organisations in the various Länder nor the various special-group organisations on the fringes of the party possess any autonomy; they are basically subject to the decisions of the party as a whole. Nevertheless, in the field of recruiting in particular, a de facto autonomy has emerged in the sense that regional and other subsidiary organisations claim certain positions. The group of socialist trade unionists in the Austrian Trade Union Federation (Gewerkschaftsbund) (ÖGB), and also the Women's Organisation and the individual Länder organisations, have traditional claims on parliamentary seats accord-ing to a prescribed formula.

The Austrian People's Party (Oesterreichische Volkspartei)(ÖVP)

The Austrian Volkspartei is the second largest party in the country. Considering itself to be a christian democratic party, it compares in theory and practice with the other parties of the Euro-pean Union of Christian Democrats, such as the Democrazia Cristiana or the German CDU/CSU.

As successor to the Christian Social Party, the ÖVP draws as before its main support from the active Catholic elements of the population. Like the SPÖ, the ÖVP is a "natural party of government". From 1945 to 1970 the ÖVP was continuously the government party and always appointed the Federal Chancellor, who was always (with the exception of very short transitional periods) at the same time the federal party leader (Leopold Figl, Julius Raab, Alphons Gorbach, Josef Klaus). Events since 1970, however, that is to say four suc-cessive defeats in the elections, suggest that the ÖVP, through too long an absence from the responsibilities of government, may well have lost its position as a "natural party of government".

The supporters of the ÖVP are mainly to be found among the farm-ers and the middle classes. The vast majority of those working on the land and the vast majority of the self-employed in commerce, trade and industry regularly vote ÖVP; the office workers and civil ser-vants groups are more or less proportionally divided between the two large parties.

As regards the distribution between men and women voters and between the various age groupings, the shares of these in ÖVP supporters is basically proportional. The important element of strength for the ÖVP is however its leading position among the "active" catholics. The large majority of active catholics identify themselves with the ÖVP and regularly vote for the Volkspartei.

The composition of the electorate which supports the ÖVP implies a certain strategical disadvantage for the party in that the main groups among its supporters are declining in numbers - the numbers of those working on the land have been regularly declining for some decades, as have the numbers of the self-employed in commerce, trade and industry. There is also a gradual decline in the numbers of active catholics. This means that the core of traditional supporters of the ÖVP is declining in numbers, and that the ÖVP is even more dependent than the SPÖ on winning support among the floating marginal voting groups.

The farming and middle class character of the ÖVP is also reflected in the ranks of the party's officials. A large majority of the officials in the party institutions, and also in the civil service (insofar as these are occupied by the ÖVP) come from the middle-class professions or from farming. In addition there is an increasing number of university trained people in the leading party organs.

This is also connected with the role of Catholic young people's organisations in the ÖVP. Thus, the Austrian Cartellverband of Catholic "Colour-wearing" Student Associations (ÖCV) is the most important reservoir for leading functionaries. With one single exception (Karl Schleinzer, 1971 to 1975) all the federal party leaders of the ÖVP have been members of the ÖCV.

From the regional point of view the incidence of ÖVP membership in the population declines as one moves from west to east. The majorities of the Volkspartei are particularly strong in the western Länder (Vorarlberg, Tyrol). In the eastern part of the country Lower Austria is a stronghold of the ÖVP, because of the agrarian character of the Land.

The Volkspartei is organised on indirect and federalistic lines. It consists of six member organisations (up until the 1977 Party Conference, five) whose members constitute the membership of the Party. The number of direct members is insignificant. Combined with the roles played by the Länder organisations this kind of membership means that the Austrian Volkspartei is made up of 54 sub-parties - 6 member organisations in each of the 9 Länder.

Total membership figures for the ÖVP are very difficult to estimate since multiple membership in the constituent organisations is allowed; but since there are no statistics as to the extent of such multiple membership, the estimate which is most likely to be nearest the truth is the one which adds together the membership figures of the three Bünde ("federations" - see below), but which ignores the membership figures of the three other constituent organisations as a particularly high percentage of those constituent organisations can be assumed to be at the same time members of one or other of the Bünde.

The degree of organisation of the Volkspartei, which has an estimated membership of between 800,000 and 900,000 out of a total of about 2 million voters, is about 41 per cent. In terms of international comparisons, this degree of organisation is unique. In multi-party systems only regional parties like the South Tyrol Volkspartei have similar degrees of organisation. Other European parties with a similar position in the political spectrum (centre-right) have a much lower degree of organisation.

The organisation of the Volkspartei is particularly influenced by its constituent organisations. The three Bünde, which can be regarded as the pillars and actual founders of the party, are: the Oesterreichische Arbeiter-und Angestelltenbund (ÖAAB - Austrian Workers and Clerical Workers Federation) which represents the interests of wage-earners; the Oesterreichische Bauernbund (ÖBB - the Austrian Farmers Federation), which represents the interests of the farmers; the Oesterreichische Wirtschaftsbund (ÖWB - the Austrian Economic Federation), which represents the interests of the self-employed in commerce, trade and industry. The three other constituent organisations are: the Oesterreichische Jugendbewegung - the Junge Volkspartei (Youth Movement), the Oesterreichische Frauenbewegung (the Women's Movement), and the Oesterreichische Seniorenbund (Old People's association) which attained the rank of a subsidiary organisation only in 1977.

The Austrian Liberal Party (Freiheitliche Partei Oesterreichs) (FPÖ)

The FPÖ (the Austrian Liberal Party), the party of the German-national camp, plays a significant role in the Austrian party system mainly because it prevents the functioning of a genuine two-party system. Hitherto excluded from participation in government because of its origins in the German-national camp, the possibility that "small coalitions" may be formed between one of the large parties and the FPÖ in the future cannot be excluded. In this connection the effort this party is making to acquire a liberal image, which stands in latent contradiction to the remains of the old, German-national image, has something to do with this. The FPÖ is in any case not to be regarded as a liberal party like the British Liberals or the German FDP, although it contains certain elements which might in future help to move the party in the direction of the liberal parties.

In the field of socio-economic factors the electorate of the FPO is largely similar to that of the People's Party. The FPO is predominantly middle class, and partly also makes some appeal to farmers.

As regards the religious question, however, the FPO is not like the People's Party. In accordance with the tradition of the German-national camp, the FPO supporters are not predominantly to be found in the field of the catholic active elements, but - largely similar to the voting structure of the SPO - among the non-active catholics and non-catholics.

Regionally, the FPO is relatively strong in Carinthia, Salzburg and Upper Austria, and is traditionally weaker in east Austria than in west Austria.

The origins of the FPO in the German-national camp can also be seen in the recruiting of the party officials. A very high percentage of the party officials are old enough for this to be possible, and were already active in NSDAP organisations - this is true of the two former federal party leaders of the FPO, Anton Reinthaller (up until 1958) and Friedrich Peter (from 1958 to 1978). Among the younger generation of party functionaries this connection can still be seen since many of them come from the ranks of the "colour-wearing", German-national, (sometimes dual-practising) student associations.

The Freiheitliche Partei is, like the Socialist Party, directly organised. Membership of the party is only by individual application. Compared with the degree of organisation of the two large parties, the FPO is relatively thinly organised. It is in any case the only relevant Austrian party which cannot be regarded as a "membership party".

The Austrian Communist Party (Kommunistische Partei Oesterreichs) (KPO)

After the withdrawal of the Soviet occupying power, the KPO dwindled to the status of a splinter party. In the last elections in 1970, 1971, 1975 and 1979 only just over 1 per cent of Austrian voters voted for the communists. Between 1945 and 1947 the KPO participated in a "government of national concentration" with the People's Party and the Socialist Party, but after that the communists were unable to win any decisive positions at regional level or in the factories and trade unions. Their attempt in 1950 to organise a general strike against the wishes of the social democratic leaders of the trade unions also failed.

Between 1965 and 1969 the KPO tried to dissociate itself from the accusation of being under Soviet domination from outside. To this period belongs the KPO's recommendation to its members to vote SPO (except for one Vienna constituency) in the election in 1966, and the explicit condemnation in 1968 of Soviet intervention in

Czechoslovakia. But at the party conference in 1969 the "revisionist"
line was decisively rejected and full alignment with Soviet policy
resumed.

It is not possible to give precise details of KPÖ membership figures, but it can be assumed that there was a strong decline in membership after the 1969 party conference.

The Verbände (associations) system

General characteristics of associations in Austria

The first distinctive feature of the Austrian associations system
is its high degree of concentration and organisation. The associations dominate large areas of political life, which means that they
are very closely interwoven with the political parties. The participation of the Austrians in this system of associations which are
closely interwoven with the political parties, but also with each
other, is very high. This is due both to the highly developed system of the associations with automatic membership (Zwangsverbände -
compulsory associations), and also to the efficient organisation of
the associations with voluntary membership (freie Verbände).

The economic associations in Austria can be divided into compulsory associations and voluntary associations. With the exception of
workers in government service, all the larger occupational groups
are organised in compulsory associations; many occupational groups
are represented both by compulsory and also by voluntary associations.

The most important compulsory associations are the Chambers of
Labour (workers and employees), the Chambers of Trade, and the Chambers of Agriculture. The most important voluntary associations are
the Austrian Trade Union Federation (ÖGB) and the Vereinigung österreichischer Industrieller (Industrial Employers' Association). There
is broad parallelism between the interests structure of the Chambers
of Labour (workers and employees) and the ÖGB (Trade Union Federation),
and also between the Chambers of Trade and the Employers' Association.

The Chambers are constituted by the State through legislation.
Their task is only partly the representation of economic interests;
they are also organisations to which the government turns for help
in its administration. The Trade Union Federation and the Industrial
Employers' Association are not established by law, but are based on
private law agreements in the form of associations. In real political life, however, the functions of the voluntary associations are
very similar to those of the compulsory associations; in particular
a political division of labour exists between Chambers of Labour and
the ÖGB on the one hand, and between Chambers of Trade and the Employers' Association on the other.

The compulsory associations are basically more federalistic in their organisation than the voluntary associations. The Chambers are each organised into nine Landeskammern (provincial or Land Chambers). Over these Landeskammer there are umbrella organisations at national level. The significance of these central organisations varies. In the case of the Chambers of Trade the central Bundeskammer (Federal Chamber of Trade and Commerce) is most important, in the case of the Chambers of Labour the Oesterreichischen Arbeiterkammertag (Austrian Conference of Chambers of Labour) is less important, and in the case of the Chambers of Agriculture the Präsidentenkonferenz der Land-wirtschaftskammern Oesterreichs (Presidents' Conference of Austrian Chambers of Agriculture) is the least important. The Trade Union Federation (OGB) and the Employers' Association are more centralis-tic in organisation, their organisations at Land level being more subordinate to the central, national organisation than is the case with the Chambers of Labour and of Trade.

The most important of the associations not based on economic motives are the churches. The Constitution guarantees the liberty of belief and conscience of every citizen. In addition, the state guarantees a number of explicitly recognised religious communities certain privileges, such as for example the right to organise reli-gious instruction in the schools, and government assistance in the collection of membership contributions. Within this group of state-recognised religious communities the Roman Catholic church is by far the most important, if only because about 89 per cent of the Aus-trian population are members of it.

The large economic associations, but also to some extent the churches, have both formal and informal influence on the political decision-making process. Their informal influence consists in the fact that they are closely interwoven with the political parties and in the many types of recruiting tasks which the associations are made responsible for. The formal influence, as far as the economic associations are concerned, is concentrated in the system of Sozial-partnerschaft (social partnership) (see below). Over and above this, the economic associations and the ideological associations also pos-sess the official possibility of exerting influence on the political decision-making process in the form of the Begutachtungsverfahren (expert advisory reporting procedure). Under this procedure, the Federal Government gives the associations opportunities to state in writing their positions with regard to draft legislation which is still in the pre-parliamentary stage. According to the importance of the interests represented by a particular association, such in-terests are through this procedure already taken account of in the legislation.

Interconnections of the associations with the parties

Relationships between the associations and the parties in Austria
are characterised by two factors:

- formal neutrality of the large associations with regard to
  the political parties;
- interconnection with the political parties in spite of that
  neutrality.

None of the five most important economic associations listed
above, nor the Roman Catholic Church as the most important of the
non-economic associations, are officially or unofficially linked to
any particular party. Nevertheless the parties play a part in the
life of the associations, and the associations are similarly politically active within the parties. There is however no monopoly
relationship between any one of the large associations and any particular political party. Within the economic associations these
interconnections with the parties find their expression in the formation of party-political groupings (Fraktionen). In the case of
the Chamber organisations, the elections which they regularly hold
are confrontations between group lists, each of which is closely
bound up with a particular party. In the ÖGB (Trade Union Federation) this competition between party-political groupings can be seen
in the elections for workers' councils (Betriebsräte) and staff representatives (Personalvertretungen). Within the Austrian Employers'
Association there are no party-political groupings, but there are
interconnections with the parties on a personal basis.

In the Trade Union Federation, and also in 13 of the 15 industrial unions, the majority of important posts are in the hands of
the Fraktion of Socialist Trade Unionists. This group is officially
an SPÖ organisation. In the central organs of the Trade Union Federation, the Christian Trade Union Group is the next strongest group,
and this group also dominates the Civil Servants' Union. This group
is closely connected with the People's Party, not formally but on a
personal basis. Also in the Trade Union Federation there are small
minority groups belonging to the communist group of trade unionists
(Linksblock - interconnections with the KPÖ), the Arbeitsgemein-
schaft freiheitlicher Arbeitnehmer (Association of Liberal Workers),
connected with the FPÖ, the "Trade Union Unity" Group (split off from
the KPÖ) and the Arbeitsgemeinschaft parteifreier Betriebsräte (Working Association of Non-Party Works Councillors).

The structures of the Chambers of Labour (workers and employees)
are basically the same as the Trade Union Federation structure described above. The interests of the workers who support the People's
Party in the Chambers of Labour are not represented by the Christian
Unionist Group, but by the Austrian Workers and Clerical Workers

Federation (ÖAAB), that is to say a constituent organisation of the People's Party. This party is therefore interconnected with the Chambers of Labour not only on a personal basis but also organisationally and formally. The ÖAAB has a majority in one of the Land Chambers, namely the Vorarlberg Chamber of Labour.

In the Chambers of Trade the majority grouping is the Austrian Economic Federation (ÖWB) which is a constituent organisation of the People's Party. The Freie Wirtschaftsverband (Free Economic grouping) of the SPÖ, and the Ring freiheitlicher Wirtschaftstreibender (Liberal employers' group) of the FPÖ have the role of small minority groups within the Chambers of Trade. The situation is similar in the Chambers of Agriculture: the Austrian Farmers Association (ÖBB) of the People's Party has a stable and strong majority, while the Arbeiterbauernbund (Farm-workers' Federation) of the SPÖ, the FPÖ and the (non-party) Allgemeine Bauernverband (general federation of farm-workers) play only minority roles.

The Austrian Industrial Employers' Association is not split up on party-political lines, but the important positions are all in the hands of officials who also belong to the Austrian Economic Federation and therefore to the People's Party. There are often also close connections with the Sektion Industrie, which has branches in the nine Chambers of Trade and Commerce in the Länder, and also in the Bundeskammer at national level. A certain minority role is also being played by the Ring Freiheitlicher Wirtschaftstreibender, since FPÖ functionaries can frequently be found in certain positions in the Industrial Employers' Association.

Interconnections of this kind with the political parties do not exist for the Roman Catholic Church. Since the Church's structure is different, there are no groupings with party-political connections. But a certain connection can be said to exist in that there are significant correlations between party preferences and Church activity. The majority of citizens active in the Church prefer their political interests to be represented by the People's Party. The SPÖ, and also the FPÖ, play some kind of minority role here. In addition the Church organisations have some significance as recruiting fields for politicians, particularly within the ÖVP.

The interconnection between the parties and the associations is however not by any means a one-sided matter. Not only are parties or party-linked groups active in the associations, but the associations are present in the parties, and important positions within the parties are occupied by the large economic associations. Thus, 50 per cent at least of all deputies to the Nationalrat, elected as candidates on party lists, have regular activities in the economic associations alongside activity in Parliament and in their party. The representatives of the economic interests are therefore, through these interconnections between associations and parties, in the centres

216

of decision in the parliamentary system. They therefore hardly need
the arsenal of traditional lobbying instruments, they do not have to
exert pressure from outside, they are themselves part of the decision-
making centres.

In the context of these interconnections the associations, and in
this case exclusively the voluntary associations, play a role of some
importance in the financing of the parties. The Austrian Industrial
Employers' Association regularly subsidises the People's Party, and
to a lesser extent the Liberal Party. The Trade Union Federation
subsidises the training activities of the party-political groupings
of trade unionists according to their respective strengths, so that
the group of socialist trade unionists gets by far the biggest share.

But it is not only through their interconnections with the parties that the associations influence political decision-making. They
have also created for themselves, through the system of Sozialpartnerschaft (social partnership) their own instruments for use in the
decision-making process. Through this system of the balance of interests, in particular through the independent system of Sozialpartnerschaft, the associations are able to influence political decision-making in a way which is separate from and basically independent from party-state parliamentarianism.

The Austrian association system is in a position to defend and
promote the interests which the economic associations represent at
two decision-making levels - "party-state" parliamentarianism and
"association-state" Sozialpartnerschaft. This means that the associations are deeply rooted in the political system. Through their
double links - through the parties in the parliamentarian system,
but also in the Sozialpartnerschaft system, the associations, which
by their nature one would expect to be on the periphery of the political system, have become a central feature of that system. The far-
reaching integration of the associations' system can be regarded as
a special feature of the overall political culture of Austria, and
as a factor for the stabilization of existing relationships through
the linking up of partly conflicting or contradictory interests.

Internal structures of the economic associations

The main economic organisations are organised on democratic lines
in a multiplicity of ways. They take part in government decision-
making processes the democratic nature of which is guaranteed by the
rules of the game of the Constitution. They are interconnected with
the parties, which also are organised on predominantly democratic
lines. And lastly they are, through their internal structures, and
also partly by law, committed to democratic forms of organisation.

Democracy in the economic associations is expressed, as far as
the three large "Chamber" organisations and the Trade Union Federation

are concerned, through the adoption of party-political structures. The formal or informal party-political groupings are endowed with varying weights from below, that is to say through their members. These different weightings provide a democratic legitimation of the decision-making organs at the top of the economic associations.

In the three large "Chamber" organisations this democratic legitimation of the top organs takes the form of free elections. The party-political groupings (Fraktionen), at Land level, draw up lists of candidates; the members of the Chambers can decide which candidates they will vote for. At Land level, therefore, a fundamentally democratically-produced image of the various preferences of membership is provided, which is also reflected indirectly in the central institutions at federal (national) level. The regularly held Chamber elections are an expression of the internal democracy of the associations, but also an expression of the density of organisation and the general significance of the Austrian association system.

The Trade Union Federation and the 15 industrial trade unions which belong to it practise an indirectly democratic form for appointing their top organs. The legitimation of the functionaries occurs at successive stages. The first stage is the results of the workers' council (Betriebsräte) elections (in the case of the industrial unions), or the staff representative elections (in the case of civil servants). The strengths of the party-political groupings in the industrial unions is assessed according to these election results; the strengths of the party-political groupings in the Trade Union Federation results from the corresponding relationships within the industrial unions.

The corresponding organisation structures in the Austrian Industrial Employers' Association are not directly party-political, since here the voting is for persons and not for party lists. But because of the predominating balance of interests in industry and the numerous personal cross-links, particularly with the Sektion Industrie in the Chambers of Trade and with the Economic Federation of the People's Party, the internal structure of the Industrial Employers' Association is after all not very different from that of the other associations.

In international comparative terms the internal structures of the Austrian economic associations are distinguished by their high degree of centralisation. This is achieved through the formal distribution of powers - in general (the chief exceptions to this are the Chambers of Agriculture) the important decisions are matters for the central (national or federal level) and not for the Land associations or individual groups (Sektionen, industrial unions). Furthermore, the Sozialpartnerschaft system (see below) strengthens this centralisation. It is the central associations which are bound into the Sozialpartnerschaft system, not the Land associations or industrial unions or Sektionen. The close interconnections of the associations, among themselves within the Sozialpartnerschaft system, and with the political parties in the parliamentary system, and in any case the strong formal bias of location of power in favour of the central bodies, endows the whole associations system with a high measure of central control power.

The associations system, characterised by centralisation and a high density of organisation, offers - in competition with the party system, although it is closely bound up with that system - a second alternative to the representation of social interests through the political system. Participating indirectly in the parliamentary system, and directly controlling the Sozialpartnerschaft system, the Austrian associations system is as important for the functioning of the whole political system as the party system itself.

C. The Socio-Economic Infrastructure

Property (ownership) structure

The first important feature of the Austrian economic system is that it accepts the principle of private ownership, even as regards the means of production. In this respect Austria is a capitalist country. But a further important feature of the Austrian economic system is that there are relatively far-reaching exceptions to this principle of the private ownership of the means of production.

These exceptions have their origin in the nationalisation Acts of 1946 and 1947. Through them important parts of the steel, mining and chemical industries were taken into state ownership. Since also three banks, of which two are large banks, are state-owned, the holdings in industry of both banks must be reckoned as belonging to the state-owned sector.

The remaining area of private ownership in industry must, to bring out a further special feature of the Austrian economy, again be split up - into the part which is foreign controlled and the part which is domestically controlled. Applying these different categories of ownership to Austrian industry means that - measured by the numbers of employed - the "classical" form of capitalist economy, the domestic privately owned part, only employs just over half of all those employed in industry; the state-owned sector more than a quarter, and the foreign controlled somewhat less than a quarter. When the property relationships in industry are further broken down according to the size of enterprises, the peculiarities of the Austrian economic system become still clearer. Taking the 50 largest enterprises in Austria, the state-owned sector is unmistakably the larger - whether in terms of numbers employed, or turnover, or

exports. The shares of the State sector in these three fields are
in each case more than two-thirds. Taking these 50 largest enterprises, the share of foreign-controlled capital is also greater than
that of domestically controlled private capital.

This spread of ownership is a significant departure from the basic model typical for a capitalistically structured national economy.
Private domestic capital has been driven into a comparatively subordinate role compared with state-owned capital and foreign-owned capital. State-owned and foreign-owned capital predominates above all
in the field of the large industrial enterprises, so that trends towards concentration must lead to a further lessening of the role of
domestic private capital.

For the political controllability of the economy as a whole, the
effects of these special features are divisive, indeed conflicting.
While State ownership means a particularly intensive interlocking of
political and economic structures, the presence of foreign-owned
capital leads to a more sharply defined dividing line between the
policies determined in Austria and the partially foreign-determined
part of industry. The State sector makes possible a central direction of the economy through government policies, which is rather
atypical for a capitalistic economic system, whereas the presence of
foreign-owned capital reduces this ability to impose central direction to more relative proportions.

The property structure outside industry, as expressed in terms
of wealth distribution, shows no very unusual features however.
Austria is similar in this respect to other comparable Western systems characterised in the political field by a multi-party system
and in the economic field by basically capitalistic property relationships: property in the form of measurable wealth is highly concentrated, that is to say, a relatively small number of natural or legal
persons possess relatively large shares of total wealth.

In spite of this concentration of wealth, the Austrian economic
system is also characterised by a pronounced small- and medium-sized
enterprise structure. In this area of small- and medium-sized enterprises in commerce and craft trades the property relationships are
closest to the type of a "classical" capitalistic economic system.
This stage of development is also reflected in the representation
of political interests: the Chambers of Trade (Handelskammern) are
in Austria traditionally controlled more by the craft trades and
commerce Sektionen than by the industry Sektionen: at least the
policies of employers and entrepreneurs are very strongly influenced
by the interests of the small- and medium-sized firms.

The special features and lines of development of the property
structure in the Austrian economic system influence the whole political system. The relative weakness of domestic capital in the field
of big industry favours the "social partnership" balance between

employers' associations and labour associations. The fact that domestic capital tends to be concentrated in the small- and medium-sized firms means that the large industrial firms are predominantly run in accordance with government policy directives, whereas the employers' policies fed into the "social partnership" system reflect the interests of the smaller firms. It is because of these underlying economic factors that, in the "social partnership" system, and especially in its independent part, the Chambers of Trade organisation for employers and entrepreneurs, which is not primarily determined by the interest of large-scale industry, has the main say, whereas the Austrian Industrialists Association plays a more or less marginal role.

Income structure

The distribution of personal income in Austria shows a long-term steadiness which has been repeatedly confirmed. All available studies show that both the relationship between the incomes of the self-employed and those of the dependently employed, and also the various relationships within these two large groups, are stable.

The figures showing the stability of the relationships between the incomes of the self-employed (share of income from property and entrepreneurship, savings of corporations) and the incomes of the dependently employed (wages and salaries) need correction, since population trends have for a long time now tended to increase the numbers of dependently employed and lessen the numbers of self-employed, so that it is the average share per person which must be considered. The relation between the shares so corrected is so stable that it is clear that the ability of the central political system to influence this income distribution is either non-existent or works exclusively in the direction of a stabilization of the existing relative share ratios.

The minor fluctuations in the relative shares going into wages and profits can be explained by the fact that in periods when the economy is doing well, profits increase at first more than average, whereas in periods of economic downswing wages catch up and re-establish relative equality.

Within these two groups of income-earners the constancy of distribution is above all to be seen in the group of the dependently employed, that is to say the wage and salary earners. This stability applies not only to the relationship between wages of workers and salaries of employees, but also to the relationship between the highest incomes and the lowest incomes.

In the self-employed group the constancy is not so marked. The various forms of industrial concentration mean that certain groups of self-employed show higher-than-average increases in incomes (the liberal professions for example), whereas other groups (such as those in the craft trades) show lower-than-average increases. In the field of agriculture the main feature is that the share of those in the lowest income groups is remarkably high. In general it can be said that personal incomes in Austria, as one would expect with the favourable long-term growth trend and a stable income distribution, have risen at a faster-than-average rate compared with other countries. At the same time it must be said that the inequalities within income groups are unchanged - there is no indication of any basic tendency either towards more equality or towards less.

This stability of distribution in the field of personal incomes is closely related to the political interest structure and the pattern of political representation and decision-making. The "social partnership" system, which largely determines economic and social policies, and through which wages and price trends in particular are influenced, helps to maintain this stability. Since under the "social partnership" system all the large organised groups capable of initiating conflicts are represented by their associations, and since under that system the rule of unanimity prevents any redistribution which would be counter to the interests of any particular group, the dominating role of the "social partnership" type of decision-making necessarily works in the direction of a stabilization of existing distribution patterns.

The way in which income distribution is handled in Austria can in any case be considered to be an important indicator of the fact that the various institutions and decision-making centres of the political system work along similar, and therefore compatible lines which help to stabilize existing relationships. Also the moderate, "peaceful" way in which, thanks to the "social partnership" system, the conflicts between employers and workers are worked out - the so-called "social peace" - must in any case be considered as an important factor in holding firm the status quo of existing income relationships. The far-reaching renunciation of powers by Parliament in favour of the "social partnership" system in this field makes income distribution a necessarily prescribed field - which can essentially only be steered in the direction of greater stabilization - for social policy as a whole.

Lines of development of the economic system

Austria is a small country, which means that the Austrian economic system depends for its development in the main on international trends Austria can go beyond or run counter to world economic influences only within certain limits.

The present lines of development of the Austrian economy are characterised by the after-effects of extremely rapid growth between 1969 and 1974 and the subsequent period of recession. The unusually fast growth of the early 1970s caused the Austrian economy to have growth rates which were well above the average for the European OECD countries, and similarly a more than average increase in industrial production. This absolute and relative increase in growth continued in the years of the cyclical downswing or recession from 1973 to 1975, and also in 1979.

The strong growth performance of the Austrian economy in the last ten years was accompanied by a particularly favourable trend of the labour market, labour productivity and real wages. Unemployment in Austria has been very much below the OECD average.

As regards the stability of the currency, the trend in Austria has also been relatively favourable. The inflation rate in Austria has always been comparatively low - only Switzerland and Germany have had better records in this respect.

The trends of these indicators - more than average growth, more than average job security, and more than average currency stability - must also be attributed to the political orientation of the economic system. Irrespective of whether economic factors in the strictest sense must be regarded as the cause of these trends, the "social peace" policies produced by the decisive forces of the party system and parliamentarianism on the one hand, and the associations system and "social partnership" on the other hand, must be regarded as a favourable model for the settlement of social conflicts; favourable in the sense of a maximisation of economic growth and a minimisation of unemployment; favourable for the maximisation of currency stability; basically unsuited, however, for the redistribution of property and income in the sense of a change in customary distribution ratios.

These favourable basic starting positions might in future be threatened not so much by changes in the decision-making process in the political sub-system as by specific structural problems arising in the economic sub-system, such as:

- the comparatively new and unconsolidated industrial structure;
- strategic mistakes by enterprises and in economic policies in dealing with structural breakdowns;
- changed selling situations through partial saturation of demand;
- structural disadvantages of small states;
- special adjustment problems of small firms;
- insufficient research;
- limited mobility and shortage of risk capital.

These development trends of the Austrian economy, which - not least because Austria is a small country - can only partially be influenced

by the Austrian political decision-making centres (the parties and
the parliamentary system, the associations and "social partnership"),
can all be brought down to one very general denominator: the Austrian
economy, partly because of a late economic and social development,
has improved itself considerably in relation to comparable systems.
At the present time, however, this catching up and partial overtaking
must be regarded - at least provisionally - as at an end. If the
various indicators permit of a plausible interpretation of the near
future, then the most likely forecast is that the improved ranking
of Austria cannot in the near future be substantially improved, but
nor will it substantially worsen. The Austrian economy must be numbered among the relatively stabilized, relatively predictable and
controllable national economies - and an important contributory factor in this is the special political decision-making models which
have developed in Austria since 1945.

2. THE POLITICAL PROCESS

A. Parliamentarianism and the "Party State"

Post-classical Parliamentarianism

Parliamentarianism in Austria has developed considerably from
its theoretical starting position. This change from classical to
post-classical parliamentarianism can be observed in the following
fields:

- the direct election of Members of Parliament takes the
  form of direct voting for party representatives who
  have already been selected within their party;
- legislation by Parliament is de facto very strongly
  influenced by prior discussion by all kinds of bodies
  in a complex pre-parliamentary stage;
- supervision by Parliament of the Executive, that is to
  say of the federal government, has become supervision of
  the government by the opposition;
- the freedom of action ("freies Mandat") of Members of
  Parliament is limited in that while they are personally
  independent vis-à-vis their voters, they are not personally independent vis-à-vis their party, their Fraktion
  (parliamentary party), their association;
- the parliamentary decision-making process is public only
  in its final phase, that is to say the discussion in
  plenary session: the whole decision-making process in
  the pre-parliamentary stage and the committee activity
  in the parliamentary stage not being public.

These lines of development of Austrian parliamentarianism are only remarkable to the extent that, while they are similar to the general tendencies of Western and Central European parliamentarianism, they have been pushed to great lengths in Austria. The fusion of legislative and executive through the principle of parliamentary systems, the linking of the parliamentary majority with the government, is reinforced in Austria by the pronounced "party-state" character of its political system.

The direct election of the people's representatives is in Austria ensured by the direct election of the Nationalrat (National Diet), the first and most important of the two Chambers of Parliament. This election is based on the principles of proportional representation and list voting. Because of the proportional representation principle, fluctuations at the base, that is to say among the voters, are not amplified as they are with majority voting. Voting for lists of candidates, combined with the relatively large constituencies, shifts the responsibility for the ranking of candidates to the competence of inner-party institutions. These two effects, the relatively narrow extent of fluctuations and inner-party responsibility for the recruiting of people's representatives, are responsible for the pronounced party-state character of elections for the Nationalrat. The personal composition of Parliament is decided by the parties in internal non-public processes; the voters' duty is to provide a weighting between the lists of candidates already selected for them.

The changes in the field of legislation mean a shift of legislative decision-making power from Parliament towards the government, the bureaucracy and "social partnership". The overwhelming majority of the laws passed by the Parliament derive from bills drafted by the government; and a very high proportion of these laws initiated by the government are passed by Parliament without any change or with only unimportant changes. This shift of legislative competence is in practice not uniform for all legislation. The significance of "social partnership" and the concentration of the economic associations on the field of economic and social policy leave the Parliament more room for decision-making in all non-economic questions, whereas in all economic questions the process of shifting the actual decisions forward to the pre-parliamentarian stage has developed a very long way.

The fusion of powers and the party-state character of the system have also considerably changed the control or supervisory function of the Austrian Parliament. Since most of the rights of supervision, in the main only with the exception of the right to put questions (Interpellationsrecht), are rights exercised by the majority, this results in supervision of the government through the government party. In practice the ruling parliamentary majority party uses these rights to support the government, so the actual supervision of the government mainly takes the form of the various questions put by the opposition - urgent questions, written questions, oral questions. The Rechnungshof (Audit Office) provides a constant stream of material for this purpose through its regular reports.

The pronounced party-state character of the system has also sapped the "freies Mandat" (Member of Parliament's freedom of action) guaranteed by the Constitution. The individual Member of Parliament is theoretically only answerable to his own conscience, but is in practice firmly controlled by his party and his Fraktion. Since his parliamentary career is already the result of his inner-party achievements, since his re-election is solely dependent on his party, and since the two large parties at least openly subscribe to the principle of parliamentary party discipline ("Klubzwang"), the Austrian Parliament is not in reality governed by 183 people's representatives as individuals who are different from one another, but by united groups of parliamentary party teams of differing strengths. The internal parliamentary party decision-making processes and discussions, the interconnections with the party and association headquarters, and with the federal government, gain considerably in significance because of this.

These internal parliamentary party processes and these interconnections with the pre-parliamentary field also lessen the importance of the public nature of parliamentary proceedings, which is also further reduced through the important part played by the parliamentary committees. Since an important part of parliamentary decisions is taken in committees and sub-committees, which - in accordance with the tradition of European parliamentarianism - are on principle not public, the transformation from (theoretically public) "classical" parliamentarianism to (in practice) largely non-public, "postclassical" parliamentarianism is reinforced. The public aspect of the parliamentarian process is concentrated, of course - and the influence of the media adds to this - on the confrontation between the parliamentary parties in the plenary sessions of the Nationalrat. The plenary sessions of the Bundesrat, for which basically the same characteristics of openness are valid, take very much of a second place in regard to the public attention, which is devoted to the Nationalrat. The lesser importance of the Bundesrat in the innerparty hierarchies and its second place in time in the parliamentary process, combined with its inferior position under constitutional law, deprive the Second Chamber of the Austrian Parliament of public attention.

Parliamentary competition

The activities of the Austrian Parliament are in practice determined by the confrontation between the government and the opposition.

The government has need of Parliament in order to put through the necessary laws for the steering of the whole system. The opposition needs Parliament in order to appear in parliamentary publicity as the alternative to the government.

This basic starting point, which is in any case typical for Western and Central European parliamentarianism, is reinforced in Austria through the particularly pronounced party-state character of Parliament and the concentration of the party system. Since in the Austrian Nationalrat of the Second Republic from 1945 to 1949 and from 1959 onwards there were only three parties operating, and hence three disciplined Fraktionen (parliamentary parties), and in the period from 1949 to 1959 only four parties and hence four disciplined Fraktionen, parliamentary confrontation was concentrated in a small number of easily visible frontal positions.

But in 1966 a decisive change occurred in this confrontation which had an important influence on Austrian parliamentarianism. Up until 1966 there was always either an all-party government (1945 to 1947), or a "big coalition" (1947 to 1966). At first there was no parliamentary opposition, and then from 1947 onwards the opposition was quantitatively very small indeed. Since the two large parties in the coalition government committed themselves in various agreements (coalition pact, working agreements, etc.), not to fight out their quarrels in legislative sessions in Parliament, but instead to use for that special conflict-regulating machinery (coalition committee, working parties, etc.), the Austrian Parliament was largely spared the tensions and disputes between the two large parties up until 1966.

It was only with the ending of the "big coalition" that confrontation in Parliament between the government and the opposition began to reflect the general confrontation between the Austrian Socialist Party and the Austrian People's Party. From 1966, therefore, in regard to the effect on the public of parliamentarian activities, it is possible to speak of a veritable revalorisation of Parliament.

This revalorisation through a role-determined confrontation between the large party of government (1966-1970, Austrian People's Party, and from 1970 onwards the Austrian Socialist Party) and the large party of opposition, did not in fact reverse the general change in functions in the direction of "post-classical parliamentarianism". The revalorisation of Parliament, that is to say in the main of the Nationalrat, did not mean any winning back of actual unrestricted legislative competence. Even after 1966 the bulk of legislative decision-making continued to take place in the pre-parliamentary area. Nor did the revalorisation of Parliament in any way mean a revival of the individually defined representative of the people, using his "free mandate" to the full. This revalorisation also did nothing to change the key role of inner-party arrangements for the recruiting of the people's representatives.

The revalorisation of Parliament since 1966 is however reflected in two areas: in an increase in the importance of the instruments of checking and supervision that the parliamentary minority, that is to say the opposition, actually and effectively uses; and in an increase in the degree of public attention given to parliamentary activities.

Since 1966, therefore, Austrian parliamentarianism has been dominated by a process pattern which in essence represents the "normality" in Western and Central European parliamentarianism: people's representatives, bound to their parties, deposit in the plenary sessions of the Nationalrat, carefully observed by a broad public, the decisions of their parties which have already been decided beforehand.

The professionalisation of Parliament

Parliamentarianism in Austria is characterised by the general trend towards a working Parliament. The most important manifestation of this trend is that those responsible for the parliamentary process, the people's representatives, increasingly exercise their political functions as a profession - Members of Parliament are becoming professional politicians. As a professional politician, the Member of Parliament is at least partially isolated from the social milieu, from the social group, which has delegated him according to the basic assumptions of "classical" parliamentarianism. Precisely because the people's representative wants to become politically effective, and also in the interests of the voters who delegate him, he cannot in his everyday life be a worker or a farmer, a civil servant or a lawyer, a student or a businessman; he must devote himself fully to his political activity.

An outward manifestation of this trend is the growing number of civil servants in the Austrian Nationalrat. The occupational group of public civil servants, officials (Beamte) in the broadest sense of the word, is by far the largest group in the Nationalrat. This of course does not mean that civil servants are in fact Members of Parliament; but it does mean that professional politicians in the Nationalrat are socially advantaged by formal civil servant status. The Member of Parliament with a civil service post is, precisely because of the official arrangements for freeing him from his post while allowing him to continue to draw his salary, a particularly generous arrangement in Austria, a typical form for the whole situation in Austria, so that the Member of Parliament with a civil service post behind him is outwardly a member of a "middle class" occupational group; but in practice he is a professional politician who divides his activities in various forms between Parliament and party, "social partnership" and association.

A further, important aspect of the professionalisation of Parliament is the interlocking of Members of Parliament with the "associations". Since Parliament is organised in a party-state way, and the parties are very closely interlocked with the associations, the importance of the associations is reflected in Parliament indirectly too. More than half of the Members of Parliament in the Nationalrat are bound not only, as are basically all Members of Parliament, to a party, but also to an association. Full- and part-time activities for and in an association are characteristic of the practice of Members of Parliament and also therefore for the reality of the whole of parliamentary life.

Another aspect of the professionalisation of Parliament is the long period of stay in the Nationalrat. Membership of the group of parliamentary professional politicians does not in principle, as it did according to the idea of "classical" parliamentarianism, have to be fought for anew by each individual Member of Parliament at each parliamentary election. Generally speaking, what matters for a parliamentary career, as for any civil service career, is the principle of seniority; once elected to the Nationalrat, the average Member only leaves when he has to on grounds of age.

Another feature of professionalisation is the phenomenon of an increasing "academicisation" of Parliament. The proportion of university degree holders in the Austrian Nationalrat is steadily increasing. About four out of ten Members have some sort of university studies behind them.

These aspects of professionalisation are valid generally for all the parliamentary parties. In particular the SPÖ parliamentary party, which, because of the proletarian background of social democracy, originally consisted much more of politicians with a proletarian background, has come into line with the academic, civil service structures of the other parliamentary parties.

In consequence politicians' careers are becoming increasingly similar to the career patterns which are usual in business. Whether someone has a particular social background and comes from a particular milieu, whether he is, say, a worker or a farmer, is not so important as the fact that he is an efficient professional politician. The Member of Parliament who, through his background and his generally recognisable links with a social group, his way of speaking and his specific political culture, is a representative of a closed, politico-philosophical camp, is increasingly being replaced by the expert in politics. And he is characterised by qualifications which no longer have anything to do with his origin in a particular camp. Origins, but also political programmes and ideological expertise are diminishing in importance; education, efficiency, functional expertise are increasing in importance.

B. Social Partnership and the "Associations State"

The development of Austrian "social partnership"

Austrian "social partnership" has a variety of social roots. The
emergence and effectiveness of social partnership, or close co-
operation between associations of employers and associations of employees, depended on certain conditions as prerequisites on both
sides:

- On the side of the employers' associations, the relative
  weakness of domestic capital is one reason for comparatively co-operative behaviour on the part of the employers;
- On the side of the employees' associations, the non-party,
  and at the same time ponderous, social-democratic-oriented
  Gewerkschaftsbund (Trade Union Federation), with its high
  degree of centralisation, is also a favourable pre-condition
  for a basically co-operative attitude.

Certain historical events and experiences have also played their
part. Early steps in social partnership between 1918 and 1920, the
experience of the civil war and Austrian fascism, and especially the
experience of occupation by National-Socialist Germany, have since
1945 strengthened the awareness of common interests and put the awareness of differences into perspective.

The concordance machinery was manifested in the field of parliamentarianism in the "party state" mainly in the form of the "big
coalition" up until 1966. In the field of social partnership in the
"associations state" this concordance machinery persisted after the
historical break which took place in 1966. The social partnership
which had emerged in the coalition era survived the demise of the
coalition.

From the point of view of the history of ideas, Austrian social
partnership has as one of its main roots the tradition of Christian
(Catholic) social theory, which emerged in concrete form in the
framework of the Christlichsoziale Partei in the concluding phase
of the monarchy and in the First Republic as an "occupational corporative" or "corporative state" ideology. The experiment of an
"authoritarian corporative state", tried out from 1934 to 1938 with
dictatorial means and with fascist tendencies, specifically and explicitly claimed that it was in this tradition. Social partnership
since 1945 can be seen as a continuation of the corporative state
experiment with democratic means.

These components from the history of ideas, which from 1945 onwards also contributed to more moderate behaviour by the employers,
finds a certain echo in the tradition of Austro-marxism. While its

theory in the framework of international social democracy was "left", the practice of Austro-marxism already in the First Republic was very much to the "right". Marxist in word, revisionist in deed, the Austrian Social Democratic Party, and in particular the parliamentary group of socialist trade unionists, began from 1945 onwards to build up social partnership, which it interpreted as co-determination at higher than factory level (überbetrieblich) and as part of an industrial democracy.

This already historically-rooted inclination towards compromise was strengthened by frontal opposition to the Communists. During the occupation of Austria by the four allied powers, social partnership also became an instrument of Austria's determination to assert herself, and in particular of isolating the Communist Party, which from about 1947 onwards considered social partnership to be a betrayal of the class struggle by the Social Democrats. The Austrian Communist Party also used the 4th Wage-Price Agreement, negotiated in 1950 on social partnership lines, as an excuse to organise a general strike against the wishes of the Austrian Trade Union Federation, and in this way to bring about a change in the leadership and in the whole orientation of the trade unions.

From 1945 onwards social partnership developed first in the form of non-autonomous social partnership, i.e. institutional co-operation between government bodies, employers' associations and employees' associations. Finally, in 1957 the Joint Commission for Wage and Price Questions (Paritätische Kommission für Lohn - und Preisfragen) was formed, and by 1966 had developed into the keystone of an autonomous social partnership, that is to say co-operation between employees' and employers' associations without the intervention of government bodies in the decision-making process.

It can be said of social partnership in general, and of autonomous social partnership in particular, that it is the complement to and antithesis of party-state parliamentarianism:

- The basic legitimation of parliamentarianism is the direct election by the people of at least one chamber of the Parliament; the basic legitimation of social partnership is agreements between the main economic associations.
- For parliamentarianism the dominant pattern for settling disputes is the principle of majority decision; for social partnership, on the other hand, every decision must be based on the principle of unconditional unanimity.
- Parliamentarianism requires an essential minimum of openness to the public, in the form, for example, of general accessibility to debates in the parliamentary plenum; social partnership requires, equally essentially,

confidentiality through the basic and complete exclusion
of openness to the public.
- The "free mandate" for Members of Parliament is one of
the theoretical features of parliamentarianism; an
essential feature of social partnership is that all
those engaged in it act, formally or at least inform-
ally, on behalf of their associations.
- Parliamentarianism is thus characterised by the principle
of competition, social partnership by the principle of
agreement.

Forms of social partnership

Austrian social partnership found its autonomous form in the
Joint Commission for Wage and Price Questions (Paritätische Kommission für Lohn- und Preisfragen). The Austrian Trade Unions Federation and the Austrian Conference of Chambers of Labour as employees' associations, the Federal Chamber of Trade and Commerce
and the Presidents' Conference of Chambers of Agriculture as employers' associations constitute this Commission; the representatives of the federal government who attend its meetings have, at
least in the final instance, no voting rights and thus no real right
to participate.

The Joint Commission has three sub-committees. The Wages Sub-
Committee discusses wage increases, the actual negotiation of which
is of course done by collective bargaining machinery; in the Wages
Sub-Committee the green light is given for wage negotiations and
approval is given to the collective agreements which result. The
Sub-Committee on Prices is responsible for deciding on price increases, which the individual industry and trade groups apply for
through the Federal Chamber for Trade and Commerce (Bundeskammer der
gewerblichen Wirtschaft). The Advisory Council for Economic and
Social Questions (Beirat für Wirtschafts-und Sozialfragen), the third
sub-committee, is the "brains trust" for autonomous social partnership, and is made up of representatives of all four associations
and some independent experts, and is concerned, in each case at the
request of the chairmen of the industrial associations,with long-
term forecasts and reports.

The umbrella body over these sub-committees is the Joint Commission itself, often called the Full Assembly of the Joint Commission. It meets regularly once a month, with the Federal Chancellor as Chairman, though he has no right to vote. The Full Assembly also meets quarterly as an "economic policy forum" (Wirtschafts-
politische Aussprache) at which representatives of the Finance Ministry,the National Bank and the Austrian Institute for Economic Research, and additional experts from the associations can be co-opted.

The central feature of autonomous social partnership is however the Chairmen's Discussion (Präsidentenbesprechung), which takes place before each full assembly of the Joint Commission. In these Chairmen's Discussions the Chairmen of the four economic associations which make up the Joint Commission work out and agree on compromise solutions. Decisions which have not already been taken in the sub-committees are decided on here; the formal final decision in the Full Assembly is then simply a formality.

All decisions under autonomous social partnership, that is to say in the various bodies of the Joint Commission, are taken unanimously and are not public. There is no majority and minority, no conflict between government and opposition. Only in the framework of the Advisory Council for Economic and Social Questions can majority and minority viewpoints be formulated in the form of expert opinions. Through this perfect realisation of the concordance principle, any of the four economic associations has the power to bring autonomous social partnership to a halt. Majority relationships in the field of parliamentarianism or election results in parliamentary elections have no direct effect on the decision-taking situation in the concordance system of autonomous social partnership.

Non-autonomous social partnership has developed very far, but of course it is, unlike autonomous social partnership, not peculiar to Austria. The many forms of co-operation possibilities which the economic associations can find in the field of government administration and government jurisdiction, enable the economic interest groups to have a direct influence on government behaviour. This form of social partnership is, although of course not so intensively established in most of the other systems, typical for advanced "western" systems characterised by a capitalism curbed by social and welfare-state considerations and by a multi-party system.

Non-autonomous social partnership begins with the legal possibility of influencing legislation. The economic associations have the right to present considered reports on government draft bills before these get to the stage of actual legislation in Parliament. The whole weight of non-autonomous social partnership is however concentrated on co-operation in administration. In more than 100 institutions - advisory councils, commissions, etc. - economic associations collaborate in the shaping of government administration, that is to say government policy. In the individual ministries (especially in the Federal Ministry for Trade, Commerce and Industry; the Federal Ministry for Social Affairs; the Federal Ministry for Finance; the Federal Ministry for Agriculture and Forestry) the economic associations co-operate on a permanent basis in the concrete shaping of policy. Even though, in accordance with the basic principles of parliamentary systems, the federal minister concerned possesses final powers, even though therefore the associations in no

way take on the responsibility of the federal government, the actual
political weight of the associations, especially when they are united
among themselves, must be considered to be very great.

Besides this activity as collaborators with the federal government, the associations also possess the right, in non-autonomous
social partnership, to operate the public social security system au-
tonomously through the social security institutes. Similarly in the
field of government agricultural policy, various Agricultural Funds
consisting of representatives from the economic associations lay down
the basic lines for Austrian agricultural policy.

Besides many other possibilities for collaboration, mention must
also be made, because of its special significance, of the economic
associations' right to collaborate in the General Council of the
Austrian National Bank, and in the various fields of jurisdiction.
The associations send their representatives to the National Bank,
that is to say to the official body finally responsible for deciding
monetary policy. The associations also send representatives to the
courts which deal with questions of cartel law and with questions of
labour law.

The political significance of social partnership

The significance of Austrian social partnership lies above all
in its manifold stabilization functions. Autonomous and non-autonomous social partnership complement each other in producing economic,
social and political stability.

The economic stability produced by social partnership takes the
concrete form of strict compliance with existing scales of ratios
for the distribution of wealth and income. The consensus principle
of social partnership means that decisions taken under its umbrella
can never harm the basic interests of any of the participating associations. Social partnership decisions must remain within the framework of the smallest common denominator, and that, in economic policy
terms, means: income and welfare distribution according to well-
established ratio scales.

The economic stabilization shows itself in the stable relationship between wage and profit ratios and in the emphasis put on growth
policy. Since a falling behind of the real income of any of the
large, powerful groups organised in an economic association would
endanger the complicated balance of social partnership and thus
threaten the internal authority of that economic association, the
raising of the real incomes of all participating interest groups is
the logical consequence. Since, however, the consensus principle
does not permit of any change in the distribution ratio formulae,
increases in real income are only possible when there is real economic growth.

234

The social stabilization takes the form of a moderation of the whole social climate, in particular of the relations between employers and employees. The regular and firmly institutionalised contacts between the leading workers' representatives and the leading employers' representatives damps down the opposition inherent in the confrontation between labour and capital. Institutionalised co-operation between the representatives of the interests of capital and the representatives of the interests of labour moderates, from above downwards, social contradictions and social conflicts.

This social stabilization results in a minimisation of the costs of social conflict. The most important indicator of this is the unusually low figures for strikes in Austria. Apart from Switzerland there is no comparable industrialised country with a liberal-capitalist economy and liberal-democratic politics which can show such a low figure for the long-term average of strike frequency.

The political stabilization consists of permanent participation by all potentially conflicting, organised, economically determined large groups in the central exercise of power. Whereas parliamentarianism is characterised by arrangements for the temporal separation of powers, by the field of tension between government and opposition, and by the possibility of having a spell in opposition, social partnership - particularly in its autonomous form - is an economico- and socio-political concentration government on a continuing basis. Whereas each of the large parties in the parliamentary field is threatened by the danger of having to go into opposition and so being excluded from the central decision-making process, each of the four main economic associations is assured of being able to play its part in this central exercise of power irrespective of other developments, so long as the rules of the social partnership concordance system continue to be observed.

This political stabilization has a very intensive, socio-political integration effect. Since each of the large parties is interlocked with large associations, which again in the framework of social partnership automatically have a say in decisions and in this sense collaborate in government, there is no large politico-social organisation equipped for the exercise of power which does not actually take part in the exercise of that power. The interlocking of "party state" and "association state", of parliamentarianism and social partnership, prevents any large organised group from actually being excluded from playing its part in manipulating the levers of central power.

3. POSSIBLE DEVELOPMENTS IN THE POLITICAL SYSTEM

A. Factors making for the continuation of the status quo

Of the characteristics of the political system and factors in the political process described above, some are clearly recognisable as making for the continuity of the system and the process:

In regard to the structure of the Constitution, it is the federalistic principle which does most to make for continuity. The division of government powers between the Federation and the Länder has the effect of ensuring that each of the two large parties, at least at Länder level, has a leading role to play in government. The confrontation between the government and a large opposition party is thus moderated, potentially centrifugal effects of this confrontation situation being damped down. Federalism means a spreading of power and the involvement of party-political groupings to a greater degree than that exercised at federal level.

In the field of the socio-political infrastructure, the high degree of concentration in the party system must be considered as basically making for continuity, as conservative of the socio-political status quo. The fact that the number of relevant parties is small, that there is little likelihood that a fourth or more parties will be involved in the exercise of power in the foreseeable future, enhances the stability of the whole party system and, indirectly, the stability of existing social relationships.

But the most important single factor making for continuity is the associations system. The high degree of organisation through the dense network of compulsory economic associations and the complementary network of voluntary associations ensures the involvement of all important economically defined interests. Any possible veto-power is thus organised and, through the participation of the large economic associations in social partnership, involved in the exercise of power. Centralisation within the economic associations, and the unambiguous dominance of a particular party group (Fraktion) at any one time, are factors which strengthen the internal authority of the association and thus again make for continuity.

Of the two central political processes it is social partnership in the associations state which has the function of ensuring socio-political continuity. The participation of all economically defined, potentially conflictual large organised groups in the exercise of power in the form of a comprehensive concordance system makes for the continuity of the existing distribution of social resources. Any breakdown in existing social conditions which harms the vital interests of one of these large groups cannot in the broad framework of this concordance system have any chance of success.

This stabilization through integration is also reinforced by the specific socio-political instruments which the Austrian associations state has developed. Over and above the representation of economic interests, the associations state has in particular established a firm influence for itself in the sector of the media. In the Austrian Radio, a government monopoly, representatives of the associations sit alongside representatives of the parties in the decision-making positions. In the field of the printing media, the press, directly or indirectly dependent on the associations, is acquiring a steadily increasing importance, bearing in mind the in any case highly developed concentration trends of the Austrian newspaper market. The associations can thus, through their indirect influence by way of the institutionalised interlocking with the parties, build up an awareness of the problems of the day in the constitutional bodies and, through the printing presses of the non-autonomous social partnership system and the independent decision-making centres of the autonomous social partner system, in broader circles still.

Clearly the concordance machinery of social partnership has one innovative aspect, in that the absence of competition and publicity, which characterises it in comparison with parliamentarianism, makes it easier for it to take decisions which are unpopular, but which are considered as inevitable by the élites of all the large groups. Social partnership as the continuation of the "big coalition" with other means - namely the "associations state" - is in a very good position to be able to decide on new policies and also to carry them through, but obviously only on condition that the new policies they decide on do not harm the fundamental interests of the large associations, that is to say when the new policies are supported by the interests of the large associations. Generally speaking, however, the stability of the system and the process in Austria must be considered to be very high. Factors making for continuity must, leaving aside possible and external economic or political influences coming from abroad, in any case be regarded as unusually strong. Socio-political steering in Austria, in the framework of existing conditions, is relatively easy; if, however, these existing conditions were to be destroyed, socio-political steering would become extremely difficult.

B. Factors making for a change in the status quo

In the field of constitutional structure the merging of the legislative and the executive, and the parliamentary system thus de facto produced, can be seen as a potential factor facilitating change. The merging of powers thus brought about makes possible a unified, central steering of the whole government system and facilitates decisions even when these are resisted by the opposition.

Tensions between separate constitutional bodies, which can lead to stalemate situations, are therefore largely excluded. This is not a system of separation of powers, of "checks and balances".

Another factor which can be regarded as favourable to change is the principle of the proportional vote. This facilitates the emergence of new movements in the form of parliamentary parties. The double threshold erected by a majority principle voting system - against small parties and against extreme parties - is avoided.

In the party system, parliamentary confrontation as it has emerged since 1966, between the large governing party (up until 1970 the Austrian People's Party, since 1970 the Austrian Socialist Party) and an opposition of almost the same size, can also be considered as a development favourable to change. The largest party, supported by a stable parliamentary majority, can in the framework of the Constitution translate its programme into political reality uninfluenced by any veto power which might be exercised by another party. This, reinforced by the de facto merger between the parliamentary majority and the government, provides the possibility at least of rapid decision-making even against opposing interests.

A further possible factor for change is the mechanics of the parliamentary process whereby political decisions are fought through competitively, in the full view of the public, with emphasis on party-political differences. This tends to produce a general awareness of social conflict, and makes people think in terms of alternatives. The revival of parliamentarianism since 1966 means also essentially a revival of this factor which is inherently favourable to change.

Social partnership on "associations state" lines can, as already mentioned, only be considered to be a potential factor for changing existing conditions to the extent that it facilitates a change on the basis of a broad consensus among the élites of all large associations, but it makes any change which is against the interests of one part of those élites impossible. The mechanics of social partnership is therefore, in all analyses of socio-political strategies, programmed as an ideal case of crisis management. If decisions with far-reaching political consequences, or extraordinary measures involving the participation of all relevant interests, have to be taken, social partnership is then an optimal instrument, and to proceed on social partnership lines is the best possible form of crisis management.

If, however, it is a question of pushing through as effectively as possible political decisions which run counter to the established interests of any of the main organisations involved in the social partnership system, this is something the system is particularly unsuited to do.

Summing up the characteristics inherent to the system itself, i.e. as if it were a closed system, it would seem that the factors making for change are more than outweighed by the factors making for continuity. Thus, for example, the effect of the power-linking and hence power-concentrating factor of the de facto parliamentary system is much reduced when considered in conjunction with the effect of the factor of federalism. And, to give another example, the pro-change effect of the whole complex of parliamentary confrontation between governing and opposing large parties is much reduced by the fact that considerable powers have been shifted away from the parliamentary decision-making process and made the responsibility of the social partnership decision-making process. If the comparison between factors making for continuity and factors making for change is limited to the forces stemming from within the political system itself, then there can be only one answer - the factors making for continuity must be regarded as the stronger.

But if external factors are taken into account, then that answer is no longer possible, and the question must instead remain open. The obvious dependence of the small state of Austria, particularly in the field of socio-economic infrastructure, on influences from abroad which the closely integrated political system cannot control, make the limitations of any mere inward-looking examination of the problem more than clear.

The political system of Austria shows a maximum of integration, of participation, and hence of guarantees for the continuity of existing interests. Impulses coming from the uncontrollable external approaches to the system - such as economic crises caused by world economic conditions, or military tensions between the blocks in Europe - are potential determining factors which must remain in the realm of the incalculable.

BIBLIOGRAPHICAL NOTES

Bluhm, William T., Building an Austrian Nation. The Political Integration of a Western State. Yale University Press, New Haven, 1973.

Bös, Dieter, Wirtschaftsgeschehen und Staatsgewalt. Untersuchungen am österreichischen Beispiel. Herder Verlag, Vienna, 1970.

Farnleitner, Johann, Die Paritätische Kommission. Institution und Verfahren. Pruck Verlag, Eisenstadt.

Fischer, Heinz, "Zur Praxis des Begutachtungsverfahrens". Österreichische Zeitschift für Politikwissenschaft, 1/1972, Europaverlag, Vienna.

Fischer, Heinz (Edit.), Das Politische System Österreichs. Europaverlag, Vienna, 1974.

Fornleitner, Luise, a.o., "Die Transformation des österreichischen Parlamentarismus. Analysen des Struktur- und Funktionswandels des Nationalrates". Forschungsbericht des Instituts für Höhere Studien, Vienna, 1974.

Gärtner, Heinz, Kein Eurokommunismus in Österreich, Analyse einer sowjetorientierten KP. Braumüller Verlag, Vienna, 1979.

Gerlich, Peter, Parlamentarische Kontrolle im politischen System. Die Verwaltungsfunktion des Nationalrates in Recht und Wirklichkeit. Springer Verlag, Vienna, 1973.

Kausel, Anton, "Beurteilung der nachhaltigen Wettbewerbstärke der österreichischen Wirtschaft aufgrund makroökonomischer Tatbestände". Gutachten, erstellt im Auftrag des Bundesministeriums für Finanzen, Vienna, 1979.

Khol, Andreas, a.o. (Hrsg.), Um Parlament und Partei. Alfred Maleta zum 70. Geburtstag. Styria Verlag, Graz, 1976.

Khol, Andreas, und Stirnemann, Alfred (Edit.), Österreichisches Jahrbuch für Politik 77. Verlag für Geschichte und Politik, Vienna, 1978.

Khol, Andreas, und Stirnemann, Alfred (Edit.), Österreichisches Jahrbuch für Politik 78. Verlag für Geschichte und Politik, Vienna, 1979.

Klose, Alfred, Ein Weg zur Sozialpartnerschaft. Verlag für Geschichte und Politik, Vienna, 1970.

Lachs, Thomas, Wirtschaftspartnerschaft in Österreich. Verlag des ÖGB., Vienna, 1976.

Mommsen-Reindl, Margarete, Die österreichische Proporzdemokratie und der Fall Habsburg. Böhlau Verlag, Vienna, 1976.

Nassmacher, Karl-Heinz, Das österreichische Regierungssystem. Westdeutscher Verlag, Cologne, 1968.

OECD-Wirtschaftsbericht Österreich, herausgegeben vom Bundeskanzleramt, Vienna, 1979.

Österreichischer Arbeiterkammertag (Edit.), Wirtschafts- und Sozialstatistisches Taschenbuch 1978, Vienna, 1978.

Pelinka, Anton, und Welan, Manfried, Demokratie und Verfassung in Österreich. Europaverlag, Vienna, 1971.

Pelinka, Anton, "Österreich". In: Joachim Raschke (Edit.), Die politischen Parteien in Westeuropa. Rowohlt Verlag, Reinbek, 1978.

Pütz, Theo (Edit.), Verbände und Wirtschaftspolitik in Österreich. Verlag Duncker und Humblot, Berlin, 1966.

Ritschel, Karl-Heinz (Edit.), Demokratiereform. Verlag Zsolnay, Vienna, 1969.

Seidel, Hans, Die österreichische Wirtschaft. Entwicklung, Erfolge und Probleme. Gutachten, erstellt im Auftrag des Bundesministeriums für Finanzen, Vienna, 1979.

Shell, Kurt L., Jenseits der Klassen? Österreichs Sozialdemokratie seit 1934. Europaverlag, Vienna, 1969.

Spira, Leopold, Ein gescheiterter Versuch. Der Austro-Eurokommunismus. Verlag Jugend und Volk, Vienna, 1979.

Steiner, Kurt, Politics in Austria. Little, Brown, Boston, 1972.

Steininger, Rudolf, Polarisierung und Integration. Eine vergleichende Untersuchung der strukturellen Versäulung der Gesellschaft in den Niederlanden und in Österreich. Anton Hain Verlag, Meisenheim am Glan, 1975.

Tichy, Gunther, Zahlungsbilanz - und beschäftigungsrelevante Strukturprobleme von Industrie und Gewerbe sowie Ansatzpunkte zu ihrer Ueberwindung. Gutachten, erstellt im Auftrag des Bundesministeriums für Finanzen, Vienna, 1979.

Walter, Robert und Mayer, Heinz, Grundriss des österreichischen Bundesverfassungsrechts. Verlag Manz, Vienna, 1976.

Wandruszka, Adam, Österreichs politische Struktur. In: Heinrich Benedikt (Edit.), Geschichte der Republik Österreichs. Verlag für Geschichte und Politik, Vienna, 1954.

Weinzierl, Erika, und Skalnik, Kurt (Edit.), Österreich. Die Zweite Republik, 2 Bände. Styria Verlag, Graz, 1972.

Welan, Manfried, und Neisser, Heinrich, Der Bundeskanzler im österreichischen Verfassungsgefüge. Brüder Hollinek, Vienna, 1971.

Annex II

STATISTICAL OVERVIEW OF RECENT ECONOMIC AND SOCIAL TRENDS

LIST OF TABLES

Table 1

AVERAGE ANNUAL PER CENT CHANGES OF GROSS DOMESTIC PRODUCT(1) 1970-1980
(at constant prices)

Country/Area	1970	1971	1972	1973	1974	1975	1976	1977	1978	1979	1980(2)	Average 1970/1980(2)
Austria	7.1	5.6	6.0	5.3	4.3	-1.7	5.8	4.4	1.0	5.1	3.6	4.2
Germany	6.0	3.2	3.7	4.9	0.5	-1.8	5.2	3.0	3.3	4.6	1.9	3.1
EEC(3)	5.1	3.5	4.0	5.9	1.7	-1.3	5.2	2.3	3.2	3.4	1.4	3.1
OECD: Europe	5.2	3.7	4.4	5.8	2.2	-0.9	4.7	2.3	3.0	3.3	1.6	3.2
OECD: Total	3.6	3.7	5.5	6.2	0.6	-0.5	5.3	3.7	3.9	3.3	1.2	3.3

1) In purchasers' values.
2) Provisional.
3) Excluding Greece.
Sources: 1950-1979 National Accounts of OECD Countries, Vol. I, OECD, Paris, 1981 (for 1970-1979); Main Economic Indicators, OECD, Paris, May 1981 (for 1980).

Table 2

POPULATION, TOTAL LABOUR FORCE, WOMEN IN CIVILIAN EMPLOYMENT, WAGE AND SALARY EARNERS 1970-1979

Country / Area	1970	1971	1972	1973	1974	1975	1976	1977	1978	1979
Austria										
Population (Thousands)	7 426	7 459	7 495	7 525	7 533	7 520	7 513	7 518	7 508	7 503
Total Labour Force(1) (Thousands)	3 013	3 011	3 028	3 042	3 051	2 996	3 001	3 038	3 079	3 116
T.L.F. in % of Population(1)	40.6	40.4	40.4	40.4	40.5	39.8	39.9	40.4	41.0	41.5
Women in % of Civilian Employment	38.7	38.7	38.5	38.4	38.6	38.4	38.2	38.2	38.6	38.5
Wage and Salary Earners (Thousands)(2)	2 389	2 455	2 513	2 608	2 657	2 656	2 686	2 737	2 758	2 774
1970 - 100	100	102.7	105.2	109.2	111.2	111.2	112.4	114.4	115.4	116.1
Germany										
Total labour Force in % of Population	44.2	43.9	43.6	43.5	43.2	42.7	42.5	42.5	42.8	43.1
Women in % of Civilian Employment	36.6	36.6	36.8	37.2	37.5	37.8	37.8	37.9	38.0	38.3
Wage and Salary Earners, 1970 - 100	100	100.8	100.7	101.4	99.4	95.9	95.4	95.7	96.9	98.8
EEC(5)										
Total Labour Force in % of Population	42.2	42.0	41.7	41.8	41.8	41.8	42.0	42.2	42.3	42.6
Wage and Salary Earners, 1970 - 100	100	100.4	100.8	102.6	103.1	102.0	102.1	102.9	103.4	105.0(5)
OECD: Europe										
Total Labour Force in % of Population	42.2	41.9	41.8	41.8	41.8	41.7	41.7	41.8	41.9	42.1
Wage and Salary Earners, 1970 - 100	100(4)	-	-	-	-	-	-	-	104.0(3)	n.a.
OECD: Total										
Total Labour Force in % of Population	43.1	43.0	43.0	43.3	43.5	43.5	43.7	44.1	44.5	44.8
Wage and Salary Earners, 1970 - 100	100(4)	-	-	-	-	-	-	-	114.0(3)	n.a.

1) These figures differ considerably from those of the data bank of the Austrian Institute of Economic Research (e.g. for 1970
   the latter gives 3 119.8; 1976 = 3 277.7; 1977 = 3 301.3; 1978 = 3 316.8; and 1979 = 3 321.6 which would change the figures
   for TLF in % of population as follows: 1970 = 42.0; 1976 = 43.6; 1977 = 43.9; 1978 = 44.4; 1979 = 44.2).
   Source: Health Insurance Statistics (According to OECD Labour Force Statistics: 1970 = 2 160 and 1979 = 2 524).
2) Including Secretariat estimates for Greece, Switzerland and Turkey.
3) Including Secretariat estimate for Greece.
4) Total labour force including Greece; indices of wage and salary earners excluding Greece.
5) Source: Labour Force Statistics 1968-1979, OECD, Paris, 1981.

246

Table 3

LABOUR FORCE PARTICIPATION RATES IN SELECTED OECD COUNTRIES(6)
by age groups

Country	Year	15 - 19		20 - 24		25 - 59		60 - 64		65 +	
		Males	Females	Males	Females	Males	Females	Males	Females	Males	Females
Austria	1971(1)	65.6	60.0	87.5	68.0	94.9	50.0	44.9	13.2	8.0	3.2
	1976	63.1	57.9	88.5	71.1	94.8	52.6	34.9	11.0	5.4	2.7
Denmark	1971(2)	55.2	43.3	84.1	70.4	94.8	61.5	79.7	31.4	22.5	5.5
	1977(2)	47.9	37.0	81.8	79.1	95.0	72.5	79.4	34.3	22.5	5.0
Finland	1972(2)	42.8	33.8	77.4	66.0	90.1	70.1	58.4	34.1	11.4	2.8
	1977(2)	38.6	31.7	78.5	67.0	88.1	74.2	37.0	24.2	5.1	1.8
France	1972(2)	32.3	23.3	81.8	65.1	95.8	51.0	63.3	32.7	14.1	6.4
	1977(2)	27.3	21.6	81.2	68.6	95.0	58.4	48.8	27.2	11.5	4.8
Germany	1970(2)	55.4	53.6	85.9	69.8	96.0	46.0	74.7	22.5	19.7	6.5
	1976(2)	52.6	48.3	78.3	69.3	93.4	49.5	56.3	16.7	9.9	3.9
Italy	1972(2)	36.0(3)	26.3(3)	77.4	42.0	93.8	28.5	43.4	9.1	10.4	2.1
	1977(2)	34.2(3)	29.6(3)	79.1	54.4	94.5	37.7	41.6	11.4	14.1	4.1
Japan	1972(2)	27.4	28.5	80.7	67.3	97.0	53.1	79.5	37.9	47.2	15.6
	1977(2)	18.0	19.8	72.3	67.4	96.9	53.9	78.5	38.2	42.3	15.3
Netherlands	1971(1)	42.4	49.6	83.7	55.5	94.9	22.7	73.9	12.0	11.6	2.3
	1977(2)	32.5	37.9	82.3	64.0	93.3	29.1	58.0	9.1	6.3	1.4
Sweden	1972(2)	53.1	50.7	76.6	68.1	93.6	66.2	76.5	34.3	17.0	4.8
	1977(2)	56.6	56.0	83.3	77.0	94.6	75.7	70.2	38.3	8.5	2.9
United Kingdom (G.B.)	1972(2)	58.8	57.1	89.5		94.3(5)	52.0(5)	87.9	26.0	17.8	5.2
	1976(2)	65.4(4)	58.3(4)		64.5	97.9	61.2	87.7	28.4	15.9	4.8
United States	1972(2)	59.1(4)	45.7(4)	84.9	59.0	93.2	50.4	71.4	35.0	23.3	8.8
	1976(2)	61.7(4)	51.3(4)	85.3	66.4	91.9	56.9	62.0	32.6	19.3	7.6

1) Census results, total labour force. 2) Sample surveys, total labour force. 3) 14-19. 4) 16-19. 5) Including age group 20-24. 6) No specific criteria used for country selection.
Sources: Austria 1976: Helmut Jeglitsch, Der Arbeitsmarkt in den Bundesländern 1971-1991, Vienna, 1978; Austria 1971 and all other countries: Labour Force Statistics 1961-1972 and 1966-1977, OECD, Paris, 1974 and 1979.

Table 4

CIVILIAN EMPLOYMENT BY SECTOR 1970-1979
(in per cent)

Country-Area / Sector	1970	1971	1972	1973	1974	1975	1976	1977	1978	1979
Austria										
Agriculture(1)	18.8	17.7	16.6	16.2	13.0	12.5	12.4	11.8	10.9	10.7
Industry(2)	40.3	40.2	40.6	40.6	41.0	40.9	40.1	40.6	40.6	40.4
Other Activities	40.8	42.1	42.8	43.2	46.0	46.6	47.5	47.6	48.5	48.9
Germany										
Agriculture(1)	8.5	8.2	7.8	7.5	7.3	7.4	7.1	6.8	6.5	6.2
Industry(2)	48.5	48.1	47.6	47.5	47.3	46.0	45.1	45.3	45.0	44.9
Other Activities	42.9	43.7	44.6	45.0	45.3	46.6	47.8	47.9	48.5	48.9
EEC(3)										
Agriculture(1)	11.5	11.1	10.5	10.1	9.7	9.5	9.2	8.9	8.7	8.4
Industry(2)	42.5	42.2	41.7	41.6	41.3	40.3	32.7	39.4	39.0	38.6
Other Activities	46.0	46.6	47.7	48.4	49.0	50.2	51.1	51.7	52.3	53.0
OECD: Europe										
Agriculture(1)	18.2	17.8	17.3	16.7	16.4	16.1	15.9	15.5	15.2	14.9
Industry(2)	39.0	38.8	38.4	38.3	38.2	37.5	36.8	36.6	36.3	35.9
Other Activities	42.8	43.4	44.3	45.0	45.4	46.4	47.3	47.8	48.5	49.2
OECD: Total										
Agriculture(1)	13.9	13.4	12.8	12.1	11.9	11.6	11.3	11.0	10.7	10.4
Industry(2)	36.9	36.4	36.1	36.4	36.1	35.0	34.6	34.4	34.2	34.0
Other Activities	49.2	50.2	51.1	51.4	52.0	53.4	54.0	54.6	55.1	55.6

1) Including hunting, forestry and fishing.
2) Comprising mining and quarrying, manufacturing, electricity, gas and water and construction.
3) Including Greece.
Source: Labour Force Statistics 1968-1979, OECD, Paris, 1981.

Table 5

UNEMPLOYMENT RATES IN SELECTED OECD COUNTRIES(1) 1970-1980

(Rates adjusted to Austrian definition, i.e. annual average of registered unemployed in per cent of annual average of wage and salary earners and registered unemployed)

Country	1970	1971	1972	1973	1974	1975	1976	1977	1978	1979	Average 1970/79	1980(3)
Austria	1.9	1.5	1.3	1.2	1.3	2.0	2.0	1.8	2.1	2.0	1.7	1.9
Belgium	2.7	2.7	3.4	3.5	3.8	6.2	7.9	9.2	9.7	10.1	5.9	10.6
Canada	6.6	7.1	7.0	6.2	6.4	7.6	7.8	8.9	9.3	8.3	7.5	8.3
Denmark	1.3	1.5(2)	1.5	0.9	2.4	5.6	5.7	6.6	7.7	6.2	3.9	n.a.
Finland	2.5	2.9	3.3	3.0	2.2	2.7	4.7	7.0	8.7	7.1	4.4	n.a.
France	1.6	2.1(2)	2.3	2.3	2.8	4.7	5.2	5.9	6.3	7.2	4.0	7.6
Germany	0.7	0.7	1.1	1.2	2.6	4.9	4.7	4.7	4.5	3.9	2.9	3.9
Japan	1.8	1.8	2.1	1.8	1.9	2.7	2.8	2.8	3.2	2.9	2.4	2.8
Ireland	8.3	7.8	9.0	8.3	8.6	11.8	13.3	13.0	11.9	9.6	10.2	10.5
Italy	6.5	7.5(2)	7.5	7.1	6.9	7.5	7.8	8.9	9.8	10.2	8.0	10.8
Netherlands	1.2	1.6	2.7	2.8	3.4	4.8	5.2	5.0(2)	5.0	5.0	3.7	5.3
Sweden	1.7	2.8	3.0	2.7	2.2	1.8	1.7	2.0	2.4	2.2	2.3	2.2
United Kingdom	2.7	3.5	3.8	2.7	2.6	4.1	5.7	6.1	6.1	5.7	4.3	7.4
United States	5.5	6.6	6.2	5.3	6.1	9.2	8.4	7.7	6.5	6.2	6.8	7.6

1) No specific criteria used for country selection. 2) Break in series. 3) Provisional.
Sources: Austria: Health insurance statistics and unemployment statistics of Ministry of Social Affairs;
EEC countries: EUROSTAT, Employment and Unemployment (for registered unemployed) and Labour Force Statistics
1968-1979 and Quarterly Supplement, OECD, Paris, 1981; other countries: Main Economic Indicators 1960-1975,
Historical Statistics, OECD, Paris, 1976 and Main Economic Indicators, OECD, June 1979, June 1980 and June 1981,
(reg. unemployed) and OECD Labour Force Statistics.

Table 6

UNEMPLOYMENT RATES(1). IN AUSTRIA BY SEX, EMPLOYMENT STATUS, AGE GROUP AND DURATION, AND JOB VACANCIES
1968, 1975 and 1977

	1968	1975	1977
Unemployment by Sex			
Males	2.1	1.5	1.4
Females	4.3	2.8	2.5
Unemployment Rates by Employment Status			
Blue-collar workers	4.1	3.1	2.7
White-collar workers	1.2	0.9	0.9
Unemployments Rates by Selected Age Groups(2)			
15 - under 20	0.96	0.92	0.80
50 - under 60	1.75	1.79	1.53
Unemployment by Duration (in per cent)(2)			
Less than 1 month	20.1	18.9	21.2
1 - 5 months	56.6	61.2	57.8
6 - 11 months	14.2	13.4	11.0
1 year and more	9.1	10.1	10.0
	100.0	100.0	100.0
Vacancies per 100 Unemployed	39.3	69.9	82.1

1) Rates adjusted to Austrian definition, i.e. annual average of registered unemployed in per cent of
   annual average of wage and salary earners and registered unemployed.
2) Related to unemployment of August.
Sources: Indikatoren zur gesellschaftlichen Entwicklung; Wirtschafts- und Sozialstatistisches Handbuch,
   1972 and 1977, Kammer fuer Arbeiter und Angestellte, Vienna, 1973 and 1978.

Table 7

TIME LOST THROUGH LABOUR DISPUTES IN SELECTED OECD COUNTRIES(1) 1968-1979
Average number of minutes lost per wage earner and salaried employee(2)

Country	1968	1969	1970	1971	1972	1973	1974	1975	1976	1977	1978	1979(4)
Austria	1.5	4	5	0.5	3	33.5	1.5	1	0	0	2	0
Belgium	62	27	231	196.5	56	135	88	94	139	103	156	96
Canada	376	353.5	459	195.5	509	350	538	625	652	183	397	421
Denmark	10	15	26	5	5.5	963.5	46	25	51.5	55.5	30	40.5
Finland	88.5	49	68.5	789.5	136.5	689	115	74.5	325	630	35.5	65.5
France	- (3)	68	53	130.5	110	112	95	110	141.5	102	61	n.a.
Germany	0.5	5.5	2	97	1.5	12.5	23	1.5	12.5	0.5	97.5	11
Japan	43.5	54.5	57	85	71.5	61.5	128.5	105.5	42	19.5	17	11.5
Ireland	269.5	578	663	177	137.5	135.5	356	193	516.5	291	405.5	999
Italy	358.5	1 445.5	684	479	791.5	861.5	695.5	949	876.5	562	345.5	935
Netherlands	2	3	33	12	17	73	1	0	1.5	29	0.5	37.5
Norway	5.5	9	18.5	3.5	4.5	4	109	4	43.5	7.5	19	2
Sweden	0	16	21.5	116	1.5	1.5	7.5	47	3	11	4.5	3.5
Switzerland	0.5	0	0.5	1.5	0.5	0	0.5	0.5	4	1	1	0.5
United Kingdom(G.B.)	97.5	142.5	230	289	519	152	311	127	70	215	199	624
United States	346.5	293	451	322	176.5	174.5	294.5	195	229	210	205	191

1) No specific criteria used for country selection. 2) Calculations were made on the assumption that normal working
   hours per day were 8. 3) General strike of 1968 not statistically covered. 4) Except for Austria and Japan provisional.

Sources: Wirtschafts- und sozialstatistisches Handbuch 1972 and 1978, Vienna, 1973 and 1979; Wirtschafts- und sozialstatistisches Taschenbuch, 1981. Kammer für Arbeiter und Angestellte für Wien, Vienna, 1981.

Table 8

INDICES OF INDUSTRIAL PRODUCTIVITY IN AUSTRIA AND GERMANY 1971-1980
1971=100

	1971	1972	1973	1974	1975	1976	1977	1978	1979	1980(2)
Austria(1)										
Productivity per employee	100	106	109	115	112	122	125	130	140	145
Productivity per hour worked	100	108	113	122	129	140	146	154	165	171
Germany										
Productivity per employee	100	106	113	114	114	125	130	133	140	139
Productivity per hour worked	100	107	114	117	121	131	138	142	149	151

1) Mining and quarrying and manufacturing.
2) Provisional.
Sources: Austria: Oest. Stat. Zentralamt, Statistische Uebersichten, Tables 4.1 and 4.3; Germany: Statistisches Bundesamt, Wirtschaft und Statistik.

Table 9

EMPLOYEES IN AUSTRIAN INDUSTRY BY SIZE OF ESTABLISHMENTS(1) 1969 and 1979
(in per cent of total number of employees)

Empl. Year	-20	21 - 50	51 - 100	101 - 500	501 - 1 000	more than 1 000	Total
1969	3.1	8.0	10.8	35.3	15.6	27.1	100
1979	3.6	8.0	10.3	35.0	15.5	27.6	100

1) Industry in the narrow sense, i.e. establishments recorded as "industrial"
   establishments. Employment figures for all employees in manufacturing
   and mining are considerably greater than those recorded under the label
   industry by the Chamber of Commerce, Industry and Trade (e.g. in 1969,
   931.800 as compared with 606.300 and 1979 938.900 as compared with
   662.600).
Source: Oest. Stat. Zentralamt, on basis of quarterly employment statistics
   of the Bundeskammer der gewerblichen Wirtschaft, Sektion Industrie (Federal Chamber of Commerce, Industry and Trade, Department for Industry).

Table 10

TURNOVER, EXPORTS AND EMPLOYMENT OF THE 50 BIGGEST
AUSTRIAN ENTERPRISES BY TYPE OF OWNERSHIP 1971

Ownership	Turnover (in per cent)	Exports (in per cent)	Employees	
			Number	in per cent
A. Federal State, Länder(1)	17.2	12.3	31 960	11.8
B. Federal State: OeIAG(2)	37.6	34.6	108 996	40.4
C. Owned by State-owned banks	15.4	23.0	49 744	18.5
D. Co-operatives	2.5	0.3	1 120	0.4
E. Private, domestic capital	11.4	18.1	32 291	12.0
F. Private, foreign capital	15.9	11.7	45 604	16.9
Total	100	100	269 695	100

1) Directly owned enterprises are for instance the State-owned railway
   system, Post and Telecommunications, etc.
2) OeIAG is the Holding Company for all nationalised industrial enterprises.
Source: Manfred Drennig, "Vermoegensverteilung in Oesterreich, ihre
   politische Relevanz", in Heinz Fischer, Das politische System Oesterreichs, Vienna, 1974.

Table 11

CONSUMER PRICES 1970-1980
(average annual percentage changes)

Country / Area	1970	1971	1972	1973	1974	1975	1976	1977	1978	1979	1980	Average 1970/1980
Austria	4.4	4.7	6.3	7.6	9.5	8.4	7.3	5.5	3.6	3.7	6.3	6.1
Germany	3.4	5.3	5.5	6.9	7.0	6.0	4.5	3.7	2.7	4.1	5.5	5.0
EEC(1)(2)	4.5	6.0	6.1	8.0	12.3	12.6	10.3	10.1	7.3	9.6	12.2	9.0
OECD: Europe(2)	4.8	6.4	6.5	8.5	12.9	12.8	10.9	11.5	10.0	12.5	14.3	10.1
OECD: Total(2)	5.5	5.3	4.9	7.8	13.2	11.2	8.6	9.0	8.3	10.9	12.8	8.9

1) Excluding Greece.
2) Calculated as fixed-weight arithmetic averages of the component country data.
Source: Consumer Price Indices, sources and methods and historical statistics, Special Issue of Main Economic Indicators, OECD, Paris, 1980
(for 1970-1979); Main Economic Indicators, May 1981 (for 1980).

Table 12

INDICES OF AUSTRIAN EXPORTS AND IMPORTS OF COMMODITIES 1970-1980
(1971=100)

	1970	1971	1972	1973	1974	1975	1976	1977	1978	1979	1980(1)
Exports											
Indices of volume	96.8	100	111.8	121.2	135.6	126.0	145.9	150.2	165.6	187.2	196.7
Indices of average price	96.6	100	101.4	107.1	125.1	129.9	129.8	133.8	133.8	139.3	146.5
Terms of Trade	101.0	100	101.0	102.9	100.8	100.9	98.7	98.0	98.2	96.9	93.3
Imports											
Indices of volume	92.2	100	115.1	126.7	130.0	121.3	149.2	163.8	161.2	178.4	192.6
Indices of average price	95.7	100	100.4	104.1	124.1	128.7	131.5	136.5	136.3	143.8	157.1

1) Provisional.
Sources: Oesterreichisches Statistisches Zentralamt, Statistik des Aussenhandels Oesterreichs.

Table 13

EXPENDITURE OF GROSS DOMESTIC PRODUCT IN AUSTRIA AND GERMANY 1960, 1970-1979
(at current prices)

(in per cent)

Country / Expenditure	1960	1970	1971	1972	1973	1974	1975	1976	1977	1978	1979
Austria											
Private consumption	59.3	54.7	54.9	54.6	54.4	53.9	56.0	56.6	57.6	56.0	55.9
Public consumption	12.7	14.7	14.8	14.8	15.3	15.9	17.2	17.6	17.6	18.5	18.1
Gross domestic fixed capital formation	24.9	25.9	27.9	30.4	27.4	28.1	26.7	26.0	26.2	25.0	25.0
Change of stocks including statistical errors	+2.6	+3.7	+1.6	-0.3	+2.5	+2.4	-0.6	+1.3	+1.4	+0.4	+2.2
Exports of goods and services less imports of goods and services	-0.5	+1.0	+0.7	+0.5	+0.4	-0.3	+0.6	-1.5	-2.7	+0.04	-1.2
Gross Domestic Product at current prices	100.0	100.0	100.0	100.0	100.0	100.0	100.0	100.0	100.0	100.0	100.0
Germany											
Private consumption	56.8	54.2	54.0	54.2	53.5	53.4	55.9	55.5	55.8	55.4	54.7
Public consumption	13.5	15.9	17.1	17.4	18.1	19.7	20.9	20.2	20.0	20.3	19.8
Gross domestic fixed capital formation	24.3	25.6	26.4	25.9	24.5	21.9	20.8	20.7	20.9	21.3	22.7
Change of stocks including statistical errors	+2.9	+2.3	+0.5	+0.3	+0.8	+0.6	-0.3	+1.2	+0.9	+0.7	+2.1
Exports of goods and services less imports of goods and services	+2.6	+2.1	+1.9	+2.1	+3.0	+4.4	+2.8	+2.4	+2.4	+2.6	+0.6
Gross Domestic Product at current prices	100.0	100.0	100.0	100.0	100.0	100.0	100.0	100.0	100.0	100.0	100.0

Source: National Accounts of OECD Countries 1950-1979, Volume I, OECD, Paris, 1981.

Table 14

GROWTH OF AVERAGE YEARLY GROSS EARNINGS OF EMPLOYEES IN AUSTRIA IN REAL TERMS(1) 1970-1980
(average annual percentage changes)

1970	1971	1972	1973	1974	1975	1976	1977	1978	1979	1980(2)	Average 1970-1980(2)
3.5	7.6	4.9	6.0	3.2	3.1	2.5	3.4	2.3	1.5	1.1	3.6

1) On the basis of deflator of private consumption. 2) Provisional.
Source: Österreichisches Institut für Wirtschaftsforschung.

Table 15

TAX REVENUE IN SELECTED OECD COUNTRIES(1), IN OECD EUROPE AND IN TOTAL OECD AREA
(in per cent of GDP 1978)

| | Total Tax Revenue | Revenue from taxes on: | | Social Security Contributions | Other Taxes(2) |
		Goods and Services	Income and Profits		
Austria	41.43	13.09	11.16	12.66	4.51
Belgium	44.18	11.54	18.14	13.26	1.24
Canada	31.13	10.03	13.94	3.66	3.49
Denmark	43.59	16.67	23.61	0.58	2.72
France	39.67	12.40	7.09	16.68	3.50
Germany	37.82	9.85	13.49	12.82	1.65
Italy	32.58	8.56	9.55	13.26	1.20
Japan	24.06	4.15	9.71	7.09	3.11
Netherlands	46.79	11.99	15.30	17.45	2.01
Norway	46.94	17.81	19.44	8.44	1.25
Sweden	53.50	12.71	24.19	14.30	2.30
Switzerland	31.47	6.41	13.43	9.36	2.26
United Kingdom	34.45	9.14	13.91	6.20	5.19
United States	30.19	5.12	13.86	7.56	3.65
OECD: Europe	37.83	11.18	14.36	10.00	2.29
OECD: Total	35.80	10.25	14.45	8.56	2.55

1) No specific criteria used for country selection. 2) Including levies on payroll, taxes on property and other tax revenue.
Source: Revenue Statistics of OECD Member Countries 1965-1979, OECD, Paris, 1980.

Table 16

PER CAPITA PRIVATE FINAL CONSUMPTION EXPENDITURE IN REAL TERMS 1970-1979
(average per cent changes at annual rates)

Country / Area	1970	1971	1972	1973	1974	1975	1976	1977	1978	1979	Average 1970/1979
Austria(1)	3.7	6.9	6.1	4.8	2.6	3.7	4.5	6.7	-2.1	4.7	4.2
Germany	6.3	4.1	3.4	2.0	0.2	3.5	3.9	3.7	4.0	3.2	3.4
EEC(2)	4.7	3.8	4.1	4.1	0.6	1.4	3.6	2.1	3.7	3.4	3.2
OECD: Europe	4.2	3.7	4.2	4.0	1.0	1.2	3.3	1.7	2.6	2.8	2.9
OECD: Total	3.1	3.3	5.0	4.5	-0.1	1.4	4.0	2.8	3.2	2.6	3.0

1) Private Savings rate in Austria from 1970 to 1979 was:

1970	1971	1972	1973	1974	1975	1976	1977	1978	1979
11.2	10.4	9.4	7.9	7.5	8.1	9.4	6.4	8.5	9.2

2) Excluding Greece.
Source: National Accounts of OECD Countries 1950-1979, OECD, Paris, 1981.

Table 17

DISTRIBUTION OF GROSS REVENUE AND EXPENDITURE OF GOVERNMENT SECTOR IN AUSTRIA 1963, 1968, 1973 and 1978

Year	Federal government		Federal Länder (excluding Vienna)		Municipalities (excluding Vienna)		Vienna (Land and municipality)		Federations of municipalities		Public funds		Chambers which are statutory associations		Social insurance institutions		Total
	Exp.	Rev.	Exp.	Rev.	Exp.	Rev.	Exp.	Rev.	Exp.	Rev.	Exp.	Rev.	Exp.	Rev.	Exp.	Rev.	
1963	51.4	50.7	7.8	7.8	9.6	9.9	6.4	6.4	0.9	0.8	3.8	4.2	2.0	2.2	18.2	18.0	100
1968	47.6	47.4	9.4	9.4	10.2	10.5	6.8	6.8	0.8	0.8	3.1	2.7	1.9	2.0	20.2	20.3	100
1973	44.0	42.9	13.3	13.5	10.6	10.9	7.9	7.9	0.7	0.8	1.7	1.8	1.7	1.7	20.0	20.6	100
1978	45.8	41.8	12.0	13.2	9.2	9.7	8.2	8.2	0.4	0.4	2.1	1.6	1.4	1.6	20.9	23.5	100

Source: Wirtschafts- und sozialstatistisches Handbuch 1972 and 1978, Kammer fuer Arbeiter und Angestellte, Vienna, 1973 and 1979.

OECD SALES AGENTS
DÉPOSITAIRES DES PUBLICATIONS DE L'OCDE

ARGENTINA – ARGENTINE
Carlos Hirsch S.R.L., Florida 165, 4° Piso (Galería Guemes)
1333 BUENOS AIRES, Tel. 33.1787.2391 y 30.7122

AUSTRALIA – AUSTRALIE
Australia and New Zealand Book Company Pty, Ltd.,
10 Aquatic Drive, Frenchs Forest, N.S.W. 2086
P.O. Box 459, BROOKVALE, N.S.W. 2100

AUSTRIA – AUTRICHE
OECD Publications and Information Center
4 Simrockstrasse 5300 BONN. Tel. (0228) 21.60.45
Local Agent/Agent local :
Gerold and Co., Graben 31, WIEN 1. Tel. 52.22.35

BELGIUM – BELGIQUE
LCLS
35, avenue de Stalingrad, 1000 BRUXELLES. Tel. 02.512.89.74

BRAZIL – BRÉSIL
Mestre Jou S.A., Rua Guaipa 518,
Caixa Postal 24090, 05089 SAO PAULO 10. Tel. 261.1920
Rua Senador Dantas 19 s/205-6, RIO DE JANEIRO GB.
Tel. 232.07.32

CANADA
Renouf Publishing Company Limited,
2182 St. Catherine Street West,
MONTRÉAL, Que. H3H 1M7. Tel. (514)937.3519
522 West Hasting,
VANCOUVER, B.C. V6B 1L6. Tel. (604) 687.3320

DENMARK – DANEMARK
Munksgaard Export and Subscription Service
35, Nørre Søgade
DK 1370 KØBENHAVN K. Tel. +45.1.12.85.70

FINLAND – FINLANDE
Akateeminen Kirjakauppa
Keskuskatu 1, 00100 HELSINKI 10. Tel. 65.11.22

FRANCE
Bureau des Publications de l'OCDE,
2 rue André-Pascal, 75775 PARIS CEDEX 16. Tel. (1) 524.81.67
Principal correspondant :
13602 AIX-EN-PROVENCE : Librairie de l'Université.
Tel. 26.18.08

GERMANY – ALLEMAGNE
OECD Publications and Information Center
4 Simrockstrasse 5300 BONN Tel. (0228) 21.60.45

GREECE – GRÈCE
Librairie Kauffmann, 28 rue du Stade,
ATHÈNES 132. Tel. 322.21.60

HONG-KONG
Government Information Services,
Sales and Publications Office, Baskerville House, 2nd floor,
13 Duddell Street, Central. Tel. 5.214375

ICELAND – ISLANDE
Snaebjörn Jönsson and Co., h.f.,
Hafnarstraeti 4 and 9, P.O.B. 1131, REYKJAVIK.
Tel. 13133/14281/11936

INDIA – INDE
Oxford Book and Stationery Co. :
NEW DELHI-1, Scindia House. Tel. 45896
CALCUTTA 700016, 17 Park Street. Tel. 240832

INDONESIA – INDONÉSIE
PDIN-LIPI, P.O. Box 3065/JKT., JAKARTA, Tel. 583467

IRELAND – IRLANDE
TDC Publishers – Library Suppliers
12 North Frederick Street, DUBLIN 1 Tel. 744835-749677

ITALY – ITALIE
Libreria Commissionaria Sansoni :
Via Lamarmora 45, 50121 FIRENZE. Tel. 579751
Via Bartolini 29, 20155 MILANO. Tel. 365083
Sub-depositari :
Editrice e Libreria Herder,
Piazza Montecitorio 120, 00 186 ROMA. Tel. 6794628
Libreria Hoepli, Via Hoepli 5, 20121 MILANO. Tel. 865446
Libreria Lattes, Via Garibaldi 3, 10122 TORINO. Tel. 519274
La diffusione delle edizioni OCSE è inoltre assicurata dalle migliori
librerie nelle città più importanti.

JAPAN – JAPON
OECD Publications and Information Center,
Landic Akasaka Bldg., 2-3-4 Akasaka,
Minato-ku, TOKYO 107 Tel. 586.2016

KOREA – CORÉE
Pan Korea Book Corporation,
P.O. Box n° 101 Kwangwhamun, SÉOUL. Tel. 72.7369

LEBANON – LIBAN
Documenta Scientifica/Redico,
Edison Building, Bliss Street, P.O. Box 5641, BEIRUT.
Tel. 354429 – 344425

MALAYSIA – MALAISIE
and/et **SINGAPORE - SINGAPOUR**
University of Malaysia Co-operative Bookshop Ltd.
P.O. Box 1127, Jalan Pantai Baru
KUALA LUMPUR. Tel. 51425, 54058, 54361

THE NETHERLANDS – PAYS-BAS
Staatsuitgeverij
Verzendboekhandel Chr. Plantijnnstraat
S-GRAVENAGE. Tel. nr. 070.789911
Voor bestellingen: Tel. 070.789208

NEW ZEALAND – NOUVELLE-ZÉLANDE
Publications Section,
Government Printing Office Bookshops:
AUCKLAND: Retail Bookshop: 25 Rutland Street.
Mail Orders: 85 Beach Road, Private Bag C.P.O.
HAMILTON: Retail: Ward Street,
Mail Orders, P.O. Box 857
WELLINGTON: Retail: Mulgrave Street (Head Office),
Cubacade World Trade Centre
Mail Orders: Private Bag
CHRISTCHURCH: Retail: 159 Hereford Street,
Mail Orders: Private Bag
DUNEDIN: Retail: Princes Street
Mail Order: P.O. Box 1104

NORWAY – NORVÈGE
J.G. TANUM A/S Karl Johansgate 43
P.O. Box 1177 Sentrum OSLO 1. Tel. (02) 80.12.60

PAKISTAN
Mirza Book Agency, 65 Shahrah Quaid-E-Azam, LAHORE 3.
Tel. 66839

PHILIPPINES
National Book Store, Inc.
Library Services Division, P.O. Box 1934, MANILA.
Tel. Nos. 49.43.06 to 09, 40.53.45, 49.45.12

PORTUGAL
Livraria Portugal, Rua do Carmo 70-74,
1117 LISBOA CODEX. Tel. 360582/3

SPAIN – ESPAGNE
Mundi-Prensa Libros, S.A.
Castello 37, Apartado 1223, MADRID-1. Tel. 275.46.55
Libreria Bastinos, Pelayo 52, BARCELONA 1. Tel. 222.06.00

SWEDEN – SUÈDE
AB CE Fritzes Kungl Hovbokhandel,
Box 16 356, S 103 27 STH, Regeringsgatan 12,
DS STOCKHOLM. Tel. 08/23.89.00

SWITZERLAND – SUISSE
OECD Publications and Information Center
4 Simrockstrasse 5300 BONN. Tel. (0228) 21.60.45
Local Agents/Agents locaux
Librairie Payot, 6 rue Grenus, 1211 GENÈVE 11. Tel. 022.31.89.50
Freihofer A.G., Weinbergstr. 109, CH-8006 ZÜRICH.
Tel. 01.3634282

TAIWAN – FORMOSE
National Book Company,
84-5 Sing Sung South Rd, Sec. 3, TAIPEI 107. Tel. 321.0698

THAILAND – THAILANDE
Suksit Siam Co., Ltd., 1715 Rama IV Rd,
Samyan, BANGKOK 5. Tel. 2511630

UNITED KINGDOM – ROYAUME-UNI
H.M. Stationery Office, P.O.B. 569,
LONDON SE1   9NH. Tel. 01.928.6977, Ext. 410 or
49 High Holborn, LONDON WC1V 6 HB (personal callers)
Branches at: EDINBURGH, BIRMINGHAM, BRISTOL,
MANCHESTER, CARDIFF, BELFAST.

UNITED STATES OF AMERICA – ÉTATS-UNIS
OECD Publications and Information Center, Suite 1207,
1750 Pennsylvania Ave., N.W. WASHINGTON, D.C.20006 – 4582
Tel. (202) 724.1857

VENEZUELA
Libreria del Este, Avda. F. Miranda 52, Edificio Galipan,
CARACAS 106. Tel. 32.23.01/33.26.04/33.24.73

YUGOSLAVIA – YOUGOSLAVIE
Jugoslovenska Knjiga, Terazije 27, P.O.B. 36, BEOGRAD.
Tel. 621.992

Les commandes provenant de pays où l'OCDE n'a pas encore désigné de dépositaire peuvent être adressées à :
OCDE, Bureau des Publications, 2, rue André-Pascal, 75775 PARIS CEDEX 16.

Orders and inquiries from countries where sales agents have not yet been appointed may be sent to:
OECD, Publications Office, 2 rue André-Pascal, 75775 PARIS CEDEX 16.

OECD PUBLICATIONS, 2, rue André-Pascal, 75775 PARIS CEDEX 16 - No. 42017 1981
PRINTED IN FRANCE
1500/SH (81 81 03 1) ISBN 92-64-12256-7

Réseau de bibliothèques Université d'Ottawa Échéance	Library Network University of Ottawa Date Due